THE UNSPOKEN AS HERITAGE

HARRY HAROOTUNIAN

THE UNSPOKEN AS HERITAGE

THE ARMENIAN GENOCIDE AND

ITS UNACCOUNTED LIVES

Duke University Press   Durham and London   2019

© 2019 DUKE UNIVERSITY PRESS. All rights reserved
Printed in the United States of America on acid-free paper ∞
Designed by Courtney Leigh Baker
Typeset in Warnock Pro by Copperline Book Services

Library of Congress Cataloging-in-Publication Data
Names: Harootunian, Harry D., [date] author.
Title: The unspoken as heritage : the Armenian genocide and its unaccounted lives / Harry Harootunian.
Description: Durham : Duke University Press, 2019. | Includes bibliographical references and index.
Identifiers: LCCN 2019006360 (print) | LCCN 2019012084 (ebook)
ISBN 9781478007029 (ebook)
ISBN 9781478005100 (hardcover : alk. paper)
ISBN 9781478006282 (pbk. : alk. paper)
Subjects: LCSH: Harootunian, Harry D., [date]—Family—Biography. | Armenian Americans—United States—Biography. | Armenian massacres survivors—United States—Biography. | Armenian massacres, 1915–1923
Classification: LCC E184.A7 (ebook) | LCC E184.A7 H376 2019 (print) | DDC 956.6/20154—dc23
LC record available at https://lccn.loc.gov/2019006360

COVER ART: Harootunian family members, late 1920s.
Courtesy of the author.

For the memory of Sena Harootunian
and to Victoria Pedersen

CONTENTS

Acknowledgments ix

ONE. **THE UNREALIZED EVERYDAY** 1
By Way of an Introduction

TWO. **UNNOTICED LIVES/UNANSWERED QUESTIONS** 17

THREE. **TRACES OF A VANISHED EVERYDAY** 37

FOUR. **HISTORY'S INTERRUPTION** 87
Dispossession and Genocide

FIVE. **HOUSE OF STRANGERS/DIMINISHED LIVES** 114

EPILOGUE. **RETURNING TO ANI** 149

Notes 161   Bibliography 171   Index 175

A gallery appears following page 86.

ACKNOWLEDGMENTS

I owe great thanks to an army of friends who read various drafts and versions. I would like to mention Kristin Ross, who read the first draft and encouraged me in this project and throughout its completion; Nancy Armstrong, who introduced the idea of turning to a form of life writing and who read an earlier version; and Leonard Tennenhouse, who participated in the discussions we had on life writing and also read an earlier draft. I want to acknowledge Anne Allison, who read an earlier version and offered consistent encouragement, as well as Rey Chow, Larry Fuchser, Tanya Fernando, Helen M. Kearney, Carol Gluck, Kim Brandt, Marilyn Ivy, Jonathan Strong, Adrian Rifkin, Denis Echard, Michael Dutton, Michèle Longino, Laura Neitzel, Holly Hudak, John Hudak, Claudia Karagianis (especially for help with the photos), Chris Nelson, Ken Kawashima, Andrea Arai, and my two sisters, Sena Harootunian and Victoria Pedersen, to whom I have dedicated this book. Sena died before the book was published but had read and corrected an earlier draft. I want to thank Anne, Charlie Piot, and others who arranged for me to discuss a draft of the manuscript at Duke University in 2017, where I learned a lot of what I should be doing, and a number of anonymous readers who made extremely valuable suggestions and comments, which they will recognize in the text. Thank you to my editor, Ken Wissoker, for sticking with this; to Susan Albury, project editor; and to Joshua Tranen, editorial associate.

All of us, without suspecting it, are the carriers of an immense embryological experiment: for even the process of remembering, crowned with the victory of memory's effort, is amazingly the phenomenon of growth. In one as well as the other, there is a sprout, an embryo, the rudiment of a face, half a character, half a sound, the ending of a name; something labial or palatal, sweet legume on the tongue, that doesn't develop out of itself but only responds to an invitation, only stretches out *toward*, justifying one's expectation.

An Armenian fairy tale from the ancient city of Ashtarak: "Three apples fell from heaven: the first for the one who told the tale, the second for the one who listened, and the third for the one who understood."

—OSIP MANDELSTAM, *Journey to Armenia*

ONE. **THE UNREALIZED EVERYDAY**

By Way of an Introduction

When I was younger I read and heard stories about the ancient Armenian city of Ani and even dreamed I walked among its discarded ruins. Ani was the capital of the Bagratid kingdom in eastern Anatolia ("Higher Armenia") that had been a powerful fortress as early as the third century but by the ninth century was the center of a large kingdom that covered a good part of the region of eastern Anatolia. Known for its architectural and artistic brilliance and as the city of 1,001 churches inhabited by a population estimated at 100,000 and even higher, larger than any medieval European city at the time, it stood at the strategic crossroads of several trade routes between east and west. In the thirteenth century it was overrun and sacked by the Mongols. A century later it was completely destroyed by an earthquake, reduced to the rubbles of ruin, where a small village that eventually disappeared was erected on the site. I never realized my youthful desire to visit Ani's ruins, but years later it occurred to me that the image of the city's remaining stone wreckage retreating back into the nature from which it was cut and pried loose captured the moment of the fateful and sorrowful destiny of the Armenians' struggle between the unyielding grasp of both nature and history, indelibly inscribed in the ruins of Ani. Perhaps more fabled and subject to romantic fantasy once it was released from history, Ani's particular fate seemed a fitting reminder to Armenians whose successive history often came perilously close to repeating its disappearance of a lived actuality. The Turkish genocide's determined attempt in the early twentieth century to make the Armenians as extinct as Ani was a continuing episode in this sad narrative. Yet the ruins still offered the trace of a historical existence, a shattered silhouette of what it had once been and thus the prospect of a pathway for returning to home and a new start.

The Armenian genocide of 1915–16 was planned, implemented, and executed by the dominant political group in Turkey's Ottoman Empire, the Committee of Union and Progress (CUP, ITTIHADIST PARTY), or simply the Unionists or Young Turks. It was neither surprising nor coincidental that in 1915 the Young Turks were an elite party, most of whose members were born and educated in Europe, principally the Balkans, the Aegean Littoral, and Constantinople. Despite its enthusiastic embrace of the tradition of the European Enlightenment or because of it, it was this cohort that committed the resources of an empire to the total destruction of the Armenian population and, paradoxically, of itself. As the German military attaché in Constantinople pronounced in 1918: "the (Turkish) government ... wishes to destroy all Armenians, not solely in Turkey but also outside of Turkey."[1] The massive program of destruction aimed at Armenians and other Christian minorities in Anatolia like the Greeks and Chaldo-Assyrians used the occasion of World War I and Turkey's alliance with the Central Powers as both the moment to inaugurate the grim labor of mass murder and the masquerade to make what clearly was a genocidal intention appear as merely collateral damage and even a sideshow to the Great War. While the genocide constitutes the inducement for this memoir of my parents and their perilous escape from Anatolia and eventual migration to the United States, I am not concerned with writing another narrative of the history of the event for a number of reasons explained later in the text.

Not long ago I began to think about how my parents separately survived the Armenian genocides of the early twentieth century and how once they were able to find their way to the United States, they encountered the unwelcome prospect of facing another challenge of survival. This had not been a question that occurred to me when I was younger and growing up with my two older sisters in Highland Park, an industrialized autonomous enclave within the precincts of the city of Detroit, at the time the home of an early and one of the larger Ford assembly plants. For me, those years were marked by a kind of voluntary indifference to anything related to Armenian life, which increasingly appeared irrelevant and would have precluded asking questions of our parents' survival when growing up; these questions now need to be explained. A contributing explanation might have been the force of the Americanizing process to which we were subjected in the schools and in daily life, the effort to make us all look like Americans or some version of WASP America but not quite. This process of disidentification required breaking down whatever identity we had and aimed at making us eager to look like Americans; it also seemed to override any consideration to retain the thinning threads of an ethnic identity. Paradoxically, the appeal to whiteness today is precisely the template of Americanness in which my generation of immigrant children had been socialized into a national and nationalist identity. But the necessity to ask such questions we neglected as children has gradually come back like an unscheduled revenant demanding compelling urgency, especially in the years I was growing older and beginning to recognize in the migrant life we lived not the glowing image so often portrayed in histories and circulated in public schools of a land of plenty and infinite opportunity, as represented in school history texts and civics classes designed to make the children of immigrant families into Americans. Instead I began to see the United States as a place that grudgingly accepted large numbers of immigrants from the late nineteenth century on but only as reservoirs of cheap, unskilled labor, and more often than not badly treated, to staff the growing industrialization that marked those years immediately before and after World War I. For most immigrants, living in their own enclaves, America was an oversized "mean streets," a vast configuration streaked with multiple forms of unevenness and deeply engraved precincts of permanent inequality, traversed by boundless combinations embracing the capitalist new with diverse cultural practices brought by different ethnic groups as a way of navigating the new terrain. There was little in the country's early history that pointed in the direction of what it would become. In fact, that early history showed it was moving the other way.

When the question arose of actually trying to investigate and account for my parents' survival and subsequent struggle to stay afloat in a new environment, it gradually pressed upon me and became an imperative in late adulthood. I rejected the idea of taking the familiar route of writing another historical account or narrative of the large-scale event of Turkey's involvement in World War I, retracing the complex historiographical controversies over the origins of the genocide, and continuing arguments over whether it qualified to be named as a genocide and the long decline of the Ottoman Empire the genocidal event it was designed to stem. There was already a mountain of scholarly literature dedicated to elucidating these themes, and I could add nothing new to the diverse controversies. I was not trained as a specialist in Ottoman or Middle East history, could not read either Armenian or Turkish as starters, and did not have the inclination to approach the genocide from a historical perspective that would always end in the call for more evidence and documentary precision to definitively determine the cause, which would happen only in the last instance; and I knew that history, as such, could not address questions of memory and experience the victims lived through. The appeal to memory expanded experience and experience in turn, as hinted by Mandelstam, enlarges memory's compass, through growth and "stretch[ing]" outward "toward . . . expectation."[2] As a supplement to Mandelstam's earlier insight, Antonio Gramsci once described this kind of phenomenal operation as an "inventory of traces" and explained that "the starting point of critical elaboration is the consciousness of what one really is, and is 'knowing thyself' as a product of the historical process to date which has deposited in you an infinity of traces, without leaving an inventory."[3] Later on in the same passage, Edward Said reminded us that Gramsci emphasized the vital importance "at the outset to compile such an inventory."[4] Said reports that the latter portion of this passage was not translated in the Hoare and Smith translation and appears in the Italian version.[5] What I have thus tried to do in this memoir is to follow the pathways offered by these two perspectives and compile my own inventory of memory traces as they've grown and expanded.

I have never been convinced that the question of the Armenian genocide or any comparable instance of mass murder is reducible to mobilizing more historical evidence to support one or another interpretation. What the endless gathering of more historical documentation produces is deferment that often overlooks the fact that a large number of people were brutally killed in the effort of another group to eliminate them. Scholarship, it seemed to me, was not the answer but perhaps the problem since the more historical information amassed, the less the prospect of achieving some sort of resolution. The process of ceaselessly accumulating additional material and evidence appeared more as some sort of delaying tactic that would permanently displace the necessity of reaching a final conclusion or a minimal consensus yet fulfill some kind of symbolic role among the contesting parties that progress toward a resolution was being made. I have always been convinced that the history of the event that continues to demand representation is not the same as those memories of survivors who became the diaspora and who were said to have "experienced the event" by later historians, even though they would not have known it at the time as historical. Yet it is the weaving of countless stories of unnoticed lives of the perished and survivors concerning what had befallen them and the questions they have raised but must remain unanswered that stubbornly comprise the subject not of a history, as such, but rather a recomposition of when such unanswered questions appeared in the interstices of the daily lives of survivors as they made their way to safety and a new afterlife. It is hard to know what they would have been thinking apart from how to get out. The appearance of such unanswerability at certain moments raises the question of what is prompting them, which is as unanswerable as the answers they offer. But it must say something about why these questions are asked throughout our lives. What I am concerned with is my parents' efforts to escape the threat of imminent death and a past that showed itself as an exhausted endgame that led to the moment of being forced to reinvent themselves in a new present and environment. In this journey they sought to repress through silence what probably refused to go away. My sisters, Sena and Victoria, and I inherited this repressed silence, which, I believe, was imprinted on our subsequent formation into adulthood. Just as I am not interested in recycling the history of the genocide as a subject of historical inquiry, I have no interest or competence to provide a psychological accounting of how the return of the repressed in our parents affected our individual formations.[6] I have found in constructing this recomposition the habitual barriers of expectation that inevitably seek to turn this retelling into the groove of the genocide's history, as if there is no other story and no other way to tell it. Because of this constant collision with habitual barriers, I believe it is important for me to pursue the question of why the experience of surviving became the subject of our parents' collective silence and our inheritance.

My decision to undertake this project thus originated not from the lure of historical scholarship but rather from an intensely personal concern in the long and multigenerational afterlife of the genocidal moment that has remained at the heart of the Armenian diasporas. For Armenians of successive generations like mine, this concern has itself become a form of heritage that obliges each, in its own way, to find adequate form to express this continuing testimony as a necessary condition of preventing the defining memory of the experience from falling into permanent indifference and forgetfulness.

In the world of immigrant studies and diaspora, making it to the shores of the United States or elsewhere meant realizing success in surviving whatever people were running away from but also receiving their ticket to mobility and a secure life. This seemed once to be the established story line. But I suspect that in most cases, like the first generation of Armenian diaspora, immigrants to the U.S. confronted challenges of survival often as great as the ones that drove them out of their natal habitat and into the land of golden opportunity. In this regard, the Armenian experience could claim no exception and was no different from what countless other immigrants endured. Where they may have differed from those migrants who came for a better economic life was posed by the problem of genocide itself, which inducted them into a life course of determined silence to never speak of the calamity and loss that befell them and from which they barely and often accidentally escaped.

What undertaking this project has provoked was the growing conviction that my sisters and I knew little or nothing of the individual experiences of our parents—Ohannes der Harootunian and Vehanush Kupalian—escaping the terror of Turkish massacres. While we knew some objective facts about where our parents came from and something of the tempos of such village lives in premodern Anatolia, we never knew or heard them articulate the actual experience of living through and escaping genocide, what they thought, felt, or believed would happen to them. We were deprived access to any experiential knowledge or even the recollection of crucial memories of that moment. All we could recall were the uncertainties they met as they made their way through the depression years of the new American environment, because we lived it with them. Once embarked on this writing project, lacking any clear-cut direction or even sense of purpose, I increasingly felt how difficult it had become. But the difficulty was also compounded by the sudden realization that I really did not know my parents, much less myself. What this practice taught me was the need to find some mode of communicating a relationship between the two registers of history and the everyday of their lives, between the conceived and the lived, as Kristin Ross has put it, and the difficulty in doing so, given the privilege accorded to the former as a natural national narrative and the transient unreliability of the latter.[7]

The problem I have had to confront is that both parents remained consistently silent on their respective experiences, rarely showing any willingness to share their memories with us and, apart from glimpses gleaned from anecdotes, never directly speaking about them to my two sisters and me. In response to the absence of extensive correspondence between each and their relatives, no family archive of photographs from that time, and a general reluctance to impart the experience of this episode in their lives, I have had to resort to a recomposing of what they might have gone through on the basis of what the three of us were able to recall or thought they had endured from the afterlives of the genocidal moment. This recomposition often resembled an archaeological exposition, sifting through fragmentary traces in order to get a clear idea of how to imagine the totality of a life-form from the remaining, incomplete pieces. While the memoir is concerned with what they must have encountered, felt or imagined, and thought, the account can make no claim to historical authority, as such, since it is about the fragmented memories of an experience of survival, reflected in their split lives, that stayed with them and us throughout the rest of their lives and ours. In this sense, the act of memoration is also one of imagination. Even though my parents rarely spoke of those earlier years when we were growing up, it is evident that the experience of genocide, loss, and escape shadowed their efforts to rebuild their lives in a new and often unwelcome environment and posed a second challenge of survival made even more difficult when they confronted the world depression. Yet, as I have tried to look back on those years, the shape or negative imprint of the earlier experience always remained present in their struggle to navigate through the times of economic and social uncertainty.

The essential point of the memoir is an "encounter with the void," in the sense of political destruction and postdestruction survival. It is driven by the "persistence of unanswered questions lasting from childhood," as well as "imaginings that have tried to satisfy them," about our parents' pasts, what they endured, feared, and even repressed; and it is trailed by an irony of how "genocide becomes reproduced on the everyday level in the form of the victims' silence." We confront the namelessness of relatives we never knew since the past was not allowed to be spoken of, and yet we recognize that "the power to name something animates it into existence." Above all else, the memoir is about the lasting effects of destruction in the lives of my parents that inadvertently became an inheritance passed on to us (my sisters and me) through their practiced silence: "the unspeakable as a heritage."[8] What was destroyed were memories of family relationships of relatives we never knew or experienced and the figure of their everyday lives in Anatolia, which I can only try to reimagine. Yet what was unspeakable, demanding a daily regime of muteness, raised a host of questions that would be repetitively asked the rest of our lives but never answered. What I have tried to do is to organize when and where these unanswered questions appeared, which was in the various phases of everyday life my parents lived from village life in Anatolia, turning inside out into its unimaginable negative; to an everyday filled with the terror of death marches to a desert inferno where those who survived the unscheduled daily marauding and ambushes would surely perish; and finally to the everyday life of permanent exile in new lands for those who managed to escape the Turkish exterminations.

When Sena died in 2017 and I attended a service for her, with my children and grandchildren, it struck me how little I knew of her. I felt like a stranger to even the place I had come to and wondered who was this person who returned to this far-flung suburb of Detroit, which when we were children would have seemed as remote as China, to pay a last respect. I had not seen much of Sena over the years, even though I had managed to visit her with my oldest daughter and her husband a year or so earlier to tap her memory of our parents. But Sena appeared to me as a mystery, like our lives, perhaps even more so than Victoria, who in the intervening years I had seen even less. The reason for this was that when I was a child I had seen and spent more time with Victoria, who had been involuntarily assigned to take me to the movies and watch over me. (On one occasion, she actually saved my life.) In later years, I saw as little of Victoria as I had of Sena. It occurred to me that the lack of contact between Sena, Victoria, and me might have reflected the work of our unwanted legacy, perhaps even stemming from it. Our years as a family unit were quite short, as I recall them, though Sena continued to live with Vehanush and Ohannes after Victoria and I left, caring for them as they aged. How the legacy of void worked was in its capacity to forgo intimacy and even the periodic warmth family relationships are said to engender and inculcate. Our parents were cruelly torn from their own families and deprived of the lasting effects of the quality that cements family life in affect and warmth. This, it seemed to me, is what genocide obliterated as definitively as it did of both of their families and a collective history. The absence of affect and warmth became part of the heritage handed down to the three of us, where, I suspect, it ended. My own children, I have noticed, were better parents than I had been to them. But this should not be taken as a last-moment confession or appeal to apology. We do not choose our legacies and heritages; they choose us, and, like history, they are always the unwanted and uninvited presence shaping our lives, without our knowing it until it is too late to do more than recognize this inheritance. What our parents were forced to forfeit in return for their survival was bequeathed to us to make our way in a land they never understood once they had seen their way to raising us.

Our lives, in this way, bore the mark of a genocide we never experienced and rarely knew or heard about when growing up. Yet, I am convinced, the event and its immense interruptions were always there, accompanying the three of us, as it still is: lives formed on the basis of a void of the silence of unanswered questions.

What I have written is a memoir of mixed forms, not a history. The result is a recomposed account relying on memory and experience, occasionally punctuated by swatches of historical narrative to place the whereabouts of my parents. In this imagined landscape, I have tried to grasp the lived experience of unnoticed lives eclipsed by the larger narratives and how it has shaped us, its inheritors. It is for this reason that I have had to resort to the form of a construction, rather than a reconstruction, which explains my decision to engage in what must be both an act of coaxing memory from its concealment into the light of our time and a commemoration of the heroism displayed by our parents' unaccounted and unnoticed lives in overcoming the immense cultural cleft and economic demands of the almost impossible transition from a premodern traditional order steeped in the reproduction of a natural economy with kin social relationships and unimaginable political oppression to a modernized society dedicated to capitalist production and "possessive individualism." I use the category of transition very loosely, since it invariably implies a distinct linear narrative and is far from the change in environment and everyday life-forms my parents experienced as they moved out of Anatolia and into the United States. Their "narrative" of transition was more like a photo montage or collage composed of different moments thrown together without suggesting any overriding causal linkage. As I now look back upon the trajectory of their lives, I cannot help but think it was frozen into an unrealized transition constituted of unconnected temporalized episodes. It is for this reason that the form of this construction should resemble a montage, whereby episodes and experiences are strung together, implying no single causal relationship but rather reflecting their broken connectedness and the offer of plural interpretative possibilities. In taking this route I have departed from the familiar narrative that predictably progresses on schedule to arrive at its foretold destination. But I will want to try to maintain the tensions of unevenness between the everyday I have imagined lived in different places by my parents and a more distant world history that eventually encroached upon it, loosely resembling the theme of Satyajit Ray's wonderful film *Distant Thunder* (1944), a history preoccupied with remote large-scale events like war and genocide, and the way they finally reach down to alter and lastingly change the village experience of everyday lives forever. The other alternative implied by history is simply to discount this register as too subjective and unverifiable, messy and irrelevant. Yet it is precisely the unverifiable family history unsteadily caught within the orbit of convulsive world historical changes that reveals the inventory of unanswered questions demanding a solution to the adequate form to tell this story. What such a compiling of what Antonio Gramsci has identified as a necessary "inventory of traces" has produced is a series of unconnected tableaux of unspoken scenes, where the principal actors have remained silent.

Reflecting on the theorization of the everyday, the French literary theorist Maurice Blanchot observed that "the everyday escapes. This is its definition.... The everyday is always unrealized in its very actualization," which no event, however important or significant, can ever produce. In fact, the everyday, for him, was "difficult to discover," initially unperceived, "what is never seen for the first time," and always unfinished and capable of escaping closure. In many ways the everyday is the event's other. If we miss its presence, it is because "it belongs to a region where there is still nothing to know . . . not yet information."[9] The everyday rarely produces events—unlike history, where events are its principal staple and everything happens. In the everyday there is only namelessness, anonymity. For the poet Fernando Pessoa it is the office, the street, cafés, homes, churches and town squares.[10] We must remember that we are speaking about a premodern or precapitalist society still retaining an uneven combination of the new and old, where people lead lives remote from their conquerors but never are permitted to forget that they had been conquered. By the same measure, if there is a subject of the everyday, it is undoubtedly the village as a whole that speaks. For me, it is everyone who inhabits the village precinct. Nothing ever happens in the everyday, Henri Lefebvre once reported, except "everything changes."[11] In the Anatolia of the Ottoman Empire, it must be asked: For whom was nothing happening? Who are we talking about? Interaction between Armenians and Turkish folk would be limited, unless one was living in a large urban area. In this environment, minorities like Armenians spoke both Armenian and Turkish and communication was grounded in rumor, conveyed by the village grapevine; everything was said and heard endlessly without ever being confirmed. In the eyes of the Turkish authorities, the everyday of the Armenian was seen to be safely under the jurisdiction of the priest, who led the *millet* system, which supposedly was to make sure that nothing would be permitted to happen. In this world empire, the minority communities like the Armenians were, for stretches of time, self-enclosed enclaves, centered on the church, until confronted by unscheduled administrative intrusions demanding revenue and pogroms by neighboring Islamic Kurds or Circassians aiming to settle land disputes by force.

Blanchot, especially, reminds us that as inhabitants or occupants of the everyday, we have "no more access to its confines" than to any moment in history "that could be historical."[12] If this observation allows us to loop back to the absence of eventfulness in the everyday—driven by a sense, particularly in precapitalist societies, that such precincts have no beginning or end, unless its inhabitants are obliterated—we know that no event, however great, can produce the actualization of the everyday. Yet events, as signified by a moving "distant thunder," can gradually overtake the precincts of everydayness. In this regard, the everyday stands apart from history, outside its eventfulness, yet strangely institutes it without knowing it has. By the same measure, history has been lifted to stand above the parochial rootedness of the everyday as its noisy eventfulness points to the spreading drama of world historical movement and meaning, where things of importance happen and begin to spill over into everydayness. Once occupying this register, history denies its relationship to the everyday and becomes a kind of "blind spot," which opens the pathway to overcoming by a process of forceful elimination. In this regard, a French observer of the Armenian genocide, Etienne Copeaux, was probably close to the truth when he proposed that the mass murders were similar to cutting off legs and limbs.[13] My difference with this is that what seemed to hold my attention is not the figure of imperial dismemberment the genocide most surely carried out but rather the wish to show that the event did not necessarily end one hundred years ago and has continued to persist as an afterlife in every present since the inaugural moment. For me, the issue was how to say something about everyday lives that no longer existed. In this regard, this desire derives from my own failure to raise certain questions with my parents while they were still alive. The heritage I wanted to unveil is the image of ordinary everyday life lived by Armenians until they were uprooted through mass acts of murder and destruction. It was this experience, not of the eventful history as such, that the diaspora has tried to recuperate in countless places the survivors have found refuge. This prior Anatolian everyday life has remained somewhat invisible down to the present, apart from its anecdotal existence recounted in Armenian households of the diaspora. In most cases, it was crowded out of the historical accounts that concentrated on the larger narrative of World War I, Turkey's involvement in it, and the collapsing fortunes of a dysfunctional empire. In this world historical narrative of eventfulness, there was no room for any consideration of the everydayness lived by countless Armenians or indeed other oppressed minorities of the empire. There was no fund of ethnographic reports, and few contemporary descriptions of the lives led in Anatolia. There was little subsequent attempt to rescue this everyday life that had virtually disappeared, and most intellectual energy was, and still is, poured into providing historical evidence of Turkey's direct initiative and involvement in the massacre as a product of the circumstances of World War I.

Not too many years ago, on a trip to Istanbul, I met and spoke with a number of Turkish anthropologists who asked where I came from, as if I were the man who fell to Earth. What they wanted to know was how my parents managed to escape and what their lives were like. I had the sense that none seemed to have much interest or ethnographic knowledge of Anatolia's murdered minorities: the Armenians, Greeks, Assyro-Chaldeans. At the time, I felt that it was almost as if they were persuaded that Armenians were an invention of diasporas, that the migration experience conferred upon them their identity, which originated elsewhere but not in Anatolia. I may have been too quick in refusing to take a trip to explore the possibility that documents related to my father's family still existed in Harput, but I still should have taken the offer to see the region in which he lived his early life.

In the end, finding a way to construct this cloaked everyday life, whose pale and often abstracted contour appeared in diaspora life, left little choice other than to reimagine it. Through the exercise of an imaginary recomposing of the memory of our parents' lives, not by means of empathic entry presuming the possibility of standing in one's place, or shoes, as hermeneutics believed conceivable, I thought it might be feasible to construct and memorialize at the same time. It is probable that this pathway of imagined recomposing is also accessible through an act of Socratic anamnesis, the rediscovery of a knowledge of the past that is within us. This would entail a form of self-excavation, digging out what we might know or has been embedded there all the time, without actually knowing it. The Dutch psychoanalyst and historian Eelco Runia suggests a similar perspective for performing a personal archaeological procedure when he advises digging into the present for the presence of the past, which coexists but remains unseen like Poe's "purloined letter," or hidden, perhaps closer to the psychoanalytic model than the Socratic method.[14] But this book's epigraph from the poet Osip Mandelstam suggests memory is about the slightest hint of recognition and growth.

The difficulty of a form of life writing that attempts to account for how my parents managed to evade a genocide and make their way to a new land was especially made evident even before I decided to undertake this project. I knew there simply was not enough material to work with, given the absence of the most basic facts they may have made known to us in daily life as we were growing up. But there were other reasons for my reluctance. It was not a subject I had ever thought about researching and writing on. As a historian, I had made a prior decision to specialize in another region of history. I had no ambition to try writing another history of the collapsing Ottoman Empire and the genocide. Apart from lacking the necessary qualifications such an undertaking requires, I was convinced that such histories reveal very little about the lives of the victims, apart from discounting them. Their existence was already outside the narrative histories and their deaths erased as instances of collateral damage resulting from World War I.

In terms of genres, I had never been an enthusiastic reader of biography, which I always saw as a fictional form that moved according to the coordinates of an orderly linear trajectory, as if anybody's life were organized so conveniently.[15] How could precapitalist Anatolian peasants be grasped within a culturally specific and temporally bound framework steeped in the formation of a specific subjectivity? Worse still, biography was usually a favored form among historians, especially, to get at the microscopic dimension of the larger history. Most biographies invariably try to address a larger subject or event or temporal referent as if the individual life will, in some metonymically magical way rarely explained, illuminate it. The usual result is to displace the very event the biography supposedly illustrates. Acts of biographical enshrinement are often misrecognized as prescient illuminations. The perspective that seeks in a biography the key to the larger contours of historical events and currents attempts to account for the relationship between the world historical level of eventfulness and a missing mundane everyday, marked by repetitive routine events, without actually articulating the connection. While Pierre Bourdieu dismissed biography as ideologizing a life, Jean-Paul Sartre discounted the genre as a genetic fallacy, but this was before he wrote his interminable account of Gustave Flaubert.[16]

Hence, all that seemed reasonably promising was an effort to record those lived aspects of our parents' lives that we (my sisters and me) were still able to recall, long after the catastrophic event brought them eventually to the U.S., carrying unwanted memories and experiences they had decided not to share with their children. Such an approach would require moving backward from I what had experienced and seen, without fully understanding, to imagine the negative imprint of a memory of their earlier life and experience—its presence in the present time. Under such circumstances, it was necessary for me to assume the fictive figure of an uninvited intruder in their thoughts and try to probe and pry them loose from their silent confinement, or imagine what they might have been, where they had been deposited for so long. This tactic comes close to Antonio Gramsci's observation that sediments and traces of a historical process are deposited in each individual, without leaving a fixed inventory. Such an approach, lacking an account of the stock, would have to look for the fragmentary signs in the thick displacements employed to conceal tracks to locate where some residue might have been left. The things remembered relate to our parents' survival in the U.S. (not the genocide), a struggle involving my sisters and me that represented, in its own way, perhaps as great a challenge to staying alive as what they faced in the midst of massacre. It seems likely to assume that the earlier experience and fears the genocide engendered were always close to them in the new environment, as if it had become a form of second nature now serving a new function. In other words, the vague figure of the genocide was always present in and shadowing the new struggle to make a secure life in the U.S., not necessarily the burden of collective guilt for having been among the survivors. It never seemed to any of us that either our mother or our father was weighted down with unrelieved guilt, even though my father's loss of an entire extended family and home were inestimable. And, in reality, I never knew what he actually felt, what memories he cherished of his lost family and vigilantly watched over and how he managed to negotiate or navigate through depths of despair to continue living. I never asked these questions, or even knew how to ask them, much less envision how they might be answered. But these unasked and unanswered questions would provide the negative print of the silence both parents had embraced. Just as we were never persuaded that our parents internalized some form of collective trauma that inhibited them from speaking of the horror the rest of their lives, even though it might have been the case for individuals who had been in positions to provide direct testimony—people such as the priest Grigoris Balakian, who nonetheless recorded what he saw on his death march. Balakian himself did not appear to be afflicted by trauma-induced paralysis but rather was driven by the necessity of staying alive, as if to provide later witness and testimony to the existence of what he knew would be denied again and again throughout the decades following the event. But it is undeniably true that the relationship of expressions of silence and a willingness to speak of trauma are not always clear-cut. Silence need not simply signify the presence of trauma, and the speech of a witness like Grigoris Balakian need not denote the absence of trauma. The gravity of our parents finding their way in American life would have taxed their collective energies and subsumed whatever guilt for surviving they may have harbored, and it assisted them to overcome whatever despair they must have experienced and endured. What they experienced separately when young seemed to have no place in a later life in an entirely different environment led together with children.

While the memoir's chapters seek to return and recompose experiences and memories of my parents at certain moments, in the manner of a photomontage without presuming causal relations, chapter 4, "History's Interruption: Dispossession and Genocide," is an attempt to show the direct relationship between massive theft and murder, what Karl Marx variously called "so-called primitive accumulation" or "original accumulation" (*ursprüngliche Akkumulation*) of capital. For Marx, primitive or original accumulation referred not to the moment of the movement of the actual process of the accumulation of capital as such, with the existence in place of the whole system of capitalist production, but rather "an accumulation which is not the result of the capitalist mode of production but its point of departure." The duration of such an accumulating process did not lead to the transition of a completed capitalism, as once believed by an older Marxism; instead, this process inaugurated the necessary presuppositions and conditions for the installation of a capitalist production program dedicated to the accumulation of surplus value. Marx saw such a time filled with "conquest, enslavement, robbery, murder, mass rape, in short, force play(ing) the greatest part." Not a blissful time but "from the beginning . . . the sole means of enrichment, the methods of primitive accumulation are anything but idyllic."[17] Thus, in Marx, primitive accumulation made visible the history of violence, bloodshed, and massive displacement of the population from its means of subsistence that ultimately accounted for capital's appearance. In *Grundrisse*, he referred to this event as the moment of separation and divorce of the producer from the means of production and subsistence. But primitive or original accumulation is not a one-time big-bang event but rather a process that is repetitive, temporally mixed in its different directions, and continuing in diverse times and places down to our own present. In fact, it is because "primitive accumulation" will occur repeatedly that there can be no singular transition as a linear trajectory leading directly to the outcome of a developed capitalism. In this way, it conforms only to a temporal moment, instead of a designated stage in the putative "transition" to capitalism. Transition, according to one historian, permits us to envision a "prolonged process of change" in societies in which capital accumulation coexists with received economic practices from prior modes of production and "political formations not yet . . . capitalist."[18] We are rightly warned that to see transition as a stage leading directly to capitalism assumes that the social process moves along a linear developmental path. Moreover, such a perspective encourages historians to emphasize socioeconomic forces that structured the development of capital but overlooks the actual consequences of the social process and what happens to the reproduction of society. In our case, this refers to the complete destruction of Armenian everyday life in Anatolia. What distinguishes the implementation of a genocidal impulse serving the interests of large-scale expropriation of wealth from others and theft facilitated by mass murder is the process that aims to eradicate the everyday lived by those targeted for elimination. I shall return to this theme of genocide and its relationship to its fateful social process and its transition to mass death.

TWO. UNNOTICED LIVES/UNANSWERED QUESTIONS

My father found job security only with the outset of World War II, which brought an end to the economic depression of the thirties. Growing up in such a "landscape," as the British historian Carolyn Steedman has described the environment of her youth,[1] we learned early that in an allegedly "classless" America, one of the great destructive myths of American social life, class was everywhere and everything—in the schools, everyday social encounters, the workforce, consumption, and so on—enforcing its distances and exclusions. Ethnicity was, as I look back at the communities it authorized, a necessity and the best defense against those class-driven distances and exclusions. What is interesting about class in the United States is not that it was allegedly absent but rather the way it was disavowed by those who represented its upper orders. Ethnicity then, and apparently even now, was used to masquerade class and displace its force through appeals of assmilationism, even though the promise of assimilation could fortify the very structure of ethnicity it hoped to remove.. It did so by an act of distancing those who were identified or marked as belonging to a different minority ethnic group. But there are ethnicities and ethnicities. In the United States, the size of the community and its capacity to generate wealth mattered and constituted assistance to successful assimilation. Size also counted for political reasons; the larger ethnic groups, like the Irish and Italians, would represent important constituencies especially in urban areas, where their appeals could be heard. Armenians in the United States were and continue to be a numerically small group, the largest wave coming in the wake of the Turkish massacres at the time of World War

I and after World War II when Armenian "displaced people" throughout Europe found their way here, usually to California. California—especially Fresno and communities in the Central Valley, and Los Angeles—was already home to a sizeable Armenian American population, and seemed to be a magnet drawing new immigrants. By this time, in the years immediately after World War II, there were ethnically based social service agencies in place to assist the new wave from abroad. And, according to my father, weather played a major role in attracting this generation of Armenian migrants to the West Coast.

As an ethnic group, the earlier wave of Armenian migrants invariably carried their minority status in the Ottoman Empire to the shores of American democracy, wearing the emblem of the unwanted, which thus permitted the continuation of how they had been considered for so long. Yet it is difficult to know whether the life of the diaspora created an Armenian identity or simply reinforced it more intensely from their history in Anatolia under Ottoman domination and the effects of genocide. Members of the earlier diaspora were usually on their own, without the assistance of social service agencies and momentarily described as the "starving Armenians," an abstract cliché and a genuine insensitive and thoughtless identification of the tragic plight of a people's contemporary fate used by American parents to elicit sympathy for their genocidal plight by trying to persuade their children to finish eating the food on their plate. Whether or not the cliché succeeded in its new assignment to induce American children to clean off their plates, it branded the Armenian into a figure of permanent helplessness and negativity. Nobody, in effect, knew who Armenians were, unless one happened to be a Greek, a Syrian, or an Assyrian. I always encountered people, as I still do, who would feel obliged to comment on my name, how "unusual" it seemed, and ask where "it comes from." When I finally identified its ethnic origin, the response usually faded into the phrase *an interesting name* or some such concluding banality. Growing up as a second-generation offspring of migrant parents, I soon learned that American racism was not reducible to the binary of black and white (the binary in American life has always seemed a favorite and convenient way of categorizing things and may have been an unacknowledged inheritance from slavery) but to the plurality of gradations of color and unpronounceable names that produce a more complex configuration of racial discrimination, which makes the generally accepted dominant racial duality look like a practically expedient but dangerous simplification. Before the Johnson Immigration Act of 1924, groups from the

Middle East, like Armenians, were all classified under the general category of Orientals along with ethnicities farther east. In national surveys carried out in the 1920s and after, designed to gauge national characteristics and how Americans felt about living among diverse ethnic groups, Armenians, like others from the same regions, were identified with Turks, who were classified low on most scales and seen as cruel, treacherous, sensual, ignorant, physically dirty, and so forth. These surveys sought to show a relationship between stereotypes and the formation of public opinion. Stereotypical national traits appeared as unsteady and unstable opinions subject to the whims of change. According to Helen McCready Kearney's valuable study of American images of the Middle East, Armenians in the nineteenth century were considered "benighted," "avaricious, "cunning," and usually not much different from Turks. But the "temporary phenomenon" of Christians being massacred brought a change in attitudes: they became "intelligent," "industrious," "prudent," and "temperate," now seen in the light of empathy for coreligionists. Once the genocide had ended and passed into collective forgetfulness, the positive images disappeared, leaving only the plaint of the "starving Armenians" as an inducement to American children to clean off their dinner plates.[2] I remember hearing reverberations of this plea a decade later. The plight of the "starving Armenians" was resituated in Depression Detroit, and perhaps elsewhere, as a metaphorical admonition reminding people of the necessity to waste nothing, resulting in the disappearance of the figure of the Armenian that had inspired it.

But these were not lessons children easily learned, as they began to mix with others who, as Steedman writes, had more of the things we would have liked to have had, social relations that disclosed to us what we lacked, and the image of a future that belonged to others by right of a historic inheritance. It should be said that linking ethnicity to class in this way actually worked to overdetermine both social and political exclusions and distances lived by most immigrants. If America, as preached by earlier generations of sociologists, economists, and historians, had no class, it was the excess of ethnicities and the racial marking that displaced the category to keep people in their place through enforced racial distance. Social science in the time of the Great Depression sought to counter the possibility of conflict by resorting to a conceptualization of an exceptionalist social formation, free from class divisions, now replaced by diverse ethnicities constituting a plural and solidary unity of difference. The desired absence of class, especially, meant that society was supposedly equipped with a safety valve that would re-equilibrate the social system when confronted by the instance disorder. From the standpoint of political leadership, ethnicity had the advantage over class inasmuch as its own sense of exclusion and inclusions kept groups separated and apart, whereas class had the propensity to bring people of different ethnic groups together into a constituency of solidarity, capable of unifying support for demands based on shared interests that, if not met, could lead to mobilized conflict. Class, rather than ethnicity, was particularly important to ethnic groups, like Armenians, who were numerically small and had no effective lever as a political constituency.

What was even worse than the unfulfilled desire to have the materiality of those who appeared far better off than us was the awful sense that they possessed something we would never have. Most of my male contemporaries from migrant families were destined for factory work in Detroit's many auto factories reproducing the lives of our first-generation immigrant fathers, while females had open to them the even narrower world of stenographic jobs and early marriage and homekeeping.

I am still not sure why our parental silence did not induce more curiosity in us; part of it may have derived from a continuing uncertainty concerning who we were, which referred to knowing we had been born and lived in the U.S., but the nature of our lives and its principal relationships came from the community of the diaspora. There is no question that this sense of uncertainty was reinforced by the identification of our birthplace and that this life, in all its immediacy, seemed to take precedence over any inquiry as to where our parents came from and what they were forced to endure. In not trying to break the wall of silence separating us, we were, inadvertently, complicit in their conspiracy and the confused conviction that all our lives began in the U.S. I think it is as if their lives started with ours; nothing else preexisted it. Our mother would have probably gone along with this origin story, as an enthusiastic modernizer before her time. It is not clear that this is a more familiar story about American immigrant life than the "inspiring" patriotic tales of what a great melting pot this place is, one that supposedly eliminated class and dissolved different identities to forge a new alloyed and unified social solidarity in the foundries and factories of industrialism that welcomed the new army of migrant workers. In fact, this unfortunately misguided but persisting mythic metaphor was finally reset in its proper place by Theodor Adorno in the 1940s when he acutely observed that "the melting pot was introduced by industrial capitalism. The thought of being cast into it conjures up martyrdom, not democracy."[3] I was only able to scratch together vague vignettes of the lives they had led before coming to the U.S., pieced together out of random shards of conversations I heard over time. But because they withheld so much about their lives, my account was destined to remain unresolvable, unfinished, a narrative without an expected plausible end or even a beginning.

Our only relatives were a few distant cousins on my father's side, and we had no archival album of sepia-toned photographs of members of either our mother's or father's families in Anatolia. Yet what few photographs we had impressed upon me the idea that sepia with the proper shade of coloring and opacity was the best way to describe the tint of those years. A few photos exist of our parents when younger, one of my father with his second cousin Avedis (see photo gallery) that must have been taken in Anatolia by the look of their age and the way they were dressed, the one holding the hand of the other; years later in Detroit this close relationship seemed more remote when we visited with Avedis and his family. There is another photograph of my oldest sister, Sena, as an infant, and a few of my father posing with her at that age. There was no fund of knick-knack remainders from the "old country," the kind of tchotchkes Svetlana Boym lovingly describes in her family's cramped apartment in Soviet Russia,[4] not even the expected Oriental rug hanging on the wall indexing a historical moment of desperate flight. The flight meant traveling light. They came with nothing and not surprisingly left with little. I glimpsed flashes of their unspeakable experience from fragments of stories overheard among their adult friends but rarely, if ever, directly from them. My father, Ohannes, was more loquacious, a born storyteller, than my mother, who apparently had no stories to tell or that she felt worth repeating. She appeared more deliberately reflective, taciturn, and reluctant to express her own witness to the prospect of unimaginable desert death marches designed to eliminate the Armenian population. She would have been younger than Ohannes at that time, and this may have been one of the conditions of her silence. But in Marash, where she was from, she would have known about the marches, as the deportees filed through the streets of the town to their final destination, and she may have even caught glimpses of them being pushed by indifferent but barking Turkish armed guards. Despite the low-level technology involved in resettling large numbers of a population in an environmental inferno where nothing grew, the resulting mass deaths by starvation and dehydration, and murder and widespread rape along the route, reflected a deliberately planned and truly cruel form of humiliation that made the actual killing fields look almost benign. I shall say more of the Turkish decision leading to not only mass murder but also the apparent enjoyment and rewards it offered in the need to humiliate that accompanied it. The deportation order was actually conceived as an instrument that provided the tactical opportunity to pursue murder, rape, mutilation, and looting along the way.

My mother, Vehanush, was a student enrolled in a German missionary school and orphanage in Marash, a city that was only one of the deportation routes to Der Zor and desert death. She acquired the status of orphan because she had been given up by her mother in order to receive an education and some guarantee of safety, as her brother was given up to a Jesuit school. The stories my father told, as I now recall them, related to what he remembered of his early years before the inauguration of the major massacres of 1915, growing up in southeastern Anatolia and village life not far from the contemporary city of Harput. At one level he portrayed an agricultural village like others throughout Anatolia, where everybody knew each other or was related to each, and the principal means of travel and transport was the mule. In fact, it was a world that measured space and time according to the "mule's way." At another level he knew that this rural scene had already been raked over by earlier incidents in the 1890s engineered by the regime of Sultan Abdülhamid II. Unlike later historians, my father had no trouble linking these incidents to a continuing chain of similar episodes culminating in the systematic murders of 1915, contrary to "scholarly" opinion that privileged the primary causal relationship of Turkey's involvement in World War I as providing the occasion for genocidal eruption. My mother had no stories of her childhood that identified some kind of village life. In fact, it was hard to imagine she had a childhood until she entered the missionary school; it is even harder to imagine what constituted this preschool time of her life. Her life began with entry into the mission school and even this environment provided few retrospective glimpses she would share with us. Her later life in the U.S. repeated the same pattern of her earlier disidentification from Anatolian village life.

It struck me that the experience of our parents' survival of the genocide might provide some kind of guide for enduring in the new environment by remaining a powerful but shadowed presence for both that never left them, despite their habitual reluctance to talk about it in front of us or to raise it in such ways as to induce in us further questions. What these two moments shared, in spite of their spatial and even temporal remoteness, was capital's force: its relentless elimination of lived cultures of reference and brutal destabilization of whole populations. It is not at all evident that our parents would have seen the relationship between the two episodes in this way. But I know they would have grasped the family resemblances between the two sequences, inasmuch as they would have recognized the similar challenge presented to their capacity for survival and how the experience of the genocide might have prepared them as a prefiguration for their new ordeal.

If the Turkish massacres of the Armenians instantiated the moment when people were robbed of their means of subsistence, which ultimately would explode in a frenzied "slaughter of the innocents," diaspora and migrant life in the United States was no more stable or secure for those who, for one reason or another, had fled their natal homes and found momentary refuge in an alien land that bore no resemblance to what they had been forced to leave. The question was how to account for the lives of my parents before they migrated to the U.S. to join the unaccounted. I would have liked to know if they saw what was coming on the horizon, if they sensed it, like a distant storm, whose tuned announcement was still barely audible. It was also related to the silence we experienced, about us and unanswerable. My father would have been old enough to make such a judgment or hear it from his elders. I believe he was politicized early in the politics of the Armenian Revolutionary Federation (ARF), which stayed with him until he died, but its politics had been replaced by the sociality it subsequently was still capable of offering in the new environment. How and under what circumstances he was recruited into its fold he never divulged. My mother was probably too young, but even in the time spent in the missionary school before 1915, she would have been filled with apprehension fueled by rumor and hearsay. Moreover, it is difficult to believe that living in such a society, as a conquered and oppressed minority sensitized to their difference from a dominant population, had not involuntarily socialized people at the earliest age to the certainty of unscheduled depredations and death. When I was older I felt that that this portion of their lives had simply vanished, enclosed in some forgotten memory bank they refused to release and that would have to be imagined from what I knew of their lives in the U.S.

What seemed important was trying to grasp an everyday for which no real or reliable record existed. It might be asked for whom such an absent everyday is to be grasped. My initial answer would have been for my sisters and myself; I would not have determined this when I was child since it would not have meant anything to me and I would not have been able to imagine it. But as I grew older and became more aware or conscious that their early lives were a mystery to me, I wanted to solve or at least fill in those blank years with their lived history. As time passed, it came to me that if what I discovered about the relationship of everyday life and genocide and what Turkey gained from it was useful to others, so much the better. My initial purpose was to look for traces or marks in the stories my father told, for some testimony of the experience and possibility of entry into it. Vehanush was more disciplined, guarded, it seemed to me, to make sure she would not involuntarily reveal anything about what she might have seen and experienced in those years. Ohannes probably had more to say from what he saw and lost; Vehanush had to live with the memory of a child who whose mother had abandoned her and would not return. But my primary concern was to provide our parents with some sort of living history before they came to the United States. Why did that strike me as important? Was it because I believed that their Anatolian past would, in some way, explain their lives more fully? What concerned me most was the question that if they shared the same kind of everyday life of Armenians in Anatolia, what allowed them separately to get out? How did they avoid perishing in the killing fields or forced deportation marches to the Syrian Desert? Diversity among victims of genocide would reflect only an expression of the narcissism of small differences. In fact, I thought that one of the major problems hindering our understanding of the genocide is the way it has been separated or deliberately bracketed from the horrors of everyday life lived by those who were caught in the programs' deadly annihilating machine. What I mean by this is that the genocide signified a world historical event inaugurated by the Ottoman state precisely at the moment it entered World War I as an ally of the Central Powers. It was thus the event of the war itself that conferred upon it historical status, whereas the lived everyday, the actual staging ground of the genocidal event and the scene of its killing fields, where it was played out throughout Armenian villages in Anatolia, was seen merely as a reflection of the war's terrible destructive power—as a secondary effect or even collateral damage. Its scale and seeming suddenness would have been unimaginable to most at the time and certainly incomprehensible but never forgettable. It seems that it is enough to find a conceptual term like *genocide* to generally cover the event of mass murder; however, this does not account for the calamitous destruction inflicted on the everyday lives of its victims apart from providing quantitative representation of the numbers killed and nothing more. Equally important is the incalculable problem of trying to imagine how the unnoticed survivors were able to pick up their lives and reconstruct the semblance of some everyday life in distant and alien environments.

What has thus prevailed and even persisted is the narrative of an other's history, which Armenians had been trying to get out of, to once more encase them within its inescapable determining logic. In this way, the everyday was only the insubstantial shadow of history, the temporary index of a negative imprint, sometimes elongated, at other times truncated, often even shapeless, but never distinct or disconnected from history, however removed it appeared, always poised at a point of disappearing yet having an autonomous presence. The separation clearly entailed a division between history (an event that happened, presumably based on facts capable of verification and measurement, that is, dating or chronology, and grounded in the "authority" of documents), and the everyday (as the domain of subjective experience and memory, neither reliably datable nor empirically certifiable, located in history's shadows). Yet the repository of affect and emotion was absent in historical narratives. This vast, shapeless shadowland, nevertheless, was the scene that produced the oversized storehouse of unanswerable questions for those who managed to survive the destruction of their everyday, which, like the scattered ruins of Ani, would remain a continuing mystery dedicated to disturbing successive generations, never able, like the randomly strewn and scattered rocks of the great medieval city, to reconstitute the wholeness that had been shattered. By contrast, historical narratives bring to light "objectively" and distinctively verifiable components of a story line usually illustrating the figure of the nation. There is no mystery here nor place for the unanswerable. By bringing to the surface measures relating to events, such as their dating and further forms of verifying their existence in time, the form of the narrative has already shaped and prefigured what will be included to constitute a national experience and what will be excluded. Left out are the remainders, the messier experiences and memories of individual lives, the repetition of ordinary lives of the nameless, which remain faded reflections clinging for identification to the national experience, like the form of their everydayness, which is presumed to be only an extension of the nation-form, the result of a trickle-down effect. Yet national history in this regard is really the site of national ideology principally because its primary object of narrative begins and ends with the nation-form. What seeps into the everyday to contain it is its ideology. For the Armenians of Anatolia, there was no national history, as such, only the more remote episodes that momentarily culminated in the achievement of Ani and the long years of shaded visibility in empire's history.

The philosopher Paul Ricoeur once asked whether history actually was the remedy to the subjective and experiential excesses of memory or its poison.[5] What he seemed concerned with was the separation of the two forms of retention and the order of their relationship. If history was a remedy, it could act as a necessary supplement, taming by mediating memory's experiential self-indulgence; if it was its poison, it would bring an end to its claims to rescue the past. But what Ricoeur failed to consider perhaps is that a little poison might be the cure. Ricoeur recognized that history, as a domain of knowledge, had, since Georg Wilhelm Friedrich Hegel, freed itself from memory, not by rejecting it out of hand but by putting itself at a distance from it. He knew that any attempt to short-circuit the relationship and forcibly bring them together could produce serious consequences for history by contaminating its own vocation committed to securing a verifiable knowledge and quantifying commensurables.[6] But the threat of such contamination of history and historiography by the spectacle of unwanted incommensurables and the insistence of memory lay not so much in its capacity to compel history in its aptitude to privilege the profoundly subjective, by making selections that often disregarded the "chronological scansions," but in its indifference to the reconstructions of a group and to identifying the global rationalizations that might ultimately explain an event or occurrence.[7] The real problem implied but not stated by Ricoeur is precisely the appearance of those unscheduled moments when an occurrence exceeds historical expectation and spills over, when history and memory are involuntarily thrown together and their differences blurred and diminished. The Turkish genocide, in spite of its earlier preparation, was such an event that swept away so many hundreds of thousands of lives and left only the rubble, residues, and ruins of a once lived everyday, bringing to the surface a long and lamentable history inaugurated by the disappearance of Ani. The genocide's fragmented afterlife conveyed by the testimonies of witnesses has consistently shown how this involuntary encounter of history and memory, and the violent collision of history and the everyday produced unanswered questions in the lives of surviving victims but also prompted their search for new ways of testimony to assert the truth of what they were able to recall and what they refused to remember. It is in such circumstances that we are forced to rely on the scraps of memory in our search to verify the unanswerable.

Ricoeur, perhaps inadvertently, also hinted at the existence of two different modes of cognition in history's reliance on narrative and the everyday as the domain of memory and experience. He did not go further than suggesting the possible toxic dangers of subjective experiences awaiting the historical reconstruction and the need for watchfulness of its excessive demands. But by considering the relationship between history and memory, he raised the question of how they might be put together in a way they are both permitted to speak their separate truths without endangering each other's respective vocational claims. I have always felt that social history was an attempt to bring historical narrative together with the singularity and specificity of everyday memory and experience. It tried to join together the two cognitive modalities only by subordinating and assimilating the subjective residues of everydayness to social history's own form of narrative reconstruction and privileging of data and chronology over experience. For our purposes, it is necessary to find a way to give both cognitive forms equal time and voice. In fact, it is important to consider them in relationship to each other because they embodied different paces and forms of time and its passage rather than constitute the components of a full story. I have found that the form that best embodies this capacity is the photomontage or collage, the juxtaposing of narrative to memory without implying a singularly linear causal chain in order to show how they may or not leak into each other.[8] Broken lives hinted at by partial memories cannot be made whole by resituating them in the context of a coherent history. But the collage captures more modestly fractured memory traces and makes no effort to connect them to a structuring story line. They exist along side each other.

What the storytelling accounts reveal is an intimate relationship between memory formation based on recalling momentary experiences and their immediate contexts in the everyday. But it should be qualified that referring to memory's capability does not mean that everything will be remembered. Selection will always prevail and some things will always remain unsaid. The appeal to stories implies a separation of the lived present at the level of the everyday from a nation's (empire's) own repetitious attempt to reorder the present according to the narrative templates of the national or imperial past's history or what it has been conceived to be. In this regard, the separation shows how the everyday meets the task of constructing a different political time that combines the past, through the memory and experience of what is near at hand, with the new demands of the present, which enables the writing of its own (the everyday), different kind of history. The way into everydayness and out of the historical as we have come to understand it was to enter the domain of experience and memory, a terrain of different forms of patterning, as the basis of putting together some kind of record. Such an accounting would increasingly become an imagined figuration, in my parents' case, even hopefully a form of personal commemoration, since the experience and memories I needed to employ were absent and unavailable. Growing up in an Armenian household with two parents who had escaped genocide and found refuge in the United States gave me no privileged perspective or supply of memories on which I could draw. Even the organization of a ghetto-like existence of migrants of a diasporic flight proved to be fictional representations of village life left behind, another kind of imagined community, the imitations of a lost life now strained to be remembered, and a homogenized averaging of the immeasurable heterogeneity of regions and locales comprised by the survivors. I have often felt that the imaging of diaspora life was based more on generalized attempts to reconstruct prior village life as represented in memory.

In any event, historical narratives that record and seek to explain the genocide have not been very helpful, apart from providing frameworks of chronology that allow tracking the movements of my parents. Involuntary slippage into the historical mode has been of little use in trying to get at the experiences of people at the level of their everyday encounters, when they have left little information to even get a glimpse of this life or no testimony at all. For people who have been drawn into the vortex of genocidal events, both those who have been murdered and those who have managed to escape, I have the sense that the event, as such, no longer exists. For the murdered dead, it is nonexistent, but for the living survivors it represents either something invisible or a jumble of fragmented and chaotic memories. With personal experiences of such magnitude and disorder, only the singularizing of its immediate experience offers a viable glance. We must remember that the loss experienced was total. The Armenians and other minorities targeted for expulsion and mass murder lost everything—home, churches, fields, relatives, friends, and environments in which they had been embedded for centuries—while the Turks, who complained that the dissolution of empire resulted in a loss of territory, faced losing local craftsmen, shopkeepers, and possibly friends. It should be noted that Grigoris Balakian asserts, in his record of what he had seen and heard in the time he marched with one of the deportation columns to the Syrian Desert, that "within Turkish society the artisans were mainly

Christians. The Turks and other Islamic peoples, generally speaking, were peasants, soldiers, clergymen, or government employees. Sometimes they were grocers, vegetable vendors, halvah sellers [*helvaji*], or chickpea sellers, but 90 percent of the Turkish people were engaged in farming, under primitive and strenuous conditions."[9] In Adana alone, Armenian artisans retained by the Turkish military authorities functioned as tailors, shoemakers, blacksmiths, coach makers, carpenters, ironsmiths, weavers, saddle makers, tinsmiths, and workers in factories that produced military necessities. Balakian was convinced that the "entire commercial life of Turkey's interior provinces was in the hands of the Armenians, and with the Greeks they shared in the foreign trade of the harbors."[10] Whatever the case, what seems certain is that Armenians, in rural Anatolia, constituted both the classes of agricultural laborers and petty bourgeois artisans and other skilled tradesmen as well as specialized professions. It is clear that in addition to ethnic and religious divisions between Armenians and Turks, there was a significant class difference that usually is overlooked in historical accounts preoccupied with ethnic and religious differences. At the same time, this does not ignore the deep divisions within the Armenian communities in cities like Istanbul and the countryside. According to the historian Gerard J. Libaridian, newly formed Armenian political parties reinforced sensitivity toward class divisions, especially between rich and poor, urban and peasant. Before that time, conflict among Armenians often came down between those in the provinces who were content to live under arrangements provided by the millet system and those who had larger aspirations of nationhood rooted in urban centers and "controlled the *millet* institutions."[11]

During moments when the state inflicted murderous pogroms on Christians, the acts were usually justified as "retribution for Christian monopolies in the Turkish economy, particularly domestic and foreign commerce, retail trade, and shipping." For this reason the "Christians were characterized as ferocious leeches that were sucking the blood of the poor Turkish people, getting rich at their expense."[12] This kind of information was later grossly exaggerated in gossip and rumor, whereby the Unionists (the Young Turks) employed countrywide communication through the "grapevine," circulating it throughout the interior provinces as a means of mobilizing Turkish peasants into complicit murderous mobs against Armenian and other Christian peasants to make of the genocide a mass movement. In the stories I remember, I do not believe my father ever mentioned Turkish friends or even Turkish and Kurdish artisans even though narratives centered on Istanbul usually dramatized a cosmopolitan environment where Armenian bourgeoisie mingled with Turks and Europeans. This is the world of Gabriel Bagradian, Franz Werfel's protagonist portrayed early in the novel *The Forty Days of Musa Dagh*, which he must eventually leave for the countryside of his childhood home and the defense of the villages of Musa Dagh. This division between urban cosmopolite and rural peasantry probably derived from the administrative separation established by the millet system, which worked to differentiate and segregate minority populations from Muslims. It was also encouraged by the large-scale population resettlements initiated by Abdülhamid II of Kurds and Circassians, especially, into agricultural regions long and densely occupied by Armenians, driven by the intention to privilege these Muslim ethnic groups as a way of forcing Armenians to migrate to the larger cities.[13] These policies would lead to interethnic conflict and to the subsequent pogroms of the 1890s instigated by Abdülhamid II. But it is evident that my father saw what Balakian later reported. His associations were with other Armenians and principally with relatives, since he came from a large family and by implication a larger extended group. But the stories do not add up to a coherent picture of life in the years before the planned genocide. The Turkish loss amounted to an unacknowledged manifestation of "collateral damage," a "sideshow," by-product of World War I, which simply diminishes the scale of the devastation and corresponding theft by naming it an accident. We know that totalizing expropriations extracted from expulsion and extermination made available more than offset whatever loss Turkey claimed it suffered. For some more recent accounts there is the suggestion that Turks lost part of themselves by branding these minorities as their enemies and Other: "Only too late came the realization that this Other was a part of oneself and his loss was like an amputation."[14] Perhaps this expression of goodwill and amity after one hundred years may be seen as a sincere gesture, but it still does not account for the violent nature of the exterminations and the willing participation of large segments of the Turkish Muslim populations to not only murder as a means of "amputating" a part of the alleged Ottoman social body but also resort to grotesque mutilations, which must symptomize another kind of morbidity and pathology. Disavowal is not simply a denial of an event but an attempt to permanently proscribe the existence of a word and its plural connotations, a silencing of an entire history, which, for Turkey, carries an indelible and unwanted association of inhuman defacement and disfigurement.

It is conceivable that the responsive reflex taken by our parents was already informed by this sense of indescribable loss. Guilt for those who had lived when so many of their relatives, friends, and compatriots perished may have played a role in this silencing, but not entirely. Our parents may have considered the event as another unscheduled interruption in their respective everyday lives, and the decision to remain silent may have been part of the effort to imagine the nature of the loss in order to retrieve some semblance of what had vanished and the necessity of its continuation. Continuity was inseparable from everydayness, even under circumstances that forced a new start in an alien and undecipherable world. What they brought to this challenge is what they had left. Yet it is interesting to note that our parents would not have been married to each other had it not been for the genocide; they would not have been brought together by the people who brokered their apparently arranged marriage and the three of us would not have existed. I have often wondered if they saw their coming together as a contingent effect of genocide and whether they continued to see the bonding of their relationship in this light, and how they thought about a relationship thrown together out of the random chaos of genocidal destruction that literally wiped out their collective cultures of reference and histories that cemented their everyday lives.

There have been writers about the Jewish Holocaust who argue, tendentiously, I believe, that the victims or survivors of world historical calamities undergo a change of status in their relation to history.[15] In other accounts this victimization conferred by genocidal catastrophe qualifies one to enter history, when before they would have remained unnoticed in an equally unseen everyday life. Steedman is concerned with the question of who owns history. On the face it, it would seem that the answer is the historian who writes up the historical account. She quotes the historian Leora Auslander, who has "discuss(ed) the power of historians and archivists of post-Shoah memory to make immortal ordinary people whose stories of suffering are a passport to the historical record in a way their everyday life would not have been. Being victim or survivor of 'a world historical cataclysm changed (their) relation to history; it both generated far more detailed documentary traces than would otherwise have existed, and made people, who would have otherwise have [sic] gone unnoticed, noticeable.'"[16] Perhaps this has been the case of the Judeocide, which undoubtedly has produced mountains of documentary testimony. But such accumulation of the accounts of suffering are not always available in other historical genocides, and does not necessarily apply to especially those examples like the Armenian massacres which represented a community caught between a precapitalist imperial order and the first murmurs of capitalist primitive accumulation with all of its destructive horrors.

But this is an archivist's and, perhaps, a social historian's fantasy and does not explain what happens when the world historical event leaves no telling traces but marks only disappearances, denials, and repressed memories unwilling to surface. More important, it keeps history at the forefront and the everyday merely reflecting the dim light it keeps cast by world historical events. It is an attempt to find a place for the everyday within the storyline of a world historical event, as if it were a natural coupling. Whether it is or not, it still remains to be demonstrated, even though a number of philosophers concerned with this problem have not been able to persuasively secure this bonding. Both the dead and the living who have no documents to offer to confirm their historical importance, as Steedman approvingly paraphrases Auslander's analysis quoted above, fail to win entry into history because they have no "stories of suffering (which) are a passport to the historical record in a way their everyday life would not have been," remain entombed in silence.[17] Despite my admiration for the writings of both Steedman and Auslander, and it is entirely possible I've misread the intended meanings of both historians, I find this to be a strange and even troubling, if not unacceptable criterion affirming the achievement of historical identity. The Jewish holocaust continues to provide the criteria for all genocides, past and present.

For the nameless, who can never be admitted into history because they leave behind no stories of their suffering and loss and their namelessness, is it necessary to secure a "passport," or a ticket to gain entry into the historical record, paid for by being obliterated by genocide? Is this key to being rewarded the prize of immortality? History becomes an exclusive graveyard whose borders require proper credentials of identification. If the victims remain nameless and without stories to tell, then their entry is acquired through some sort of quantitative measure—they will still be (bureaucratically) validated, not as individuals who once lived but because now they are counted among the multiple dead of a genocidal event. They remain nameless. We know that Walter Benjamin saw in the nameless the necessity of constructing a history not yet written.[18] Quantifying the numbers of dead, like those African populations who died en route or survived the horrendous voyages across the Atlantic to spend the rest of their lives as slave laborers, may be important to grasp the scale of an event but it also works as an abstraction to undermine the individual experience of nameless lives, their differing subjectivities, designated as fodder—mere data—to constitute the statistic. In the absence of names, ordinary individuals are denied the extraordinary status of being recognized and thus immortalized by history. If, as ordinary individuals, they fail to be included in a quantitative measure, they are simply forgotten, the homeless dead, wandering endlessly outside a historical paradise housing the counted who had gained a passport for recognition, resembling the unrequited spirits of the Buddhist or Shinto dead who must be attended to and brought home to their everyday. It is precisely the domination of quantitative measure that will lead to such meaningless conclusions that propose that one death is not as great as countless deaths. By the same token we are faced with the obverse proposition that history is now the exclusive pantheon of the immortalized victims of genocides who had the proper credentials for entry. Whom do these abstractions console? Not the dead who became part of some gross statistic and for whom history no longer matters. The living? They always remain imperceptible since the faint light of world historicality never reaches them. What did it do for them? Or for those who lived but remained outside the historical record? It is interesting to note that the statistical figure invariably becomes the basis of claims and counterclaims, denials and disavowals bent on reducing the numbers involved and those killed in order to diminish the significance of its eventfulness, or to satisfy some arbitrary definition, whose measure is now indistinguishable from quantity. What does it mean? If there is no archival authentication, do the dead remain wandering in an endless and indeterminate zone between a visible history and and a hidden everydayness? What do the dead gain by securing membership to the "historical record"? Whose record? The state's?

Yet there is a striking ironic symmetry or even asymmetry between the obsessive Turkish persistence to deny giving the mass murders the name of genocide and the namelessness of the dead who disappeared in the killing fields, the deportation marches, and the final destination of a desert inferno. In this parallelism, are we to assume that the refusal to name the event and the namelessness of the victims share a conviction that seeks to reject their claim to enter history as an effort to remove the historical altogether, as if it never happened? I believe this is an important dimension of survivor's experience, as I will try to show; these survivors rarely, if ever, mentioned the names of their dead in an act of disavowal that matched the Turkish denial of the event itself. But the silence regarding the act of namelessness and the denial of genocidal responsibility are really two different orders of muteness: while the former honors the dead, the latter makes mockery of both their lives, which never existed, and their deaths, which could not have occurred.

The importance of ordinary people who have been murdered on the occasion of or by a world historical cataclysm requires no authentication or official archival recognition from history; their ordinariness and their sudden collective disappearance should be the condition of their qualification for historical identity and enough to grant them the claim of historicity. Too often the apparent extraordinariness attributed to the historical trumps the mere ordinariness of the anonymous of everyday life; even Benjamin tried to reverse this particular catalog. Counting the nameless derives from the historian's imperative to collect 'objective' evidence that the event occurred, as a necessary exercise in verification. But when such large numbers seem to disappear virtually in a short span of time from a particular place, why is it not assumed that this qualifies as proper evidence? Where did they all go? Mars? It was precisely this ordinariness and their everyday lives that mass murder aimed to eradicate for what it could yield in theft and expropriation. Religious and ethnic differences, and the threat they are often seen to pose to a dominant group, have always been transparent alibis. Removing ordinariness from the historical account, denying its claims to qualitative consideration, leads to merely throwing the ordinary into categories of quantification. What is being suggested is that by gathering the nameless into numbered quantities, historical practice denied their claim to qualitative subjective agency. The act alone implies that historical practice still appears in thrall to the great men or personages who represent the extraordinary in history, the real makers of history, rather than the nameless rest and numbered masses who merely follow. It is surprising how older perspectives manage to capture new leases on life through the discovery of new interpretative methods and strategies announcing new vistas promising to look at historical practice and its world in an entirely new way.

Mass murder of an ethnic group confers on the act its world historical status, its new status of genocide. It was not the event that won world historical status of war but the unaccounted elimination of a whole population of individual ordinary people and their everyday. What I mean is that an immense number of ordinary people who were simply wiped out without credible explanation and acceptance of responsibility was absorbed into the world historical event of World War I, which meant that the enormity of erasing one and a half million people was diminished and permanently eclipsed as collateral damage. In genocidal episodes it is never, if rarely, the case that the dead are left with their possessions and property intact. What impelled Turkey to desperately efface such ordinariness from their world or the Germans or the Rwandans or any ethnic group bent on removing from its midst another, usually a minority (but not always, as Cambodia demonstrated), whose presence appeared to be so unbearable and intolerable that only complete annihilation would offer the chance for release or relief? The intense mutilation of Armenians by Turkish mobs in the countryside and their Kurdish and Circassian supporters seemed to supply overdetermined reassurance that the dead really are dead, this time. What drives such frenzy and why it is repeated is the problem that escapes historical reason and certainly the abstract figuration of a statistical count. In many ways, genocides point to the regularity of historical repetition as one of the commanding rhythmologies of historical time. It is possible that the ordinariness of Armenian everydayness was the offense agitating Turks, who then sought to demonstrate its opposite, the extraordinary hidden in the ordinary and the discovery of its capacity for violent destruction, at risk of momentarily leaving or being separated from the human community by their willingness to act in senselessly inhuman ways by effacing the everyday that is the basis of human existence. At an earlier time, the Armenians in the empire were considered as "faithful" subjects, undoubtedly reflecting the important positions they acquired in business and trade, artisanal professions (i.e., architecture), and scientific, literary, and educational spheres. Yet this reputation for fidelity was inverted into ressentiment and hatred to fuel the widely shared conviction circulated by the Young Turks leadership that what they enjoyed derived from theft and deception. Perhaps this resentment toward the empire's Christian minorities was more deeply seated, embedded in a Muslim political unconscious. But the Young Turks instigating of the genocide were modernizers who saw in a backward peasant majority the roadblock to Turkey's capitalist modernization and in the attainments of minorities like Armenians a worrying hindrance to their aspiration for Turkish national renewal spearheaded by a policy of "Turkification." Expropriation, dispossession, theft, murder, and expulsion offered to resolve the backwardness of Turkey's population and opened the way to Turkish capitalist modernization by removing the Armenians and appropriating their material wealth: an early expression of the "dialectic of enlightenment"?[19]

But because history is a narrative, a conceived construct rather than the account of a lived experience, it is never able to tell us how life was really carried out. And for this reason, this event would, like all genocides, exceed history. It would constitute a tear in historical time, one so complete that its restoration would never remove the terror of the caesura, its blankness; it would never bring back the prospect of what it was like before and what might have been. A history that fails to work out a mode of articulation with everydayness is fated to simple repetition of its narrative exemplars.

THREE. TRACES OF A VANISHED EVERYDAY

Just as I never knew my parents, I never really grasped the enormity of their ordeal of survival and endurance when I was growing up. This project was in some ways a belated attempt to know parents I had taken for granted while growing up in their household, never questioning them about their early lives, and never even thinking of what kind of lives they had led that brought them to the United States or inquiring about close relatives like grandparents, uncles, and aunts whom others grew up with. Our father, Ohannes (John), was the warmer of our parents, at least I thought so, and in possession of a bigger sense of humor of the two, but he was around less often and did not spend as much time with us as our mother, Vehanush. He seemed more accessible than Vehanush, who always struck me as more distant, self-enclosed, almost enigmatic (if I knew what that word meant when I was a kid), and whose cheerlessness added to the mystery. She was not always easy to like or, at times, be understood, at least for me. While Ohannes made his way through the ups and downs of the labor market, from one factory or foundry to another until he was able to land a secure and lasting job, Vehanush was the homemaker. Yet I could not help thinking that coming to the U.S. had become a learning experience for her, a work in progress. It was here she learned to cook Armenian dishes but also how to speak and read English, on her own. She became an avid reader and an extremely well informed person in time, intelligent and sensitive to the rhythms of American society, interested and interesting. In this regard, America was a continuation of the education she first received in the German mission school in Marash.

Considerations of history and memory were of no consequence to my parents. There was no reason for them to raise questions, especially while they were in the midst of getting out. This interpretative perspective comes too late, after the event has spent its ferocity. It is evident that one of the most difficult problems to confront is to imagine and thus construct what their everyday lives must have been like. How did each of our parents live before they were forcibly uprooted? It is hard not to conclude that they saw their everyday as a routinized and repetitive present that the genocidal events simply interrupted forever. But at the time, it was not clear to me that they thought their daily life was at its end. What appears certain is that Armenian everyday life remained anchored in a historical homeland that had weathered waves of invading conquests from the east and whose people lived as a colonized minority under Ottoman hegemony for more than five hundred years. This everyday began to experience challenging changes in the later half of the nineteenth century with the "wholesale destruction of home industries due to increased imports from an industrializing Europe," the penetration of money economy into the countryside and the monetization of taxes, growing disorder and lawlessness, and struggles and conflict over landholding claims among different ethnic groups in areas inhabited by Armenians, increasingly agitated by the influx of Turkish refugees from wars in Russia and the Balkans to create a continuing crisis.[1] Armenians were thus forced to forfeit a settled everydayness they had known for centuries for flight to new environments like France, the United States, and elsewhere and directly confront the spectacle of capitalist modernity when before they had only come to recognize its appearance in the introduction of new economic practices.

Yet the first experience of flight for so many was long homelessness, separations from close relatives and friends that would take long durations of time to reconnect or never, which must have imprinted a mental scar in their subsequent conscious and unconscious lives, as manifest in my parents' anxieties. My father was from the southeast, my mother from the mountains in Cilicia. He was from a large family, presumably secure in a number of ways owing to the priestly vocations of his father and grandfather. Many of these villages were predominantly inhabited by Armenians and administered by clergy of the local church. This did not exclude the presence of a mixture of other Islamic ethnic groups: Turks, Kurds, possibly Arabs in the south (according to Franz Werfel), Assyrians, and others.[2] Werfel provides us with an appreciation of the everyday lives of the villages in the south at the Syrian border before the siege of Musa

Dagh. The novel *The Forty Days of Musa Dagh* was written after Werfel's 1929 trip to Damascus, where he first observed the wretched conditions endured by young Armenian orphans working in a carpet factory who had miraculously survived the death marches to the desert, which led him to investigating the plight of the seven villages of Musa Dagh and their tragically heroic defense against a numerically overwhelming and German-equipped Turkish military that lasted forty days until the remaining defenders were rescued by French naval ships.[3]

The impression gleaned from Werfel's novel of Armenian villages is not necessarily a sunny, serene, idyllic daily life (even though Grigoris Balakian romanticizes Cilicia as a natural paradise). The constant interaction of different ethnicities was always explosive and conflict producing, especially among the empire's minorities. It was surely at the same time one suffused with continuing traditions, stretching back centuries to a time even before the Ottoman conquest and routines relating to agricultural cultivation and cooperation, centered on family, kin, and religion. Under the Ottoman Turks, life could not have been idyllic. (Perhaps comparable to the Irish, whose colonized burden under the British lasted as long.) Armenian rural families and clans were largely patriarchal and exogamous, inasmuch as marriages were made with prospective partners outside the village, establishing clans composed of mixtures from various villages that widened the community and probably reinforced the prospect of greater social solidarity. Yet it would be difficult to distinguish Armenian and Greek rural life in Anatolia from Turkish in the domains of food, folklore, agricultural production, architecture, customs, and superstitious practices like the evil eye (which I remember I was warned against by my mother) and reading the leavings of the grounds in a cup of Turkish coffee as a guide to the future of one's daily life.

In the Ottoman Empire these village communities were relatively autonomous, essentially administered by priests who, in theory, represented village interests to regional officials. Despite Werfel's sympathetic portrayal of a strong and selfless village priest in Musa Dagh, I think many of them were not always in sync with the communities' interests. These communities, like most, were centered on the church, the religious calendar punctuated by seasonal work, and the temporal cycles of production and reproduction. We tend to forget that temporal accountancy differed from the more disciplined and routinized form of measuring working time in capitalist societies and how this would have shaped its inhabitants. By the same measure, it would be wrong to underestimate the problem of adjustment immigrants encountered once they left the village for modern America and the working day in capitalism and the effects this would have in altering the character of traditional family life formed in precapitalist villages.

In these communities, the religious prevailed, while time spent in work followed seasonal patterns. But it is important to note that there was nothing like a working day with its fixed hours. Ohannes rarely spoke of the work he was required to do while growing up in his village, and it is not clear to me if he did any regular work in those years (he probably tended fruit trees). It is not surprising that when he was old enough, he signed up for contract work in the U.S. (working on the Great Northern Railway), which he disliked because the company seemed to feed its workers only beans. Nevertheless, after a brief return home, he signed up a second time for work in the United States. There are thus two possible reasons prompting this desire to emigrate: either the insufficiency of land at home, which would probably go to older brothers; or the policy of resettling Kurds, Circassians, and refugees from the Balkans on lands occupied by Christian minorities. But regardless, our father joined the first, large wave of immigrant workers before World War I to migrate to the U.S. to eventually become a member of the generation that a decade or so later confronted the Great Depression.

I think daily life was often organized around certain foods and dishes, or foods and meals constituted the particular event rather than the reverse, especially its preparation, notably baked breads and rolls at Easter that signified something of the nature of village daily life and its yearly repetitive cycle by investing specific meaning to it according to the importance of the religious observance. The whole drama of the yearly cycle culminating in the Easter resurrection was embodied in the making of certain breads that were, after forty days of eating unleavened flat bread, permitted to rise (with the help of yeast). As a child I began to associate the appearance of certain dishes with certain holidays. Even in the diaspora, the older Julian calendar was still observed, especially religious holidays and feast days. Easter was by far the most important observance in the religious year, with Epiphany after it—Christmas appearing as a more modern and Euro-American holiday. There were dishes that usually involved a large group of women, organized as an informal kitchen assembly line; this was particularly true of the making of *lahmajun* and sweets like baklava. I mention this form of cooperative activity since it probably reflected practices in village life, carried over and retained for special occasions in the new land. But Armenian dishes, especially, momentarily reminded the inhabitants of the diaspora of home and village, its smells and tastes and affective relationships.

Unanswerable questions reached back to village life, which lingered as an unnoticed and usually unspoken puzzle whose parts were missing. What regularities and rhythms were interrupted and lost forever? It seems that Armenian village societies were organized on the basis of a calendar constituting the special days of the religious year. This would mean feast days, days commemorating martyred saints, and other occasions important to the Christian calendar. We can get a modified version of how dense this religious year appears by looking at the days of observance still recognized in European Roman Catholic countries. Since the Armenian Apostolic Church was the principal religious and political institution in Armenian communities during the Ottoman period, its presence virtually saturated daily life, exercising both religious and political authority, which often were indistinguishable from each other. The church regulated the spiritual and political lives of village community through the millet system. Whatever one's personal belief, it was probably difficult to escape the constraints imposed by the church on village communities. Once the dispersed diasporas were formed and settled in foreign lands, much of this religious domination of the calendar over the village community disappeared with the destruction of village everyday life. In these new migrant settlements, the diaspora had to submit to the primacy of other institutions, as in the U.S., that were mainly secular, civic, and public. While the church followed the diaspora to new lands, it lost its privileged position as the central binding force of the village community and its religious and political hold over its members. What bound diaspora solidarity was political affiliation, then language, custom, and memory of an indefinite past.

My mother's rejection of that place and past and the apparent absence of any shred of sentiment or nostalgia toward what had been lost was what I remember most about her. In a sense, what she had to lose occurred while she was still a child and the toll was climaxed by her mother's abandonment of her and her brother. Unlike my father, she apparently had not been raised within the Armenian Apostolic Church and seemed often to hold it responsible for its commitment to backwardness. In later years, I think this different orientation explains the difference in outlooks and adaptation between Vehanush and Ohannes toward life in the United States. Sometimes, it seemed to me that she almost looked upon the genocide as the occasion to transport her out of Anatolia. But it is true that this past-present was locked in some secret mental vault, never to be spoken of or recalled. If this appears somewhat unfair, it partly explains why I was always struck by how readily she acquired an enthusiasm for life in modern America by contrast to what she had been forced to leave behind. Unimaginable terror of the experience as a young girl would explain why she might be eager to simply get out of that place. But migrating to a modern society imposed serious alterations in the division of labor and organized the household around the primacy of the working day employed by industrial factories. In this respect I thought she had probably made a quicker adjustment to the socially normative time of capitalist society than my father, even though he was the one who had to submit to the discipline of a working day once he found a job. Frequently, it appeared she was convinced that Anatolia—what both she and Ohannes called the "old country"—was simply a place, and empty and timeless space, she had been forced to pass through at an early age, and that her family, mother, father, brother, and relatives were somewhere else, where she also once lived. Getting out must have seemed like a release or perhaps even a reprieve.

When old enough, I began to think she had always been in this place, in Highland Park, Michigan, because she remained obdurately silent on what came before it. My father was perhaps more of a romantic and could spin stories of days in the village; he described a geography dominated by mule travel and transport, which actually exaggerated the distance to be covered, but rarely much about his siblings, parents, and grandparents or how he spent his days. It seemed that his reluctance to speak about his family might have affected how we envisioned our own family unit, cut off from extended relationships, trying to navigate its way in a new life without the emotional support and guidance of the larger familial group. It certainly must have persuaded us to not inquire too closely on the fate of relatives he rarely spoke of. He might mention how one of his grandfathers (probably paternal) had lived to a grand old age that would have continued had it not been for the massacres. I suggested that since he, my father, had no accurate proof of his own date of birth, it was probably true that ages were inflated, either overcounted or its reverse.

These accounts might have been an effort to portray a life that may never have existed as he recalled it, a motionless image stranded in an indeterminate timelessness, and that he may well have dreamed up or embellished out of grief for what he had lost—I do not know—but, like my mother, there was no apparent desire in him to return and no expression of permanent nostalgia for the disappearance of an everyday he would never know again. If there was, he kept it hidden to himself. Nostalgia for place was rarely an option for Armenians who survived the genocide since it was still inhabited by Turks and Kurds, and the idea of returning to the scene of a cataclysmic crime would dampen any enthusiasm encouraged by impulses of longing and homesickness. He once reported to my oldest daughter upon a brief return to his village as a fighter with the Armenian Revolutionary Federation (ARF) brigades, to find nothing left of his large, extended family. They had all either been killed on the site or forced to join one of the many deportation columns. He never said and perhaps did not know. But on his return entry to his village, he did remark, "Even the fruit trees had died." I cannot help believing that this image of dead fruit trees served as a trope capable of standing in for the totality of destruction and death that remained with him until he died. Here, Ohannes confronted the most unanswerable question of his life, which was how and where his family vanished, murdered. This question would undoubtedly remain with him the rest of his life and was comparable to Vehanush's childhood desire to know why her mother never came back for her. Unanswerability turned them into witnesses of silence, which they bequeathed to three of us.

I have often thought about why so little attention was paid to the countless lives that perished at the end of the deportation convoys, whether any systematic effort was ever made to account for the nameless piles of bones once embodied in living individuals, strewn and entombed in the desert. I always questioned if he—Ohannes—knew or had had a feeling of where and how his parents, grandparents, and siblings died. I have tried to imagine the scene of his return and entry into his village. Other members of his brigade must have accompanied him. I have been particularly concerned with how he must have reacted upon observing the quiet, dead silence of a familiar site where he heard no voices and observed on entry empty homes, many destroyed, and, of course, dying fruit trees. What were his thoughts at that moment and how did he incorporate the shock of recognition without falling apart, what had he anticipated, and when did he realize that his family had disappeared forever? And at what point did his acknowledgment of the aimlessness of the act pass into the formation of grief? His time in the dead village of his former life must have eventually forced upon him his decision to permanently leave the region and perhaps Anatolia once the war ended. It must have been in this circumstance that he began to formulate thoughts of returning to the U.S. The scene imposes limits on my capacity to imagine what he must have gone through, felt, and decided. To move beyond the obvious questions that ask themselves would be to fictionalize and violate a scene that has set its own limits of a private hell for him alone. He never spoke of or described the scene to my sisters or me, only talking to my oldest daughter about the tragedy when she was a child; her delayed recall of the conversation came years later. I have repeatedly asked myself, as I still do, why he never reported this episode to me or to my sisters. I am certain he never recovered from it, yet I have wondered whether he chose his granddaughter to momentarily release a lifetime of pent-up remorse and repression, condensed in a metaphor recalling dead fruit trees.

I keep returning to one of the few photos I have of him. Photos have been effectively used to fill in what has not been recorded in writing or in remembered conversations. The few photos we have of our parents match my own meager talents to use them as substitutes for absent letters and documents. In the end, they represent indices of particular historical moments in their material lives—how they looked, dressed, what kind of lives they were living. It is hard to visualize that they would elucidate or reveal the silences they had both embraced. In one photo, he is dressed for combat, with two comrades, bullet belt strung over one shoulder, standing at ease with a long, primitive-looking rifle, against a fake background supplied by the photographer (see figure G.3). Where was the photo taken? Was it in Eastern Armenia, Van, Kars, Erzerum, Bitlis, Tiflis (Tbilisi), somewhere along the battle line between Turkey and Russia? How old was he? Late teens, early twenties? Who were the other two comrades—friends, relatives?—and what happened to them, all nameless? The back of the photograph was inscribed in Armenian script: "This photo I present as a gift [*knvirim*] to Avetis Petrosian in memory of our unforgettable love. Hovaness T Harutynian, 1915, July 13." I do not know who Avetis Petrosian was, or ever remember meeting someone with that name, and I am not sure if he was a close relative, a friend he grew up with, a former comrade. The expression conveying the "memory of our unforgettable love" is an even greater puzzle. It may be that he was also a member of the ARF brigades who eventually was killed or died, men like himself, to be honored. In any case, Ohannes eventually left the brigades and war zone along the eastern front and got out of Anatolia for what would be the last time. He would never return. He had some stories about this episode in his life, that he had been in Persia and in Eastern Armenia, Van, Kars, Ardahan, and Georgia, and he claimed even to have seen the ruins at Ani. What has interested me about his complex itinerary is explaining his thinking, that after spending time in the U.S. on two different occasions, he came back to Anatolia as a recruit in the ARF brigades and was sent to the eastern front to fight with the Russian forces against the Turks. There are a host of question concerning how he was able to get to the eastern front and where he was trained and equipped that will have to remain unanswered.

The Armenian Revolutionary Federation was organized in 1890 and became the principal Armenian political organization dedicated to the realization of an independent Armenian nation-state and continued its existence after the genocide as the leading political group in the Armenian diaspora. Whatever prompted Ohannes to make this herculean journey from the U.S. to the eastern reaches of Anatolia to fight with Russians against the Turks? While he must have joined the ARF as a young man, and remained faithful to its goals most of his life, his decision to return must have been driven by a singular conviction. It is conceivable that he, like so many of his contemporaries, saw in this struggle the spark capable of igniting the final liberation of the Armenian people from centuries of Ottoman oppression. He must have believed it was his moral duty to fight for this cause and its realization and that with its achievement Armenians would have had an independent homeland after the war, a nation-state to house its village communities without the incessant and imminent threat of state extortion, or the violence of marauders and murder. This meant that he probably intended to stay, like so many others of his generation, but ultimately changed his mind or events changed it for him. The decision must have been made in the inaugural wake of the genocidal fury that overcame his whole family and village and his own sense of the conduct of the war in the east. He had nothing to go back to even if Armenians won independence. But he may have also reasoned that the tide of battle was increasingly less encouraging and it was best to return to the United States to join the American Expeditionary Forces (AEF), which would have given him citizenship. Yet I do not want to exclude the possibility that he was still persuaded that joining the AEF promised a possible victory over the Central Powers, a definitive end of the Ottoman Empire, and the prospect of an independent Armenian state. What would it have meant to him to return when there was nothing left to a life he had once known?

There was a short-lived Armenian State after the signing of the Versailles Treaty (1919) that was dissolved by the refusal of England and France to see through the terms of the Treaty of Sevres, in order to check the advance of the Kemalist forces that were continuing the killing of Armenians and Greeks in 1920 and as late as 1955 in Istanbul, and beginning in 1930 to target the Kurds. By 1920 Ohannes, who had been injured in a gas attack spent the remaining war year in a field hospital in St. Aignan, France, had been discharged from the AEF, given U.S. citizenship, married in France, and was trying to get our mother into the United States. Ohannes's flight from eastern Anatolia took him through Russia. He most likely took a northern route, where he could have caught a ship to England and then to the U.S. But it should be noted that he probably traveled through Russia in late 1916, perhaps early 1917, and passed through a country that was quickly disintegrating into political and social revolution that took it out of the war. If he chose a northern route, he would have gone through Moscow and St. Petersburg and witnessed signs of the unfolding revolutionary breakdown of Czarist society. He might also have stopped en route in several places. Yet I have no testimony other than his remarking that he went through Russia. It is possible he went through a Black Sea port and then to England, in which case he would not have seen much. It seems plausible that he, with other comrades, withdrew with the Russians and received some sort of safe passage. The northern route is more feasible. As a former member of the ARF brigades, fighting with the Russians, it would have been less dangerous than traveling through the Black Sea and the straits.

In any case, his stories resembled a jumbled archive testifying to the wreckages of folk village life and the splintered shards of his own personal fragmentation but never any expression depicting the coherence and wholeness of rural life or a desire to return to it. This might have been inhibited later by the struggle to make a living in the land of permanent uncertainty and golden opportunity. It also derived from knowing there was nothing left to return to. But I cannot help thinking that the failed promise of an independent Armenian state (and he never explicitly considered the Soviet version as independent), and I suspect that until early years of the World Depression he had mixed feelings about Soviet Armenia, claiming he had distant relatives who had made it to Yerevan. Still, the loss of his entire family meant a different kind of future in the U.S. that, in many ways, was not the one he would have wanted. He would continue to wage war in the U.S. through his dedication to the ARF, whatever that came to mean.

The circumstances of Vehanush's early life were significantly different. She also came from Cilicia, but not the small village life filled with family and relatives my father had known. All I know is that she came from Marash or close by and was "orphaned early," with her brother, by their mother, who put both in religious mission schools. By the time of the massacres of 1915, and in Marash, there had already been massive earlier massacres in the 1890s; it was common practice that parents would put up their children for adoption in the orphanages, as adoptees for safekeeping until a parent would come back for them. Few parents ever returned. Her mother was no exception. In the case of Vehanush's mother, who made this decision, she ended up in Beirut, which suggests that she and her second husband got out in time. How and when this occurred I have no idea. It must have been before the beginning of the massacres and deportations and somewhat after she placed her daughter in the school.

When younger, I knew little about our mother's early past, virtually nothing since she was even more closemouthed about it than my father. By the same token, what would I have understood if she did recount her history to me? What I did manage to learn in those early years came by way of isolated events I heard. But much of it never really registered with me until years later. When I was four or five I learned that her mother lived in Beirut, even though I had no idea where it was. What compelled this impulse in her to close off any information concerning her formative years? I knew this because it was at the time my mother received a letter informing her of her mother's death.

It was only when I was a teenager that I began to fill in some blank pages of Vehanush's life by conjuring, in a process no longer explainable, imagined scenarios of how she had escaped. The blank periods in her life became the occasion or supplied me the opportunity to simply make up stories about her. In fact, the appeal to the device of imagined scenarios and staged sets became the principal form of my youthful desire to fill in the empty spaces produced by unanswered and unanswerable questions. Why did I think she escaped? I really do not know and cannot remember where these stories came from. It is possible she may have said some things I completely misunderstood or deliberately misconstrued that I then cobbled together into an explanatory story. All of this may have been the product not of actual interest in her life, as such, but to make her into a recognizable figure, even a heroic one, to give her a "history" that would make her look like the mothers of my friends, as well as something she clearly was not. The most enduring among these imagined scenes was a heroically romantic tale of flight, with her mother, into the Syrian Desert, where they were rescued by Bedouins and made their way to Beirut. In this story, her brother did not accompany them. I am not sure I knew she even had a brother at that time in my life. It was another plotline out of *The Arabian Nights*, a pure fantasy made up on the basis of things heard or misheard, put together from my imaginings to become an actual and believable account. But it was wrong and well off the mark. Yet it seemed at the time as a satisfying narrative that actually worked against any further or even later attempts to inquire into her early history. This was especially true of my adulthood, when I still seemed content with fables of her life I had constructed as a child that had no basis in fact. After all, I never had the inclination to ask about her years in Marash and her early family life. I am still not sure why. But to construct imaginary scenes, in the absence of an explanation, must have been a personally satisfying way to fill the void of silence with meaning, however wildly off the mark it was. It seemed like a paradox: just as she never spoke of that time to us, I never was induced to inquire further. A further paradox or contradiction is that while I showed no interest in trying to ascertain a reliable account of her early years out of some sort of disinterest and even indifference, I nevertheless made up stories about her that I relentlessly held on to until I learned they were simply fabrications dreamed up by the exaggerated imagination of a child. I could have just asked her. Why I failed to do so is still a mystery. But resorting to imagined heroic scenes out of Hollywood movies seemed like a viable substitution. Truth be told, it was never, or rarely, possible to picture her anywhere else but in Detroit, the now-time we shared when growing up. In fact, the present was her time and tense.

She came to us without any history, or interest in history, as such, or a recognizable curiosity about the past, unlike Ohannes, whose anecdotes at least testified to an index of documentary historical traces from an indeterminate time. Vehanush seemed to be a person who accepted things as they were or as she found them, which may have been a reason why we were never encouraged to ask questions about her early life. On her part, she controlled that subject of conversation by rarely calling attention to her early years. She survived because of the school, which saved hundreds of children like her. It is difficult to know when she left the school in Marash, but it is certain she left with some teachers and other students and, according to my sister Victoria, ended up in Greece. How they got through and what port they left from is unknown, though it is conceivable they went south to the port of Alexandretta (Iskenderum, as it was then called). The problem of time is also unknown. It could have been in 1915 or even before or, more likely, in 1918 and after the Armistice. Even in 1918, Turks were still killing Armenians and Greeks in some areas and Marash was not a safe place. A year later some of those Armenians who miraculously survived the forced march to the Syrian Desert tried to come back to their homes in Anatolia to reclaim their land and were massacred. If the later date was correct, and I believe it is, the school would have been a refuge protecting the children under the sanction of the mission and the German government. She must have spent a certain amount of time in Greece, but none of us know how long or where. From Greece, she must have ultimately left for Marseilles, again by what means and with whom I have no idea—probably by ship. It is clear that the teachers who accompanied these girls (there may have been boys, as well) were Armenians who taught in the school. One of them, with whom she apparently was close, was named Bedrosian, whose name Vehanush eventually took, dropping her biological family name of Kupalian. This woman and others probably accompanied her on the trip to Marseille, which would have been a terminus for the Armenian flight from the Ottoman Genocide. It is a credible long shot that the Petrosian to whom Ohannes inscribed his photo might actually have been the husband of the teacher whose name Vehanush adopted. They are the same name and mean "son of Peter" (Peterson), and only the orthography differs since the *p* is often pronounced as a soft *b*. The transcription from *p* to *b* depends on how it is heard, regional dialect mediating it. I never knew his first name.

I do know that the woman Bedrosian, whom I met and even knew when I was a child, settled outside Detroit with her husband. (I have a photo of her taken with her husband in their Inkster Road farmhouse.) My sister Sena reported that the Bedrosians were actually our "godparents." What I did not know was that she had been both my mother's teacher who accompanied the girls out of Marash and possibly the go-between in the marriage that brought my mother and father together in Marseilles, where they were married in 1920. Ohannes was twenty-seven when he married and Vehanush may have been around seventeen or a little older. It is not known how Ohannes was contacted for the marriage and by whom, how the negotiation was carried out, or the circumstances in which he made this decision and the channels of communication and contracting he employed, but apparently it was accomplished by somebody who knew him and the Bedrosians. According to Sena, Vehanush always claimed the marriage had not been arranged and that she had received several previous offers because of the scarcity of marriageable Armenian girls at that time who had been able to escape the genocidal horror of systematic rape and murder. But it seems likely that it was arranged, inasmuch as Ohannes and Vehanush had not met until they wedded in Marseilles and the Bedrosians must have been the agents of their coming together. For a putatively arranged marriage, it was remarkably modern since there were no families on either side to satisfy and no demand for bride dowry. This coming together also remained a subject they never discussed. It could have been because it was an arranged marriage, which would have been fairly common among immigrant groups in the U.S. at that time; inhibiting discussion on the nature of the marriage may have been encouraged by the fear that it would have branded them as old-fashioned, unmodern in modern America. Or it simply could have been more commonplace than I have thought. Both could have also seen the marriage as a contractual arrangement, which in reality it was, that would develop into something else once children appeared. The practice of arranged marriages strangely continued and I remember hearing in my late teens and early twenties instances of families arranging marriages with ethnic Armenians raised in Lebanon, Palestine, and even Istanbul.

My parents used to take us to the Bedrosian farm off Inkster Road, not far from the Detroit Metropolitan Airport today. But I had no idea of their history with our parents and did not learn of it until I began asking my sisters about Vehanush's itinerary out of Turkey. The last time I saw the Bedrosians was when I was about ten or eleven and we stayed overnight since my father was painting their house. My sister Sena has a picture of him on a ladder, with a do-rag wrapped around his head, looking down at the camera, where I was standing, pretending to hold it. The camera must have belonged to the Bedrosians since I do not recall our having one at that time. I had a sense that our father was repaying some sort of debt. I vaguely remember spending other times out there with our parents but nothing else, apart from a fruit tree I usually climbed for refuge.

According to Sena, the school was formative for our mother. She apparently loved it, even though she rarely spoke about this experience. For it was there that she began a lifelong habit of reading novels and undoubtedly acquired her Germanic work discipline. This makes a good deal of sense since it was an environment in which she developed over a period of several years, one that seems to have contributed to repressing or displacing what she might have remembered or experienced in the years before entering the school. That portion of her life remains a void, apart from the death of her biological father when she was still a toddler of two years and would not have remembered and understandably about whom she never spoke. Yet there was a story about his death that circulated over time that Sena recently confirmed; it explains he died of rabies, that once bitten by a rabid dog, he was thrown into a lake. She must have heard her mother speak of him as she became older or spoken about him with her brother, who was probably older than her. But, unsurprisingly, she never referred to her mother's second husband as a stepfather or as a figure in her life.

Some combination of Vehanush's youthful age and experience colluded in such a way that those early years were all consigned to forgetfulness. Whatever else it was, it must have been difficult and unforgettable only in the worst way, which would qualify it for permanent omission. But it does not necessarily explain what in those early years with her biological family accounts for her silence about them. It could have been an unpleasant household dominated by her mother's second husband. Because she never referred to him, it seems clear that she felt no affection toward him or received any from him. By the same measure, her love of the school explains a form of liberation from the household and the experience of an aborted family that offered the possibility of a new life. Evidently, the orphanage school was anchored in a group of children who came from similar experiences of being put there for adoption and offered her an unprecedented feeling of belonging to an affective community that dramatically contrasted with what she had left (see figure G.4). In Vehanush's case, we know that her mother worked in the school for a time before she left for Beirut. At the same time, it is difficult to know whether she recognized in the school a refuge against the certainty of elimination or understood the precariousness of the position she shared with her classmates. Perhaps the older children had an intuition of the peril that lurked on the outside. Nobody could have lived in that world at the time of World War I or even before who would not have been daily haunted by premonitions of worst things to come to their ethnic communities and villages. For my mother, being installed in the orphanage/school must have seemed like the safety of a walled fortress, where inside it she and her classmates might have had the possibility of routinizing and normalizing their everyday lives with regularly predictable rhythms of play, study, and work while on the outside the world was falling apart and people were simply disappearing. One wonders what these children knew of the world outside the school's precinct of safety, what they thought about and discussed among themselves and what kind of gossip was produced within its confines and circulated and spread throughout like dry brush fire. In a strangely remote way, it reminded me of the nonconnectedness (*muen*) and security of free unfettered play offered by and identified with Buddhist playgrounds in Japan's late middle ages.

I have suggested that Marash was on one of the routes of the large de-in the German mission school created a template of imminent fear that never left her, and that could flexibly change its content, whether it was Turks bent on murdering Armenians or unemployment and economic insecurity, which was the leitmotif of my parents' life in Detroit until after the war.

School also offered her the prospect of a future and a project dedicated to learning she would not have had the opportunity to acquire if she had remained in a village. It was in school that she learned how to write Armenian, and speak and read Turkish and German, even though she did not use these skills once she was in the U.S. But it must have enabled her to learn English on her own more rapidly than others I know of, many of whom never really learned the language after decades of living in America. It is unclear what she would have done if her mother returned for her and took her back to Beirut. But it is evident that the separation from her mother must have been met with severe uncertainty, ambiguity, incomprehension, and fear driven by a sense of being abandoned and left alone. Her brother was orphaned elsewhere, and she apparently had no relationship to her mother's second husband. Just as Ohannes's confrontation with the devastating recognition that the destruction of his home and village and the disappearance of his entire family is impossible to envision, Vehanush's separation from her mother (as well as from her brother) and the ways it must have defined her are impossible to envisage. Any attempt to conjure up the circumstances of a little girl who can understand the words that are being said to her by her mother as she left but would have little capacity to assess what they consequentially meant in such indeterminate surroundings is an impossibility that no claim to empathy can grasp. It must have resembled the terrors of a living death. Initially, it is reasonable to consider that her response would have been to depict the awful spectacle of a vacant future. Even though her mother assured her she would return for her, the promise depended on the unstated conditional qualification of whether or not she lived. Vehanush would have known about the conditions that might result in her not coming back for her or her brother. But would she mull over the possibility that her mother would not voluntarily return? While parents who put their children in the safekeeping of mission schools in Anatolia often never returned because of untimely deaths, many were also convinced that they were doing the right thing by making orphans of their children since they had no intention of returning for them. In Vehanush's case, I'm persuaded by the thought that her mother had decided to not come back for her and her brother.

Once the immediate shock of fear and panic wore off, it is imaginable that Vehanush had already developed a distrust of the explanation; driven by anger, she was convinced her mother would never return. This thought must have accompanied her for the rest of her life and it is not unthinkable to question whether she ever forgave her mother or actually expressed gratitude to her once she learned she was alive in Beirut. The experience resulted in a lifelong conviction she held that only the worst could happen when confronted by dire situations, what years later I saw as a general characteristic in other Armenians, which has also passed on to me as what I have named "Armo thought."

The additional problem Vehanush must have faced is how and when she learned her mother, who never came back for her, was still alive in Beirut, and what she subsequently thought of her when she never returned. Her mother's desire to return could have been delayed or interrupted if Vehanush did not leave the school until after war's end; if it was before the actual massacres early in 1915, she might have believed that she would see her mother again once war ended. Whatever the chronological options, Vehanush would have been told by Mrs. Bedrosian, her teacher, who probably was in contact with her mother, that her mother was not coming back. In this splintered narrative, she must have thought about her brother and his prospects. How and when did she learn he had been killed or died and would she link his death to her mother's decision to remain in Beirut? Why had she never spoken about him to us? But it seems clear, as a friend suggested, that it was Vehanush, perhaps more than Ohannes, who suffered from this episode that must have combined the experience of early abandonment—being alone as a child—and the uncertain future she was forced to confront dominated by the Ottoman determination to eradicate all Armenians. This experience became the possible foundation on which she actually "rebuilt her life," in order to claim some purchase on a life for herself and the life of her as-yet-unborn children. In this regard, the education might have worked as a form of "cauterization effect" that allowed her to move on to re-create life anew.[4] Despite functioning as a persuasive narrative explanation I really have no way of knowing. As for the reasons her mother decided to never return, there are no clear justifications. She remarried, as suggested, a third time, and it is entirely possible she and her new husband started their own family in Beirut. While this may have persuaded her from coming back for Vehanush, it would not have accounted for the reasons that induced her not to bring her to Beirut once the war in Turkey ended.

It was not a story worth recounting to her children years later, perhaps, but one she was actually obliged to divulge because her survival also involved the mobilization of a psychological attitude and stamina to withstand the debilitating knowledge that had been inflicted on her for the rest of her life—that as a child she had been abandoned and thus orphaned by her entire family, thrown into a world she scarcely understood yet forced to make her way on her own in it. What I have been able to piece together from disparate fragments of information and hearsay is not, by any means, her complete story and is at best an outline. For this reason alone, it must stand as much as a recomposed narrative as a verifiable account. This was her contribution to the heritage of the genocide, unquestionably experienced by numerous children whose lives had been almost permanently interrupted and damaged and who would have to embody this disruptive experience for the rest of their lives as they made their way into an entirely different world. The imprint of this experience in later years surfaced in Vehanush's hesitant but consistent skepticism toward things said to her, too often a reluctance to take things at face value, and an expression of a rather fierce autonomy that refused to rely on people. Where she differed from our father was her conviction, certainly relayed to me, that you do not ask anything of people or rely on them, while our father believed that "blood was thicker than water," which meant that you could count on other Armenians but on no one else, despite his own experiences to the contrary. Yet the real difference was Vehanush's early separation from family life and the experience of relying on it, which, I believe, resulted in her reluctance to have expectations of people, perhaps the world itself, whereas Ohannes's upbringing embedded him in a thick web of familial relationships. In her relationship with me, she was often right to distrust what I might have said by way of an explanation concerning why I came home late or where I had been or where I had acquired unaccounted money. She was, I believe, suspicious to a fault and in our daily dealings. I cannot honestly say I ever knew what she was thinking and too regularly felt that I burdened her with endless disappointment. Frequently, her excessive suspicion exceeded reasonable assessments of what was being said or an understanding of situations. But she always showed, at least in my memory, a certain uneasiness in her relationship to the world around her, a remoteness that kept it at arm's length, and an unbending reliance on her own counsel. It is important to emphasize that a certain sense of affection was a luxury that had been taken from both Vehanush and Ohannes. And while they acted as caring parents trying to provide us with what they believed were the necessities of life in America, they sacrificed more than they could acknowledge or even know. But the absence of affection was indelibly stamped on all three of us, as if it refused to be erased or even speak its own truth, an unwanted sign, stamped but unseen, always present, marking the continuation of what our parents had been so cruelly deprived of ever knowing.

As a child, I cannot remember Vehanush ever reading to me, or any of us, even though by that time she had a good command of English. Ohannes told us children's stories from an Armenian folkic storehouse, but I do not remember them now since they comprise only a jumble of unrelated phrases in Armenian. Perhaps this was an expectation that came from the future of an American society where parents were supposed to take a proactive role in virtually everything their child did, especially in their educational formation. My sister Victoria often complained how our parents favored Sena and even me. She may have been right, but when we were growing up I believe we were treated equally when it came to the object of distributing resources like what little affection either could actually give. Later in life, it was evident that Sena, who lived with them, was treated differently from Victoria and me, undoubtedly owing to the fact that they had increasingly become dependent on her in a number of ways. This loss or absence of affection among survivors of genocides must be calculated as one of its greatest consequences, resembling an emotional emptying out and, perhaps, the principal condition of surviving its inhuman excess that demands unyielding silence. For those, like us, who came after, this inheritance became inexpressible rage.

One thing that seems clear to me is that school provided Vehanush with an environment that had little to do with the precapitalist village life she may have come out of, as had my father. The mission school was a condensed microcosm and preview of modern society that actually prepared her and her classmates for a future life they could not have conceived at that time. It made the later transition to modern America much easier since she had already begun to disconnect from traditional village life in the empire and it is not likely she would have returned to it on her own had she stayed in Anatolia. Whatever else she remembered of that moment of life was put behind her, just as she disposed of her Anatolian past as unusable, stored away in some unapproachable place. She was already familiar with modern time and the image of societies that were on some sort of linear conveyer belt moving endlessly toward progress. Village life for her, if it had any residual meaning, belonged to a past—indeed it was the definition of the past—that had brought only uncertainty, scarcity, anxiety, and pain and to which it was even pointless to think of returning. Or at least she had no desire to return to it. I recall a dinner table conversation after World War II on the topic of Soviet repatriation of ethnic minorities and her response to my father's report that he knew of several families in Detroit who had decided to return to Soviet Armenia. My father, who had no real interest in returning, nevertheless defended the decision as possibly beneficial for some people, insofar as he understood the feelings that might have prompted the impulse to leave. Vehanush registered disbelief when she asked what there was to go back to and why anybody would want to leave the U.S. after living here for decades. This was not a prescient Cold War political anticommunist reflex but a conviction that probably originated in her experience in the missionary school and grew throughout the decades she lived in Detroit. In such moments, Vehanush often appeared as someone who had made a willful effort to discredit and discount virtually everything associated with Armenian life in Anatolia as she had known it. If she had any politics, it was nothing more than that.

It is easy to imagine that she, like her classmates, already embodied the ability to make the successful transition to a life she had partially experienced and read about but had not yet confronted in its fullness. Yet this particular involvement in a mission school was undoubtedly replicated everywhere Protestant missionaries, especially, established their programs. In Japan, for example, some of the most progressive intellectuals and politicians came out of the missionary experience, which, if it did not always succeed in implanting the Bible and the word in these precapitalist societies, it certainly accelerated the process of modernization. Apart from this valuable socialization in modernity, whose value Vahanush could not have known at the time, she probably expected her mother to return for her. But in many ways, perhaps not known to her, she was preparing for a life in which her mother would not be returning or playing a role.

It was in school that she also learned how to crochet and make lace with one sewing needle and regular thread, distinctively Armenian and different from the established practice. She also made crochet items with heavier thread and a crochet needle (thicker at one end with a hook). This work was genuine art, drawn from artisanal skills, that few people were able to make; it was in demand by many who knew her work and were convinced, as I am, that what she produced was frankly masterful and beautiful. The needlework was, I believe, her one concession to preserving and identifying with something of a collective past of an artisanal material culture that was in fact destroyed by the genocide. Her creations constituted a reminder of who she was and where she had come from, marking an Anatolia that remained absent in her speech. She never saw herself as a professional artisan who went into the business of selling her work; instead, she saw in the needlework a link to another form of life she had forcibly abandoned but still embodied during her youth. In her capacity to reproduce older forms and intricate designs whose retrieval could only be remembered, not learned or preserved in books, she was, in her own way, able to keep alive the vitality of a traditional material culture. Because she had trachoma when young and a continuing inventory of eye ailments as she grew older, her capacity to produce the intricate designs on her doilies became severely hampered.

I do not know how many years she spent in the mission school, but she must have been there until her midteens. It is impossible to know what her thoughts might have been during these years, or her pleasures, complaints, and expectations for the future. I often wondered if she ever thought about the whereabouts and fate of her brother. Did she ever visit him with her mother in the vicinity before 1915, speak with him, or even exchange letters with him? What had been her experience when living with her brother in the family unit? What was his name? Why had she persisted to hold back his name from us? In all the years we lived together, and even after in adulthood, I never heard her mention her brother or even refer to him in conversation. Did she actually know him, share childhood experiences together, or were they really young when separated? Did she keep his name to herself, like my father did of siblings and parents, because they had been killed? Worse, as an adult it never occurred to me to make up for the deficit of my youthful incuriosity concerning the lives of our parents and force the question on them. I cannot explain this continuing silence but guess that it might have stemmed from long years of successfully keeping the episodes of their earlier lives unsaid and explains my acceptance and satisfaction with fantasy explanations I had conjured.

Vehanush's mother, I have already described, had made her way to Beirut and lived there until about 1934 or 1935, when she died. I have a photo of her that must have been taken in Beirut, sitting beside a standing man wearing a fez (see figure G.9). His name does not appear or sound Armenian; I wondered if he were Arab or some other Middle Eastern ethnicity, or merely an Armenian who changed his name. Vehanush apparently communicated with her mother, who must have known of Vehanush's whereabouts, and Sena reports that Vehanush's mother actually sent her a "handmade" gift when she was young or an infant. I have wondered whether she kept up the correspondence, but if she had, the letters have never surfaced. In Vehanush's mind, the past consisted of her original family, a father who died when she was an infant, a mother, a brother, a stepfather for a time, and herself (she would never have known the third husband of her mother)—three of its members definitively gone, vanished, never, it seemed, to be a part of her world of the missionary school and then the United States. She never mentioned her mother, much less uttered her name to me; she never referred to my "grandmother" or spoke the names of her father, stepfather, or brother. In fact, she never spoke of the dead brother as somebody who once had been a living presence. My childhood fables gave her a family with histories, even though the stories would have been unrecognizable to her. In her world, the nameless were the dead. She also seemed to be completely without relatives, another subject she never discussed or even raised; if she had any, they must have perished among the nameless masses denied entry into the historical record. It was not enough for their identity to have once lived and to have been part of some contemporary historical experience. I even constructed an account for myself in which her brother became a Jesuit priest living in Jerusalem. This was another family fantasy I came to believe to be true until I learned a few years ago he had died young in Turkey. The circumstances surrounding his death are unclear. Because our mother never seemed to have any relatives, I may have wanted to invent one, even an untrue one, for her and us. Yet it seems odder to me than even before that she remained so guardedly tight-lipped about her own family—so much so that it seems as if she were either trying to hide something from us so terrible that she would have no way of divulging it or that, more realistically, she had given up on them because she was convinced she would never see them again. How much time she actually spent with her brother and even her mother is unknown, but it could not have been either very long or intensely intimate. Her life looked as if it started in earnest with the school, even though the details of that experience were held back from us. Clearly, she must have had reasons but never provided even hints of what they might have been. In the case of Ohannes, it is unknown what and how much he knew about her youth or if he merely accepted her as he met her, without interrogating too closely. He would have learned something about her from Mrs. Bedrosian, who would have described her to him as part of the marriage arrangement. In any case, he never said anything that I can recall about her youth or her family, which he never knew.

It seems obvious now that she was more right than wrong to look upon that part of her past as a void. Nothing was left of it worth keeping. School represented a real start and the making of a different past from what she had known in her youthful years at home, but even that remained lodged behind walled-off memories impossible to ascend. She had a good friend in Detroit named Mary, who always called her Vehan, who was a sister of a woman who was part of the same school group that left Marash with Vehanush. I suspect she would speak about that experience with her friend, who had a stake in it, but not with us. Her silence was not unusual among survivors. I do not believe some wave of trauma inexorably swept over Vehanush and Ohannes that may have dragged them under and permanently anchored our parents in a paralysis of silence by holding them in its thrall for a lifetime. Because there was nothing left, apart from repetitiously reflecting on the staggering numbers who were killed and disappeared, there was nothing left to talk about. The survivors scattered to different parts of the world were compelled to carry out the titanic task of starting all over again, bringing nothing but themselves in most cases, and their names (even though Vehanush had no trouble changing her name), and immediately forced into finding places to live, jobs, negotiating daily with people who did not speak their language, struggling interminably with communication, and, for some, the endless search for members of their families, relatives, kinsfolk. Among survivors like my mother, especially, remembering a world that so wantonly was destroyed when she was so young would raise problems of understanding that would return to her as she grew older and perhaps reappear in forms of unwanted flashing revenants reminding her of people she knew who had been murdered. It was not a world to get nostalgic about and to bring back in words. But how else to bring it back? I cannot help thinking that these were years of peril for her. I have tried working through what she may have thought about, how she looked upon an indefinite future, and whether she ever believed she would have one—how in fact she and others with her were able to hold themselves together and function on a daily basis, constantly under the uncertain prospect of an imminent death sentence. What ambitions, dreams, and desires accompanied her, or were all these sentiments simply bracketed or indefinitely deferred until she understood her circumstances and had an idea of what she might expect, what she might be able to realize? What thoughts would she have of her mother and dead father and brother and what role did their ghostly figures continue to occupy in Vehanush's undescribed dreams or secret ruminations? To ask such questions and know beforehand that they would only elicit other unanswerable questions but never bring us closer to some sort of explanatory responses made of our parents' lives a blank tableau and turned ours into a life with strangers.

Until fairly recently, I had never been aware that the Armenian community with which we were involved when growing up was actually a community composed virtually of survivors. When thinking about it, you are struck by the odd fact that every adult you know and have some sort of contact with had come there for the same reasons and at the same time: their presence attested to their surviving. The mark of the genocide was permanently embossed on the diaspora's social body to signify what held the group together. And this fact must have been a powerful mediating force in its composition and how it looked upon the larger world of American life and its relationship to it. There were always people who believed they might one day return to Anatolia and, once abandoning that dream, to at least the eastern Armenian state in the Soviet Federation, who believed that they were only in the U.S. as temporary residents. But this proved to be a necessary illusion that contributed to their resolve to finding their way in the new society. For most, though not my mother, this attitude lasted until they died. At the same time I looked upon the people with whom we interacted through the lens of an American kid, desperate to be more American than ever, disliking many of them as weird and unintelligible and failing to understand all of them and the survivor effect that must have been a principal dimension shaping their makeup. The irony here is that Armenians always referred to non-Armenians as other—*odar*—which I used to describe Armenians.

The problem with the rhetoric of diaspora communities like this one, as I understood it, is that it made too much of the world before the genocide. It subsisted more in a past that had not yet passed into a present, if it was ever likely to do so, than a present no longer bound by the demands of a catastrophic past that could envision a future. My mother's silence notwithstanding, as a child I was subjected to a good deal of chatter and conversation among older folks about the "old country" and their preoccupations with particular villages and what seemed to me at the time an endless celebration of time and place. The village remained their world, even as they adapted to the complex and wider world of American society. I did not know where these places were, had only the most indefinite sense of the time frame of their discussions, and found them repetitious in their invariable return to social and kin relationships and food. Rarely did conversations turn to Turkish or Kurdish neighbors who lived in the vicinity or were friends. Occasionally, my father, in despairing tones, referred to the presence of "whirling dervishes," and what he considered to be a spectacle of religious insanity that served as a blanket judgment covering the Islamic majority. I only learned later that he was referring to Sufi Muslims who embodied a mystical tradition not really any more irrational than the desert saints of early Christianity and the diverse hallucinates of late medieval Europe. Yet Armenians, Greeks, Assyro-Chaldeans, Jews, and other minorities who had inhabited Anatolia long before the coming of the Ottoman Turks lived under unbending constraints and in constant nervous apprehension and fear of arbitrary killings that have carried over into modern Turkish society. Premodern empires, which today have made something of a comeback among some historians because they supposedly exemplified multiethnicity and heterogeneity, unlike the nation-state, were actually prison houses for minority populations. If these ethnic minorities were not always invisible, like slaves and women, their visibility invariably called attention to their exemplification of a heterogeneity that signified only the scandal of different otherness and the necessity to keep them segregated and under surveillance and ultimately to eliminate them. Even after the Kemalist takeover, massacres of Greeks and Armenians continued into the 1950s, with the addition of Kurds down to our present.

Despite the appearance of ethnic heterogeneity, such empires as the Ottoman, the Czarist, and even the Hapsburg resembled spaces dedicated to permanent hunting seasons against minorities as well as reservoirs of violent expropriation, that is, theft and dispossession, sanctioned in the Ottoman case by Islamic customary law. We tend to forget this history these days and especially attitudes as expressed in the following declaration that circulated throughout the Anatolian countryside and provinces in 1915: "God has created the Armenian for sacrifice [*kourban*]."[5] What this obviously meant was that Armenians were put on Earth to be exploited by the true believers and destroyed. There is nothing equivocal in the sentiment. In the Ottoman Empire, the received religious anti-Armenian racism was always expressed in the form of hatred within Anatolian Muslim communities, large numbers of which would eventually participate in the massacre. The genocide was merely the last attempt and the most comprehensive of these unscheduled pogroms and the most ambitious episode in a long history that suggests a final plan determined according to the task it was supposed to resolve: save the empire by removing troublesome minorities—erasing the stain of heterogeneity—who were said to comportation convoys that would pass through the town, and I have wondered if she and her friends had an inkling of them or even were able to catch glimpses of them as they made their fateful journey through the city. The deportations, as I show later, were themselves a moving killing field, and it was estimated that only 20 percent of the hundreds of thousands driven on these forcible marches made it to their final destination, which would be an even worse ending, as Chris Bohjalian's novel *The Sandcastle Girls* graphically portrays.

As suggested earlier, the Marash region was already marked by the memory of massive murders inaugurated by Abdülhamid II in the 1890s, and by some counts the number of people killed has reached as high as 300,000. It was my sister Sena who emphasized that our mother's mother (why is it so difficult to call her grandmother, a woman for us who was nothing more than a nameless abstraction? I have never been able to answer that question and never observed either Victoria or Sena referring to this disembodied relative as "grandmother") worked in the school/orphanage for a time before she left and she must have heard things from the outside world she conveyed to Vehanush that would have made her anxious and put her in a state of permanent fear and panic. But her mother would have also made her way out of Marash to the safety of Beirut before or by 1915 and the beginning of the genocide. None of us knew anything about her life at this time, much less her name, about her resourcefulness in getting out, or whether her reaching Beirut was the end of a long process of escape or simply a direct arrival. She apparently lost her second husband and remarried a third time in Beirut. I do remember the years in the late Depression in Detroit and our mother's anxieties about economic security since my father worked sporadically on Works Progress Administration (WPA) road projects, when he worked. This sense of worry carried her through the war and into postwar American life, when my father had a secure job and they were eventually able to buy a small house on the southwest side of Detroit, off Five Mile Road. Conceivably, she transferred the intensely real insecurities and anxieties produced by the specter of impending genocidal murder outside the school and her mother's disappearance over to the fear of permanent economic uncertainty in the United States.

Vehanush died reasonably young in 1967 (in her early sixties) from a heart attack, and as she lay in a hospital bed she was worrying about the consequences of Charles de Gaulle's threat announcing that he was going to corner the world's supply of gold. In a certain sense, her early years mand considerable wealth and a storehouse of skills that could have been productively used when Turkey decided to become a modern nation-state but rather was presented as the means by which minorities would dominate and enslave the Turks. Instead, the Young Turks resorted to the political appeal of national renewal, based on "Turkism," which simply was another name for non-Europeans, both Christian and Islamic. In the end the genocide brought the empire down.

In the Armenian diaspora community of the U.S., when the past came into conversation, it was usually an embroidered, romantic image employed to contrast it with an unfavorable contemporary life in an alien land. I can recall how my mother called these made-up stories flights of nonsense. But they were stories that nevertheless moored people to a strange land and offered the future prospect of return, even though it was delusionary. Vehanush could be harshest with our father, who would frequently slip into the groove of an almost involuntary and unyielding but momentary nostalgia. Vehanush never showed a hint of nostalgia for the world she forcibly left. These differences appeared to show the importance of their experiential backgrounds: Ohannes, raised to adulthood in a very traditional, virtually clan-dominated religious village environment; and Vehanush, whose formation began in a foreign Protestant missionary school and who became a woman who seemingly forgot nothing but who revealed even less. In these discussions Vehanush always reflected the position of someone who simply could not understand the romantic hold of traditional life, even though she knew the reasons prompting these flights. After all, one of her favorite movies was *Gone with the Wind* (1939).

I keep returning to the troubling problem of names and that both Ohannes and Vehanush never uttered them, at least before us. I have felt that this decision might have been part of a strategy to close off discussions on things they did not want to speak of; it effectively worked to foreclose any questions from us since it is difficult to speak of nameless people we would never know and see. But it seems strange now, as already acknowledged, that none of us ever sought to open discussion concerning their early years. Was it because we were here, not there, which, for us, was nowhere, filled with questions never asked and answers deferred for a lifetime and for our parents only part of an aborted past that was cut short and taken from them? Whatever their intention, silence seemed to discourage further questioning and set up a permanent barrier against expressions of curiosity. I have never really managed to successfully explain the reasons for this absence of curiosity to others or to myself. My father mentioned only one of his many sisters by name, Catherine, apparently his favorite, who, significantly, died of pneumonia before the massacres, while the rest of the large family was murdered and their names never mentioned, if I recall correctly. I have often thought about the reasons why the names of the dead or those who have disappeared were never invoked, and speculated on whether there had been some deeply entrenched traditional practice that demanded the removal of such names in everyday conversation.

Some writers have seen this absence as evidence of a broader "psychological trauma," a theorization that gained greater acceptance after World War II.[6] In the interwar years after the genocide, apparently people were not encouraged to recount their experiences. It is not clear to me why such experiences were induced to remain untold. Thomas De Waal quotes from the published account recording the horror of Leon Surmelian's childhood and the loss of his parents: "Neither my brother nor sisters spoke about their most painful inner experiences, which, like myself, could not be told. In fact I could not tell them anything about myself, nor did they question me. By a sort of silent agreement we took care not to mention our parents, and other relatives whom we dearly loved. Their names, or anything to remind us directly of them, were barred from conversation."[7] While it is not conclusive that anything like some sort of "communal fate" or collective mass trauma explains this silence, it still must have been a widely observed individual disposition. In Surmelian's account, there is a similarity to our own later experience, a generation removed, when our parents remained silent on their relatives and names and we were thus barred from further questioning. If it is said to mark the behavior of survivors of different genocidal episodes, and I am not at all sure it does, are silences a reflection of a commonly shared reason that points to the unbearable pain of speaking the names of beloved relatives who have perished in a cataclysm? Striking out the names of the dead relatives and loved ones means they no longer inhabit the everyday, as we do. In fact, the everyday for them longer exists. But it also implies they are only remembered in silence and that their presence has been removed from the record of public memory as if they never existed. This may, in part, explain the consistent practice of never uttering the names of those who have perished, as if it were a way of quarantining the lived from the dead. By contrast, the historical was all about names, usually names of the dead, who apparently still have stories to tell, fueled by it, attesting to the power of subjectivity to survive beyond death, preserving the names of the dead who apparently still have their stories for the living. One thing appears obvious: the extreme suppressing of the names of loved ones who perished is determined by the nature of the event that took their lives. If they did not die like Ohannes's sister Catherine, who died of an illness, and whose name lived on in utterances, the names of those who were inhumanly and obscenely murdered are erased.

For us, there is the additional question that asks for an explanation of the circumstances that prompted the three of us to agree to a compact of silence, as if there were no question to our acceptance that nothing ever really happened. Is it the same for those who experience an overwhelming natural disaster and have lost members of their families? What has interested me is the behavior of parents who refused to refer to their parents and children by name and its effect on us: the refusal worked to prevent us from further inquiry. We were denied even the memory of belonging to a kin group of departed relatives. I have already reported that our mother mentioned none of the names of her smaller family, not even her mother, who survived in another country, much less friendships made in school and cemented by the journey to Greece. It came to me that perhaps her life with them was too brief, not worth recalling it through their names. Nor did my father mention his family's names, with the one exception. Here was a paradox: not only did historians define the nameless by omitting from history the large numbers who sacrificed their lives to make history, but the survivors, who were part of this historic cohort of nameless people, redefined the category in order to also exclude their dead.

In many ways the silence of survivors like our mother is condensed in the act of namelessness, as if cutting out that portion of the past that no longer exists requires repressing names of people who once inhabited your world but who actually disappeared with it. This whitening out of a portion of the past is, I suspect, a kind of preparation for a new life in a different place, or no life at all. It was strangely in keeping with America's own habitual allergy to history and forgetting the immediate past as if it never happened, and it was dramatized by Vehanush's speed in adapting herself to modern American life. Vehanush's release from genocidal Anatolia seemed to relieve her of the burden of history. She had been assisted by exposure to a modern life encouraged by German Protestant missionaries who, like other Protestant missionaries in Anatolia, could juxtapose a figure of modernity in contrast to the Armenian Apostolic Church organized in the fourth century CE. The trace of our mother's training was manifest in her adaptability and decision to not affiliate with any religious institution once settled in the U.S. It is as if a Protestant missionary school

Traces of a Vanished Everyday

inculcated in her a sense of secularism as a vital dimension of a modernizing society and the necessary requirement to live in it. That decision could also have induced a disapproving response to the religious discipline imposed on the young students of the school. Hollywood continued her education into modern life. She had no trouble dropping her family name for the name of a woman who had a lot to do with saving her life. (In actuality, the Bedrosians sponsored her entry into the U.S., which resulted in taking on their name as their "daughter" and keeping it.) In all this, the real difficulty I have encountered derives principally from my recognition that my parents' complicity was necessary in shielding us from this sorrowful history, the kind of social relationships provided by a community of survivors whose members were just like our parents, and how few reminiscences I could actually (if not reliably) call forth of their willingness or unwillingness to speak about their experience to me and my sisters. Sometimes, I felt we were all passing strangers to each other.

An additional problem was my education. Second-generation children of immigrants who, like myself, were the first to have attended college discovered that one of the unintended consequences is that you lose and eventually are cut off from your earlier life and associations. When I went to graduate school, I left Detroit, never really to return, except on infrequent occasions to visit my parents and Sena. Victoria married young and moved to another state, while Sena remained living with our parents and developed a better sense of them than I possessed. And they, as they aged, depended more on Sena since Victoria and I were no longer around. But this decision also gestured toward a kind of mimetic reversal of our own mother's experience of having been separated and ultimately abandoned by her mother. In fact, the respectively different trajectories of my sisters and me suggests a significant disclosure of what our family was about or like and, perhaps, something larger concerning the dynamic of migrant American family life in the interwar period. But there does not appear to be anything in Sena's longer experience with my parents that sheds further light on their earlier years. What I have found especially disquieting by our parents' decision to remain silent about their early lives is that coming to America represented a new start that seemed to have canceled out their other pasts in order to begin again. They continued to live with these traces of that past all around them in their everyday, which remained there, in their present, in one form or another as permanent revenants no longer bound by unscheduled appearances.

While our mother was a booster of American life and Americanization, a modernizer "before the letter," she maintained a set of associations with Armenian groups like the Armenian Red Cross, the Armenian General Benevolent Union, and my father's ARF or Dashnak associates, as much for the sociability they offered as anything else. She loved movies and probably learned a great deal concerning the materiality of American life from them, as did other late-developing capitalist societies. My father seems to have had deeper roots in Armenian village life. He never described the physical conditions of home or even the village, apart from some vague remarks that it was near a "sea" or probably a lake or pond I could never locate on any map of the region. As he and my children grew older, he seemed obsessed with providing them with money for shoes, suggesting, perhaps, the recovered memory of their absence in his childhood.

In spite of his own religious agnosticism, even though he came from a priestly family or because of it, Ohannes, not my mother, insisted on my being baptized by the Armenian Church. Hence, my connection with the Armenian Church began and ended with the momentary trauma of baptism by a black-bearded, deep-voiced priest, which entailed being dumped into a large washing tub filled with water and crying my head off, as much out of fear of the imposing black-bearded priest, draped and hooded entirely in black, as from the actual immersion itself. Regardless of this disagreeable experience, throughout my life the church remained imprinted on me and on my real name, which was Harutun der Harootunian, a redundancy, to be sure, but filled with my father's hopefulness since it meant "Resurrection, son of the Resurrection." I have thought that, despite his break from the Armenian Church and religion in general, the decision to provide me with a redundant name evoking the significance of resurrection and new life must have been prompted by his desire to indelibly stamp or imprint on me my Armenian identity, which the church had historically assumed. But its overdetermination also suggests the possibility of some sort of rebirth, renewal, or conviction that hope springs eternal out of both the ruins of Ani and the ever present threat of historical extinction permanently closing off the future, interrupting Armenian dreams of an expectant and fulfilled future. Needless to say, that futureless void was actualized by the most recent killing fields of Anatolia that nearly succeeded in turning dreams into a final nightmare. It is hard to know what my father had in mind since he rarely, if ever, referred to me by the given name, and my mother never did. But my mother had no use whatsoever for the Armenian Church, looking upon its priests as freeloaders and the reservoir of all backwardness, probably because of her exposure to Protestant Christian-

Traces of a Vanished Everyday 67

ity in the orphanage. She never maintained an affiliation with any church but led, according to my sisters, an exemplary Christian life.

I did not learn about the massacres from my parents. It was gradual, and always tempered by what I overheard and could understand, which usually was calibrated to how old I was. In this way I learned about its existence in fragments gleaned from incomplete conversations overheard between my parents and Armenian friends, who had undergone similar experiences. These amounted to fragments and unconnected accounts that accumulated into an unstructured collage of statements, hearsay, half-remembered stories that could only be randomly thrown together to form a large pool open to demand plural readings and interpretations, without any coherent story line. The collage-like components could be used or selected to tell whatever story one wanted to recount. Yet, in retrospect, the fragmented conversations I had overheard as a child conveyed what proved to be the proper form of grasping the genocide and its afterlife, an episode that was itself experienced in unrelated fragments and whose survivors lived its fractured afterlife of existences in diasporas that strove to realize the lost coherence but rarely succeeded.

What I was able to gather came especially from those large-scale gatherings organized by the local ARF-Dashnak chapter, either in a building they owned in Delray (southeastern Detroit, not far from the Michigan Central Station) or at the Azadamard (Freemen's) Club closer to where we lived. In the summers there were outings (*khunjoogs*) in parks, large-scale picnics with varieties of Armenian dishes, and music and dancing; and in autumn there were expeditions into the countryside, searching for "errant" grape leaves growing alongside roads from nearby farm fields to be picked, pickled, and bottled for *sarma*. As I was growing up, I began to notice people inevitably returning to the same themes discussed in previous socials, exchanging experiences and their own memories and those they had heard. Often, I saw a woman or even a man break down in tears and I watched attempts on the part of the interlocutors to console them. It was from these discussions I heard that I began to learn that something really awful had befallen these people and resulted in the loss of people they were close to. But these disjointed conversations never supplied encouragement to interrogate either of my parents; nor were they ever prompted to explain such episodes to us. Why did I suppose that my parents, who had come to the U.S. for the same reasons and at the same time as these people, were exempt from such experiences? It was only in my early teens, I now recall, that my father began to relate his wartime experiences in Anatolia, fighting with the Russians under Dashnak command along the eastern border. These were anecdotal reminiscences concerning places he had visited. But I did not know where or when he signed up to join an ARF brigade and where he was trained. In the early years when he lived off and on in the U.S., he was clearly involved in ARF politics, an Armenian version of a bund, for which I have a few photos, taken in and around the time of World War I. One of the group photos reveals a young man in the front row in a nicely cut three-piece suit, with a watch on a chain hanging in the upper pocket of his jacket (figure G.5). (In precapitalist societies moving into capitalist modernity, the gold pocket watch was often seen as a sign of the modern.) This modern man—confident, self-assured—had a swaggering look, stylish air, and interesting face topped by thick, black wavy hair, and appeared relaxed and in possession of a serious countenance as many of the others in the photo, all dressed in three-piece suits. They were posing for a photo that must have been of some local chapter of the ARF. Two of the men in the front row are holding hands, a pose I have noticed in other photos of Armenians from that era. Was this a sign of camaraderie? What I remember of him when I was young is that the swagger and confidence had left him as he aged; the uncertainties of job security and sporadic welfare work in the U.S. had begun to imprint deep lines in his face. And years later, when I returned to that photo, I thought that his youth and his escape from a premodern village to the modern world of America must have energized him with the promise of a hope and possibility that dissipated with time and experience. In the photo, he looked like any young modern man. But it was clear that as he aged, the trappings of modernity merely concealed deeper habits and reflexes belonging to another culture from a different time. Unlike our mother, who never expressed any desire to return to Anatolia, it seemed that Ohannes in his later years had embraced an aspiration of his youth, which was the conviction that life in America was a temporary adventure and he would return home. By the time of the depression and the certainty of insecurity, all youthful energy had abandoned him—he was now in an unwanted history belonging to somebody else, still looking for steady work to feed his family, which a broader family in the vanished world of kin and clan might have taken care of in another place. At the end of his life, he went to Fresno. But in all these years I never once heard him utter any of the delusionary offers associated with the equally classic ideological promise of the "American Dream" that still continues to lure people with its false hopes. What he did often say is that people in the United States worked harder than workers in any other place.

But it is interesting to reflect on how ungenerous Armenians of the diaspora appeared to me, as if the experience of getting out with little or nothing had frozen them into the figure of Shylocks and hoarders dedicated to constantly watching over their money and possessions before they were taken away, sacrificed. I remember an Armenian family who lived in one of the upstairs flats of our building: the head—Boghoz—was seen by everybody who encountered him as a model miser and classic cheapskate; his wife, always dressed in black, was no better and incessantly poor-mouthing their situation; and their son, Vartkes, became an untalented petty thief. (Our parents thought otherwise and were convinced they were sitting on a large hoard of cash.) I generalized this image of Armenian life in the U.S., concluding they were a people of small ambitions and were petty, niggardly hoarders. I felt that whatever solidarity and resilience under Ottoman oppression imposed, the rural community was no longer operationally embodied in the diaspora, only its form remaining empty. I would learn later, and perhaps better, that they were not all like that and that it was wrong to view them from a contemporary American perspective of expectations to recognize that the experience of living in Anatolia and leaving without anything had been force-fed into migrants and shaped their personality. Most of them reached the U.S. with few resources, if any. Many made up the deficit caused by loss, whatever it may have been. Still, it should also be remembered that most Armenians who managed to get to the U.S. were from peasant families, who had already been socialized in an imperial regime devoted to ceaseless expropriation and theft. With our parents, they had little or no real resources once they returned to the U.S. from France, and it is not even clear how long they spent there before making their way to Detroit. But they never suffered from the affliction of niggardliness or succumbing to the expectations generated by false hope.

This observation of niggardliness may also have stemmed from conditions peculiar to the diaspora, which was made up of survivors who were all Armenians yet coming from different regions, towns, and villages, where the bonds of solidarity no longer operated. What had once been a regionally heterogeneous society had become homogenized in the U.S.; paradoxically, this homogenization seemed to alienate people into divisiveness who were still trying to retain their sense of a different regional or village affiliation from each other in a place where these local attachments no longer existed. This sense of division was especially intensified by the competition over scarce resources. It may have also been the case that the survivors carried with them older habitual patterns of behavior formed under Ottoman oppression, such as taking care of themselves in this uncertain environment by hoarding for the future. Clearly, the subsequent dispossession and theft encouraged and enabled by genocide exacerbated these older reflexes and impulses. It is also true that the church, which had been so deeply embedded in village life, and the millet system, which provided the fiction of semiautonomy, were no longer a force in diaspora life: the church was usually distant from its parishioners and had lost its political function, and the millet system disappeared with the empire. Where the appeal of regionalism persisted was in ways it was used to discount people from, say, such and such village, as if they had always been known in Anatolia as backward bumpkins, wretches, or whatever. This practice may well have been devised by and in the diaspora, for all I know. But it must also be recognized that empires and their spatially distant administrations create the conditions of semiautonomy or, at least, its function as a necessary illusion in spatially far-flung regions.

Into this unwelcome history of migrant life in the U.S. that excluded large numbers of people, my father and mother were actually without historical identity. To be discounted in this way led to living a diminished life, which I will return to. Diasporic migration meant leaving one's history behind because it was or is in the process of being destroyed. Arrival in a foreign and alien environment demanded involuntarily entering somebody else's history without knowing the coordinates of this new space-time. Assembling in ghettoes with coethnics is the response and leads to living the double or comparative life mentioned above. The settlements of the Armenian diaspora throughout the world were attempts to remain connected to that lost history—however imagined, abridged, and symbolized by Ani's once greatness—in the midst of a larger urban configuration that belonged to others. But the history these settlements embodied was a congealed montage representing now combined regions of Anatolia constructed out of recalled everyday lives that had ended with the genocide and flight. The diaspora became the unanticipated instrument of homogenizing the heterogeneity of Armenian life. This homogenization of Armenian life was powerfully reinforced by the genocide itself, which made no observance of regional differentiation. I recall that at social events, people would proudly appeal to the preparation of certain dishes as a sign of retrieving regional identities that had been lost in the forcible homogenization. Apparently, there was nothing like the *kufta* (a baked, stuffed meatball, made of ground lamb, bulghar, onions, and walnuts), which any number of villages claimed to having produced the best.

Over the years I have returned to that group photo in which my father appeared with his comrades and wondered about it: he was unmarried at that time and it may have been taken before the U.S. entered the war; how early is not clear, nor where it was taken, or where he lived, perhaps in Chicago. Who were the others and what happened to them? I am not able to recognize any familiar face from the friends of our father I met and knew while growing up. What happened to the men gathered in the photo? Did they join up with Ohannes to fight in the ARF brigades? But I may be wrong about the dating since in the photo of him and two comrades during his time in the ARF brigades, dressed for combat and armed, he appears to look younger, and that photo must have been taken in and around 1915 or even a bit earlier. My son still resembles my father when that photo was taken.

In those early years, how did Ohannes spend his spare time when not working? I know he made his first trip to the U.S. with a cousin, when they actually lived in Canada for a while, who eventually lived near us when we were in Highland Park. But by that time we never saw him and his family because of an earlier quarrel. My mother claimed he had cheated our father out of money or a small business venture in which they were partners. The incident put the lie to my father's favorite phrase, "blood is thicker than water." He rarely spoke of his cousin, who surprisingly physically resembled my father and who, economically, was far better off than we. In his early trips to the U.S., Ohannes must have communicated with members of his family in Anatolia—his parents, grandparents, brothers, and sisters. Why is there no record of this time or even a body of recollections he could have relayed? Where are the exchanged letters? What did he do and did he send money back? What did he aspire to? Hope for? What did America mean to him at the time he was a contract laborer? The absence of letters between my parents in the U.S. and their relatives and parents in Anatolia, exchanged in different times, is baffling, and I have no explanation concerning their disappearance, if they had actually existed. But it is evident that this kind of documentary material could have told us a good deal about how they felt and thought, what problems they encountered, what expectations they brought with them, and their observations of America, as well as reports concerning the current situation in Anatolia. The few photos we possess fail to fill in these blanks. It is not at all clear if such material was deliberately destroyed or lost in one of their moves or simply seen as not worth saving. Our mother was not known to either save or collect things. Is it that the pattern of working as contract labor in the U.S. and returning home and coming back suggested that Ohannes eventually intended to settle permanently in Anatolia? Spending time in big American cities would either gradually diminish the attractiveness of rural life in a precapitalist village society dominated by Turks and administered by Armenian priests at the local level or contribute to romanticizing it. It is interesting to speculate on whether his American experience would have induced him to migrate to Istanbul, away from village life to an urban complex already committed to forms of modernization and the actualization of modern life. That question was definitively answered when he left the ARF brigade and returned to the U.S. in late 1916 or early 1917.

The growing crisis leading up to World War I and the worsening conditions in Anatolia, especially for its minority populations, would have been worrying to Ohannes and his friends and comrades, who knew the history of the region. Maintaining steady communication with their families in Turkey must have become a subject of anxious concern, as well as what lay in store for Armenians, especially, since the community was already expressing and acting on the aspiration for independence.

Ohannes had scattered relatives, distant cousins in the U.S. who had managed to escape the genocide. I had always felt that he tried to maintain some connection with this dispersed group of distant relatives, as if frantically clasping the branches of a dying family tree to prevent falling alone onto an unfamiliar ground. These cousins and more distant relatives once constituted for him a larger and more solidary kin group in Anatolia. But now they only represented the remaining slivers that had already set their different trajectories and lives after survival that he was desperately trying to pull together. In this endeavor, Vehanush was an involuntary participant who happily accompanied him on these expeditions but always armed with the perspective of a skeptic who, having no relatives to speak of, brought no corresponding experience of living in an extended kin group to my father's attempt. Her perspective was often insightful and I found her judgments more unerring than not. Some of Ohannes's relatives were in Waukegan, Cleveland, and Detroit. I think he felt closest to the Waukegan branch, whose head of the family—my father's first cousin—ran a liquor store later inherited by his oldest son, Ashod. Ashod was probably a second cousin who would visit our father from time to time, and he had an obvious affection and respect for him that, I always felt, was not extended to the rest of us. He was not high on my list. My favorite was Nvart, another of my father's first cousins, and her husband, Garabed, in Cleveland, whom I looked upon as aunt and uncle when I was a child. They had two sons; the younger was hit by a car at age four or five and died. The oldest son, Richard, became a lawyer with whom my sister Sena and I lost contact after his parents died. And there were more distant cousins in Detroit we visited regularly, two brothers who ran a corner grocery store. In this cohort the only one I really liked was a third or fourth cousin, Berjui, who was about my age, and quite beautiful with green eyes that matched my father's. She was one of two daughters of the eldest brother, Hagop. Our mother had little use for our father's relatives and especially this branch. I often wondered about the source of this animus and thought it might have derived from the envy of one who had no relatives. I think this also may have been the case regarding Nvart, who, as a first cousin, was close to my father—they had literally grown up together. Nvart frequently referred to my mother as her "sister," which evidently rankled Vehanush. But Vehanush was wrong about Nvart and right about the Detroit branch, the Aznavourians. She believed they had treated my father badly, in some instances perhaps exploited him, and had never done anything for him when he was in need of help during the depression. I do not believe he ever asked for help. But I came to feel that the issue was related more to pretensions of social class and hierarchy within the Armenian community and possibly the zero-sum game inhabitants of the diaspora had made into a life principle. I distinctly remember that the Detroit relatives never visited us. Perhaps it was because we lived in a rather cramped four-family flat at the edge of Highland Park where it bordered Detroit. It was a working-class neighborhood of mixed ethnic groups and contrasted with their single-standing house in a middle-class area of Detroit. But I suspect that our mother had it right when she complained that they had social airs in addition to their single-standing house. The brothers Hagop and Khosrov were probably from the same village or nearby where my father came from. In other words, they were peasants. As grocers, they were upwardly aspiring petit bourgeois merchants in Detroit—probably less affected by the depression than most. As it appeared to me, the problem was Hagop's wife, Anahid, and her mother, who lived with them. Apparently, both were from Istanbul and were already socialized into the Armenian bourgeoisie of that large urban center. Anahid and her mother seemed to claim the status of inheritors of Istanbul's urban and developed cosmopolitan culture that must have trickled down among bourgeois Greeks, Jews, and Armenians. I found her mother (Nazanik), especially, an unknowing bore; she spoke of nothing but how good life had been in Istanbul, and I often wondered why she had left. Years later it occurred to me she spoke of the glories of Istanbul as if the genocide had not taken place or was simply a distant, barely audible echo of a past event. Yet, the genocide actually did reach the Armenian community in Istanbul, where the first round up and execution of professional men was carried out. Some scholars of the genocide have proposed that middle-class Armenians in Istanbul had become more assimilated to urban Turkish life than village peasants of eastern and western Anatolia.[8] This would have grated on my mother's nerves, as she literally came from nothing and understandably would have had great difficulty in believing the repetitious descriptions of the good life in Istanbul. My father was treated like a poor country cousin whom they suffered from time to time but with whom they made no effort to establish a closer relationship. In fact, they had different associations within Detroit's Armenian community and I never saw this particular set of relatives at any of the larger social functions we were made to attend with our parents, which suggests a class differentiation that often aligned with specific political groups within the diaspora. The prevailing atmosphere of these moments was shot through with thick condescension and patronization. I also think that our father's Armenian politics, his earlier involvement in the volunteer brigades, and his continuing affiliation with the Dashnaks might have contributed to widening the distance between him and the two Aznavourian brothers, whose politics seemed oriented toward a more bourgeois party, called *Ramgavar* (Liberal Democratic Party).

By the time I reached my early teens, I stopped accompanying my parents on such visits since I could not tolerate the repetition of stories about an imagined world the older woman had fantasized and felt entitled to regale us with and about which I had no desire to learn more. I also was able to liberate myself from Anahid's insistence on singing Armenian songs (or whatever they were; they sounded Armenian) before us, often sounding like a crow in deep distress. It is entirely possible that my perspective on accompanying my parents on such visits I really did not want to make, spending a whole day among older people speaking of the old country—a place I had no knowledge of or interest in—as if it were some sort of prelapsarian golden age, reflected the unintended impatience of a bored kid. But I recall sensing similar displeasure in my mother's attitude toward them, which may have reinforced my own indifference. I do recall that I rarely, if ever, saw these people once I entered my teens, with the exception of Berjui, who died young, and have no idea of what happened to the rest even though Sena maintained some contact with them after our parents died.

I mention these relatives because I never felt that we were actually related to these people who either rarely (if ever) showed up periodically or who we only occasionally visited. With few exceptions they were not close, excepting Nvart, nor particularly friendly when we visited with them. They always acted as distant acquaintances of my father, especially, and showed little affection in any way one would associate with close relatives. Unlike relatives who would have been part of our lives as we were growing up, they were distant, rarely in evidence: people who may have had some sort of blood tie to our father and prior associations but had no meaning for us. Not only were we deprived of close relations with grandparents, aunts and uncles, and cousins, sharing with them the intimacies of our lives or theirs, these distant cousins of our father seemed to treat him and us as outliers, intruders whom they felt obliged to tolerate on the few occasions we showed up. I have often thought that what reinforced this experience of distance and strangeness, if not exactly estrangement, surrounding these alleged "relatives" was the form of the occasional visit itself we made to see them. As I look back on those times, the visits appeared more like a pilgrimage whose ritualistic purpose and meaning remained a mystery to me but an unexplained necessity for Ohannes.

I have been convinced that our experience among Armenians was not particularly exceptional and that growing up and living without relatives had its own drawbacks on the formation and development of one's affective facilities. What bothered me has been the knowledge of a grandmother with whom we had no contact or even the faintest idea of her existence until she died. In this respect, the three of us reproduced the emotional world of our mother. The principal lesson learned from experiencing regular contact with estranged relatives of my father is the rapid uprootedness that occurs among people who were both closely related to each other and shared a solidarity of intimacy when they inhabited a premodern village society, which the move to a modern capitalist urban society thoroughly diluted. I suspect my father understood the effects of this momentous spatial (geographic) and temporal (capitalism's socially normative) time and tried to overcome the widening gulf between himself and his relatives through our periodic ritualistic visitations. My mother accepted the displacement as a deliverance and had no need for visits to Ohannes's increasingly remote relatives, which she saw as a waste of a good Sunday's time and another missed movie. Apart from the suppressed antagonism such visits produced, and the distinct impression I had that we were not welcome when we did show up, it occurred to me when recalling those moments that the encounters represented a projection of the microcosm of the city/countryside division in Turkey, with its entailing conceits, which would have played a much greater role in the time of the genocide, if for no other reason than the city folks had greater opportunities and resources with which to get out.

In the presence or absence of a large family group is reflected the relative intensity of affect and especially what might be called an affective division of labor. In this structure of thick relations, aunts, uncles, grandparents, and cousins all play specific roles not necessarily carried out by the immediate parents. This was entirely missing in our experience and perhaps explains why Sena sought out a broader group of Armenian friends as if they constituted a surrogate extended family, when Victoria and I took different routes. It also explains Vehanush's own indifference to the few tattered threads of relatives our father tried to pull together as a substitute, which she imparted to us. In this respect, the three of us replicated her own experience, not my father's. I also think that when catastrophes occur and remove all those other people, many of whom were relatives, they are no longer there to do what they might have had they lived, as relatives, to fulfill their various roles in the structure of an affective division of labor. But they also missed out as much as those who would have been the objects of their affective and emotional investments. Is this what happens to Pierre Bourdieu's incisive proposition concerning the reproduction of a habitat when there is no longer a larger unit to enforce a traditionally unquestioned requirement that "anything goes without saying words" in order to carry out its reproductive imperatives?[9] None of us benefited from the wisdom and love of that vanished world, and I believe that while our parents did what they could, there was always that missing piece in our upbringing. I saw it also reflected in the way my parents related to my own kids—especially in my mother's remoteness.

As for Ohannes's military training, it must have been somewhere in the eastern provinces or in the Russian Caucasus. In this respect, he spoke of having spent time in Tbilisi, Georgia, but I do not really know why he was there and for how long. As I explained earlier, I have a photo of him and two comrades armed for combat that might have been taken there. He often spoke of an Armenian general named Antranik (a favorite name given to Armenian sons), known for his heroic leadership on the eastern front and under whose command my father and his comrades must have fought. I do not know which battles he experienced in the east, where he was posted, fought, and retreated, or even how he was able to momentarily get to his village, which was at a distance to the west from the eastern front in the vicinity of Harput, to discover its destruction and the disappearance of his family. Once there, did he speak to anybody, if there were still survivors? Or did he learn of the village's destruction through reports passed on by others? If he made a trip to his village, he must have made his way back to the east because he finally left the region, traveling through Russia, where he caught a ship to England and ultimately the United States. What prompted him to leave the struggle—some sort of settlement between the Turks and Russians under whom the Armenian brigades were fighting? When did he leave? The Treaty of Brest-Litovsk in 1918 brought an end to the Russian involvement in the Allied cause and its withdrawal into a civil war between the Bolsheviks and their White adversaries. But Ohannes must have been induced to leave Anatolia and the war in the east by what he saw and felt when he returned to his village. He knew that his family had perished. What he did not know was whether they were murdered on location or driven into one of the deportation marches, which surely would have had the same effect. There was nothing left there and he knew that his entire family was gone. He must have left the region before 1918 and returned to the U.S., where he joined the AEF, apparently briefly trained, and was sent to France in 1917. He probably made this decision sometime in late 1915 or 1916. There is a photo of him in a rather large group of American soldiers, taken at some hospital for the wounded in France and dated 1918. The chronology of his movements is really skewed and at times contradictory in light of what is known of his trajectory. If he discovered the destruction of his home and family while still in the Armenian brigades, as I am convinced he did, he must have decided to permanently leave the region. The occasion was also provided by the course of military events in the east; it must have been late 1915 or early 1916, during the Russian victories and a momentary hiatus in hostilities, that Ohannes was able to make his way to his village and his parents' home to see what had occurred there in his absence and made his decision. A ceasefire prevailed throughout 1917 but by the end of the year, it was ratified by an armistice in December that brought an official end to combat between Russia and Ottoman Turkey. As a result, the remaining Russian forces withdrew, leaving approximately one thousand Armenian volunteers to face the 3rd Ottoman Army. Under such conditions, it is imaginable that my father might have left with the Russians.

As for my mother, she might have eventually left the orphanage/school she attended and lived in and where, I believe, her mother worked for a time. Her disciplined silence on all things relating to her family, as well as her years in the school, have been increasingly unsettling as I began the effort to unravel its secrecy and the reasons for it. What was she shielding us from by not referring to her brother, father, or mother by their names? Why did she choose to say nothing about them? What on earth did she have in mind? And for whom? Was she protecting someone? Her father had died earlier and well before the massacres. If her mother put her children into the safekeeping of mission schools or simply because she was no longer in a position to take care of them, it is difficult to know if she herself thought she would return in the future to collect them or had planned to abandon them. Perhaps she thought that this was as much as she could do for them under the circumstances. But when and what actually motivated her are not clear. Vehanush's mother remarried twice after the death of her first husband and ultimately found her way to Beirut, where she died sometime in the early 1930s.

I know she was in communication with Vehanush during the years of their separation, but I have no idea of its extent or regularity. Someone in Beirut who knew about the separation and the addresses of mother and daughter informed Vehanush by letter that her mother had died. At the time she received the news of her mother's death, we were living in a basement of a building owned by an Armenian name Calouste, an energetic and generous small businessman with a strangely twisted ear, who lived upstairs with his wife, daughter, and son. My guess is that little rent was being paid; our father had a good relationship with Calouste, liked him, and might have done some work for him. I do recall they regularly made *raki* in a washtub basin. This place was a block from where we lived when I was born, and it is really the first place I can remember. I was about four or five when Vehanush heard about her mother's death, which means that we had not been there too long and her mother must have known of the change of address. I remember when she received the letter, while both of us were in the front yard, and where she began to cry. This is really one of the few bits of evidence available concerning the question of communication between mother and daughter. What is not at all clear is when this communication would have started, its mode of regularity, and whether it was actually between Vehanush's mother and the teacher Bedrosian or whether she knew of the name change. It is not too plausible to assume that Vehanush continued to communicate with her mother once enrolled in the school, given the external circumstances of the mother's flight to Beirut. She certainly knew of the marriage to Ohannes and the birth of Sena.

But the motives of Vehanush's mother remain unclear. My best guess is that she had no intention of returning, even though Vehanush and her brother, given their ages, probably initially believed she would come back for them and were reassured by their mother. She must have believed they were better off where they were and/or she was better off without them. But what about the brother/son? Her response to that would depend on the time she learned when and how he died. Somewhere in this indistinct history, Vehanush must have concluded that she had been abandoned by her or she had perished, which explains why she retained the name of the Bedrosians. When and how did she learn of the death of her brother? Why did she retain Bedrosian as her maiden name even after she discovered her mother was still alive in Beirut? In some manner, Vehanush must have known that her mother was not killed or disappeared. Almost fifteen years had passed between the time Vehanush married Ohannes and the date of her mother's death, and an even longer period of time elapsed in which she never saw her mother. I have wondered what kind of contact mother and daughter managed to maintain in this rather long duration. Was it sporadic with long intervals of no communication? What did Vehanush think and how did she respond upon learning that her mother, who never returned for her, was alive in Beirut? How would her mother explain to her the decision to remain in Beirut? Did Vehanush leave the school with her classmates before she knew her mother was still alive and not returning for her, or was there no reason for the mother to return because her daughter was no longer in Marash? While the teacher was initially the communicant to the mother and conveyed information to Vehanush, in time Vehanush established direct contact with her biological mother. But it has been impossible to envision the terrors that must have invaded her thoughts, the fears that seized her throughout the years of the separation, and how she was able to come to terms with the knowledge of abandonment. How did her feelings change after she learned her mother was still alive? Was the experience of this episode at the heart of the stubborn silence on all matters relating to her early childhood, her parents, and her brother? Was it driven by unforgiving anger or did she simply pass over it and put it aside with the past she had already cut off from herself? As for her mother, our putative "grandmother," she remains an ambiguous abstraction. For Vehanush, a young life already filled to the brim with unanswerable questions, some of whose answers she must have known but kept all to herself, made of her mother the abstraction we were obliged to construct that could not offer any meaning or understanding.

The U.S. must have seemed like a second start. But that was a conclusion derived from the perspective of those of a later generation. For our parents, coming to the U.S. was simply a continuation of lives lived elsewhere after being forced to leave or die because of the genocidal interruption. They knew they would never return to the Anatolian abattoir of murderous frenzy and were now required to resume the unfinished business of making a living, which demanded the labor of persevering in an entirely new and alien environment where they could not even negotiate the language. My father had some command over English since he worked in the U.S. for several years on two different occasions and served in the army for a few more. The enormity of how he was able to navigate several times through the labyrinthine matrix of this alien environment, with limited resources and only a cursory grasp of English, still remains a puzzle of missing pieces to me: traveling from one place to another, contracting for work, and dealing with the requirements of a different daily life necessitating urgent responses. This suggests that his English was serviceable—I knew he could read, slowly but well enough to understand what was being communicated. But I never saw him read a book in English. He could understand spoken English better than speak it, even though his spoken English was comprehensible but somewhat broken. But that was in the early 1920s and my observations of his English competence derives from the late 1930s and early 1940s. At home, we spoke Armenian, but that changed as all of us got older and more deeply committed to the ambience of American life and school. Then we would switch on and off between Armenian and English, even as both parents continued to address us in Armenian. In those circumstances, both parents heard a good deal of English. Yet I cannot help thinking that language acquisition constituted an enormous challenge, if not crushing obstacle, one lived daily by countless migrants when they first came to this country. In those days, there were no programs in English as a Second Language, and communication was in English. Ohannes read as much as he could, in Armenian, given the long work hours he put in, added to the staggering amount of time spent on public transportation to the workplace and back.

If the safety of the U.S. comprised a marked departure from what our parents had experienced and knew of Anatolia, the new environment was still a struggle for survival in a different register. While they no longer lived with the constant fear of unscheduled raids and murders by marauding gangs, economic and material security was undoubtedly as great a problem for them as it was in the villages of Anatolia. There would have been a difference in the forms of economic livelihood and uncertainty between village Anatolia and urban America. Ohannes's earlier decision to find work in the U.S. and what he learned from this complex set of navigation and negotiation gave him an edge when he settled in Detroit after the war. It also provided him with independence and a fund of experience relating to the workplace and labor market. My own experience of life from the late 1930s on taught me that what sustained them was the ethnic community. I understood the importance of these enclaves and neighborhoods, which tried to recuperate the binds of social solidarity they had known elsewhere and that would eventually dissipate and disperse the diaspora in the second generation.

But we should not romanticize these ghetto-like communities: they were usually in run-down areas captive to usurious and extortionist landlords; unsanitary, often rat-infested homes; isolated locations; and places whose inhabitants were always at the edge of deprivation and poverty, especially in moments like the Great Depression. Yet they brought to American life something that is still distrusted and discounted: different histories and their importance in the present. I mention this because American life from the beginning was always oriented to a permanent present, or free of the past, everybody's past, always presuming an end of history in the new land and its dedication to endless progress. In part, this presentism reflected what looked like the promise of endless movement in the drive across the continent; in time it may well have been continued by the confrontation of too many different pasts.

In these ethnic enclaves, the history people brought embodied a different sense of time. The presence of the past always accompanied the present and actively intermingled with it. Urban America had no history, as it still demonstrates in its countless ways of forgetting and in the unrelenting tense of presentism that dominates daily life. In fact, history is only indexed in such places when the infrastructure has been so run down that it requires immediate rehabilitation. In the Armenian community in which I was raised (and I did not speak English until I went to a public school), we literally lived in a present-past, negotiating between different cultural forms and at least two different registers of time as we were obliged to move from one social milieu to another. This is what comprised everyday life and the multiple times that traversed it. History, as a national narrative and experience, really played no role in these lives. I remember thinking, when in school, that the history—the past—being taught belonged to somebody else and had no recognizable affiliation with the life we led. It was impossible for me in grade school to relate and identify with very "white" Anglo-Saxon "founding fathers" of the eighteenth-century colonies, who owned land and often slaves, an absurdity still, in part, reverberating in constitutional law and the fantasy of an interpretative "Originalism." The constant interaction and play of past(s) and present often made it difficult to distinguish between these two time tenses. Time was both reversible and irreversible—not linear, progressive, and irreversible. My father and his generation simply did not think historically—where would this consciousness come from in the world of Anatolian villages and Ottoman Empire? What time awareness may have existed would have been the identification of a moment before the conquest. Anecdotes and stories performed the labor of "history," which centered on an indeterminate time of daily life. Experience of those moments and memory were the means to retrieve the everyday in its singularity and specificity but they were pure constructions; perhaps they were allegories whose repetition reinforced meanings, or vaunted historical reconstructions testifying not to the truth of history but to a natural history. This was particularly pronounced, as it still must be, at moments of commemoration, when the celebration or observance reverts to a different calendar.

Historians who once performed as cheerleaders of immigrant history and the success of the melting pot valorized the rapid socialization of such migrant groups into American life and what they considered as their successful assimilation into it. Upon later reflection, my experience of growing up in an industrial environment taught me that they had not looked closely enough in their investigations and simply enhanced an expedient image of America that still persists, even as it is disclosed daily as an ideological fiction. This was of course the principal function of public schools during the years I was growing up; we spent compulsory time learning how to be Americans, which involved a panoply of practices from how to wash your hands after relieving yourself to learning how to properly set a table for dinner, without considering the content of the meals themselves, whether they they were ethnic or American. There were the inevitable and mandatory civic courses that taught myths as living unimpeachable truths of the exceptional uniqueness of American political society applicable to all. Behind this socialization process was a pervasive racism, which, as students, was immediately recognizable and now seems to have persevered from a distant past down to the present. In my case, I was assimilated to contribute to the process of reproducing an immigrant labor force, as were others from different ethnicities, including African Americans. Living in the U.S. at the time under the conditions differentiating and marking some as migrants represented, at least for my parents, a continuation of the struggle for a secure life that had forced them to leave Anatolia. If Anatolia promised certain death, the U.S. signified permanent uncertainty. Socialization into American life displaced the problem of economic security (and claims of ideological equality) or passed over it with confident declarations of the inexhaustible opportunities the country made available. For many, the socialization was supposed to work as a hedge against the future production of conflict generated by class divisions and permanent inequalities. But I never experienced full socialization, like so many of my contemporaries from migrant families; it simply never took in some instances, and I have always felt different and would remain as the child of migrants who were never able to comfortably situate themselves on the "city on the hill."

What is worrying are the reasons our parents chose to remain silent in this new environment on the central historical event of their lives, sheltering us from what they believed they were sparing us. Perhaps this was a received way of remembering the dead, who can no longer remember. If so, who must remember them? For us, it involved people we never knew, names we never heard. Undoubtedly, the knowledge of that silence and what it has come to mean in our lives has fortified this distance of difference. For Armenians—already a minority ethnicity in the U.S., strangely replicating an earlier status in an empire—the experience of the genocide and having survived it is what brought people to America, and the magnitude of loss they endured has to be considered in preventing the community as a whole from achieving a more effective assimilation or at least one that comes close to some imagined ideal. It is conceivable that the Depression and its demands for survival were overwhelming, hoisting up its roadblocks to successful assimilation and replacing the horrors of the past with the new ones of the present. But the lives of our parents did not loosen up until years later, when my father found a secure job and the quality of our material lives improved. I had concluded that perhaps the silence was not as important to them as it seemed to others. Yet it was their heritage and ours, whether they recognized it or not. Silence may have been our mother's way of relieving us from what she considered a debilitating heritage. It was better if we knew nothing of it that might interfere with our becoming modern and American. Benjamin observed that in "all mourning, there is a tendency to silence,"[10] and this is infinitely more so than the inability or reluctance to communicate. Mournfulness makes the mourner mute.

It must have been from my mother that I inherited the conviction that what she had abandoned was an other world, a form of alterity that she believed conflicted with modern life. In actuality that world of the past had abandoned her. In her mind, there was nothing left of that world worth preserving as a heritage. For Ohannes, this may also have been a factor in his decision to hold it back from us, with the exception of a few anecdotes and stories that he sprinkled us with, usually of a humorous nature to remind us something of that world and perhaps its immense difference. The stories he told featured the mule as the dominant figure in his world, symbolizing both time and space in its capacity to cover great distances and the time it takes to do so, which was completely absent in ours. But it is important to suggest that Ohannes differed from Vehanush in this respect: he clung to his memories of that other world, cherishing those of his childhood and his relations, set in his ways but still belonging to him. In time they morphed into his private natural history, but not for us, since they were now part of a past he had lived without us that had vanished. The difference came out in his reluctance to share it with us. While Vehanush had little to share, her memories could only remind her of homelessness. But Ohannes had some things he could have related about himself. His memories were about home and belonging. It seems that between our parents there may have been the divergence between a lived experience wiped away and its absence, one that never existed in the first place or was not worth remembering. In both cases, it became evident that something was being concealed, and it could have been because we were growing up as Americans and could never be part of his world that had become extinct. I am now convinced that I had stumbled into the realm of mourning and did not understand its imperative demand for silence.

In those days it became apparent that my desire to be only an American was constantly challenged every time I was asked to pronounce my last name and explain where the name came from and what nationality it represented. And in school, despite the regular socialization to which we were all subjected into becoming American, I was made to feel I was not quite the same as those who were not from immigrant families, whose names were usually unpronounceable, made worse by the orthographic damage inflicted at Ellis Island, where names changed with the blink of an eye and a bad ear for foreign sounds. This particular episode of confronting mispronunciations and misspellings of one's name became a metonymy of migrant life in America, as it still is. The inevitable question of asking where you came from seemed to stem from some exotic expectation (or maybe not) that was invariably disappointed with notations of the complexion of one's skin coloration. But you learn early in school that for your nonimmigrant schoolmates, skin color and the pronunciation of name were never brought up to elicit the question of origins and nationality. I came to the realization that like our names that are more often than not incorrectly transcribed, the children of immigrants are rarely ever thoroughly Americanized. At the time I couldn't figure out why they were exempt from this kind of interrogation. In later years, it became evident that they never saw, or were made to see, that they also derived from an immigration experience several generations earlier that time had safely concealed. For many of us, and I include myself, our assimilation into American life was never complete, indeed could never be completed, as the failure of completion strengthened both our further experience of exclusion and our outsider status. Parents and children experienced living half lives, incomplete lives, hybrids spent negotiating interactions in different registers that rarely, if ever, came together to make a whole.

Vehanush, Ohannes, Sena (*left*), and Victoria (*right*), late 1920s.

Vehanush in her mid-teens, probably taken in Marash.

Ohannes (*center*) with two unidentified comrades of the Armenian brigades in Eastern Anatolia or, possibly, Georgia.

Students of the German Missionary School in Marash. Vehanush is in the front row, second from left.

Dashnak group photo, possibly taken in Chicago (1915). Ohannes is in the front row, fourth from right.

Vehanush with oldest daughter, Sena, Detroit, late 1920s.

Ohannes (*left*) and unidentified friend, probably a member of the ARF, date and location unknown.

Ohannes (*right*), with cousin Avedis, probably taken in Anatolia, date unknown but possibly around 1910–13.

Vehanush's mother (name unknown), with second or third husband, taken in either Marash before the genocide or Beirut in late 1920s, date unknown.

FOUR. HISTORY'S INTERRUPTION

Dispossession and Genocide

As pointed out earlier, the experience of the Armenian genocide resembles what Marx has named "so-called primitive accumulation" or "original accumulation" and whose effects he describes as a violent history of expropriation written in blood and fire.[1] He is referring to those moments in history that always come down to igniting explosive forms of frenzied looting resulting in large-scale theft, dispossession, and genocidal murder of a group, inaugurating the twin origins of both capital and the nation-state form. My argument is that the quest for accumulating precapitalist wealth to underwrite the formation of capitalism is invariably accompanied by what can only be described as a formula combining genocidal murder and massive theft, sanctioned accumulation and directed by some form of political authority, whether an emergent state or failing empire. Specifically, the number of people killed by the Turkish military and general population, who willingly cooperated, was paralleled by the extent of theft of Armenian material wealth they were able to carry off. In both cases the totals were extraordinarily large. Mass murder meant mass acquisitions, and looting was carried as far as mutilating and picking over individual bodies and their parts in the pursuit of money and jewelry that may or not have been swallowed by the victims. The Armenian genocide, like all such events, was an exercise in the massive accumulation of money wealth, which in large part had been acquired before capitalism and would be transmuted into capital to serve the subsequent modernization of Turkish society. Whatever else the attempted murder of an entire race of people represents, its principal purpose is to carry out the forcible expropriation, theft, and dispossession of what belongs to somebody else. In this narrative, too often finessed by easy appeals to religious differences and traditional hatreds, seizure and violence remain at the throbbing heart of the genocidal adventure and cannot be separated from it. It was for this reason Marx directly linked what he saw as the necessary slaughter of the innocents to the massive theft of property and labor belonging to others that would become the basis of a process to pursuing the creation of value and its reproduction. Dispossession of a mass of people of their means of subsistence, through enclosures, expropriation and theft, murder, or all, leads to genocide, as a necessary instrument of carrying out the process of capitalism's primitive accumulation.[2]

While the conventional Marxian narrative has sought to bind the episode of "original accumulation" to a narrative of transition leading from the political form of feudalism to the formation of a capitalist order, this is an overstatement based on the example of England employed by Marx in *Capital* and described as only a "sketch" to exemplify how massive forms of expropriation—inaugurated by state violence, leading to what was called enclosures and the releasing of large numbers of people from their means of subsistence—brought about the eventual establishment of a new economic system (capitalism) aligned with the nation-state form, but not as a result of linear transition trajectory. Once in the hands of successive Marxian theorists and activists, this narrative of transition became an orthodox explanation of the process of capitalism that appeared from the contradictions of feudalism. It is evident that the narrative's purpose sought to supply a model for charting the transition yet to come to socialism. In time, Marxists would become preoccupied not so much with the question of the narrative story line itself but rather trying to reach some sort of agreement on the crucial conditions and circumstances that might more persuasively account for the move from feudalism to capitalism that would be repeated in the future transition to socialism. It is important to notice that the vulgate version of the transition narrative precluded the possibility of envisioning other routes to the development of capitalism in other times and places, since the appearance of capitalism could only follow the linear example of England in the sixteenth and seventeenth centuries. By the nineteenth century the imperialism and colonialism Marx had noted in *Capital* that sent capitalism overseas beyond Europe and maturation of the world market regulating the economic interactions of nations combined to open new and different paths to the establishment of capitalism that did not have to rely on imitating the model of sixteenth-century England.

So powerful was this model that it was replicated in historiographical controversies in China and Japan in the 1930s, and elsewhere when signs of capital accumulation began to appear. The transition narrative mandated a gradual, linear historical development, one stage replacing another, that displaced considerations of the nature of the social process and its violent, epical consequences.[3] Yet such an alleged transition was not gradual, linear, or capable of explaining the specific nature of the changes that "paved the way to the advent of capitalism" and the diverse and aggressive "forces that shaped them."[4] In most cases there was no such transition, a fantasy as such, but instead long, temporal processes characterized by intense expropriation and seizure, theft, enslavement, and mass murder that accompanied coexisting forms of capitalist and noncapitalist economic practices alongside political formations, like Turkey's Ottoman Empire, that were not yet capitalistic.[5] In *Capital* Marx proposed that "the nature of capital remains the same in its developed as it is in its undeveloped forms."[6] In Marx's reckoning of history, pasts always lay behind presents, or on top of each other, like geological strata, often in relations of coexistence and coextension, even though the figure of the past was not always immediately visible or recognizable. For Armenians caught in the Turkish vise of "original accumulation" and its enabling genocide, the only hope for transition was escape to another country willing to offer refuge.

It should be repeated that Marx, in later writings, warned that his account of "original accumulation" in *Capital* was nothing more than a "historical sketch" limited to Western Europe that offered little more than an illustration of its principal purpose to separate workers from their means of production and subsistence and make them into wage earners.[7] Moreover, it is not a stage of capitalism "associated with the transition from feudalism" but "a process that continues to this day."[8] In other words, original accumulation was constituted as a form, not as a one-time event, as implied in earlier interpretations, but as a "constantly concurrent combination" of the "three moments and temporalities of origin, development and crisis," as well "as an always-present method of extortion of surplus labor."[9] Original accumulation is thus repetitively produced by capitalism itself, avoiding a singular history of capital and its origins for the production of plural histories of capitalism in different times and places. Under the Nazi regime, the German theft of Jewish material wealth, the seizures of property and widespread expropriations of all forms of value, but especially forced slaved labor, must count as an instance of how primitive accumulation is repeated in putatively advanced industrial states.

What is important to grasp of the Armenian genocide of 1915–16 was the degree to which it shared this genealogy as the jump-start of a capitalist sociopolitical strategy that failed to save the empire but laid the foundation for a successive Turkish nation-state. Undoubtedly, the episode became a template for subsequent genocidal programs, utilizing differing forms of exploitations and mass murder, depending on historical time and place. Rosa Luxemburg saw in the Turkish Empire not capitalist modernization but combined different forms of "European capital and Asiatic peasant economy," with the empire "reduced to its role, that of a political machinery of all Oriental states in the period of capitalist imperialism."[10] According to her analysis, what destroyed the empire's economy was the introduction of a money economy, a large portion of which was undoubtedly in the hands of minorities like the Greeks and Armenians.

What this massive transformation managed to carry off with its terminating machine is the lived everyday of Armenians in Anatolia. In many ways, colonization, as Marx had foreseen, announced the inaugural moment of primitive accumulation. Colonized for more than five hundred years by Ottoman Turks, the Armenians in the late nineteenth and early twentieth centuries were targeted for elimination to make available the total confiscation of their wealth by any means. The massive theft of land and other forms of wealth betrayed the religious appeal to jihad employed to mask it. In this regard, the historic destruction of Ani, first by Mongol conquest and then by earthquake, was something of a prefiguration of the cataclysmic violence of the genocide and its determination to finally rid Anatolia of an Armenian everydayness. The only difference between the distant episode of Mongol looting and later Ottoman theft and expropriation is that the former did not serve as a form of primitive accumulation of capital.[11] This contrast reflected the difference between a society based on communal proprietorship and one already shot through with slivers of private land owning, symptomizing capital's aptitude for inducing permanent unevenness. It should also be said that the destruction committed by the Mongols was no match for the Ottoman decision to eliminate an entire ethnic group. Ani vanished as a living history into rock and rubble that had once given it life, testifying to both its moment of greatness and its permanent disappearance. But in its deathly moment of historical extinction, the ruin aspired to become an allegory filled with multiple meanings.

Since then it became the scene of a vacated history. Yet the loss of its thriving everyday life must have taken on a new role of an unwanted and untimely revenant that would continue to make unscheduled appearances in Armenian communities in times of trouble. A ghostly reminder of destruction, death, and disappearance, this equation pointing to a final ending must have prevailed in the midst of the genocide and its determined drive to empty the Armenian everydayness and return its remainders back to nature. It was the ending of Ani's everydayness, not the present's inexorable movement of world historical capitalism, that showed Armenians the image of their lost future. What other kind of thought would be provoked by the knowledge that another group is trying to make your ethnic group extinct when history already provides the answer?

Eliminating minorities like the Armenians and Greeks in Anatolia by murder and mutilation was actually unnecessary since the quest for capitalist modernization would have been more easily carried out with their involvement and cooperation. But harnessing this goal to an ideology of Turkism or Turkification made such an arrangement impossible by its incapacity to displace and conceal its real desire. What is interesting but unsurprising is that the Young Turks who planned its implementation left a large part of its execution to peasant Turks, Kurds, Circassians, Chechens, and a variety of other miscreants released from prisons specifically to carry out the labor of death and destruction.

There seems to be an inescapable logic to all planned genocides, which the Armenian episode early dramatized: the helplessness of the minority earmarked for ethnic cleansing and the duplicity of local officials. The other side of this logic is the willing complicity of larger powers, actually their indifference, to step in and stop the massacres before it is too late. We have seen the repetition of this pattern too many times in recent history in Rwanda, Cambodia, the former Yugoslavia, and Indonesia. One of the consistent themes of my father's discourse on the genocide was the hypocrisy of Western powers like Great Britain and France and their failure to intervene in the genocidal carnage and bring it to an end—what he described as a form of complicit cooperation designed to serve their own national interest. The Germans, of course, were not excused since they were directly implicated in the implementation. What this means is that Armenians have had a long history of having been persecuted and subjected to periodic and often unscheduled pogroms.

It often seems that the price of being a minority in an empire or nation-state dominated by a majority ethnic group is, in addition to suffering from unfair economic exactions, to serve as the object of regularized arbitrary attacks by official and unofficial groups, resulting in looting and murder. This chronic experience is probably elevated to acute status when empires or regions seek to turn into nation-states as a response to the imperative of capitalist modernization, and are persuaded to base their claim of social solidarity by falling back on religious or ethnic purity; minorities are thus seen as pollutants and contaminants to the national body, corrupting their history and fouling the idea of racial purity and religious homogeneity that requires some form of drastic act of removal. The Armenians in the Ottoman Empire had five hundred years of this experience, as did Jews under Czarist Russia and in some of the "new" nation-states of Eastern and Central Europe. One of the lessons learned from such a long, repetitive, and painful experience is that sometimes the wiser course is not to raise resistance against the marauders, which can often invite even greater measures of destruction.

There are accounts that suggest that Armenians were faced, as many such groups, by a dilemma: resist or acquiesce, neither of which necessarily guarantees a good outcome. But the same dilemma exists for outside powers without the surety of such a dire forecast. Hence, the Armenians, it is said, made no effort to put up some sort of resistance (which is untrue) and in the end chose a strategy informed by "blind submission." It is also said that they had no foresight into what was going to be a policy of total destruction of the race. But one wonders how this would be the case since they had always, and especially in recent memory from the days of Abdülhamid II, been confronted by unanticipated massacres in places like Adana and Sassoun—massacres that surely represented a dress rehearsal for the main act to come. There were too many signs indicating the direction of the Young Turks policy and what the occasion of a broader worldwide conflict was capable of supplying in terms of cover and opportunity. The Young Turks policy was also known by the European powers, which since the nineteenth century had acted as protectors of Christian minorities in the Ottoman Empire. These states were constantly warned by their own people in the field of the looming troubles between the Turkish government and their minorities, and the best they could come up with once the murders and rapes began on a grand scale was to declare that the guilty parties would be tried and held responsible for having committed "crimes against humanity." They did nothing in the end, despite earlier promises, like contemporary states when confronted by the prospect of yet another genocidal episode. Little wonder my father constantly excoriated the roles played by the English and the French.

The same could not be said of Germany, Turkey's principal ally in World War I. They did too much to encourage and sanction the murders and too little in dissuading Turkey from embarking on this course.[12] Had he at the time known, my father could have made a better case against the Germans, whose enthusiastic complicity in the massacres seems to have drawn a pass in the scholarly literature until recently. It was far from accidental that some of the principal planners of the genocide fled to Germany after the war, in hope of finding a safe haven, which apparently did not dissuade Armenian assassins from their appointed mission to rid the world of officials who were responsible for the commission of genocide. If the promises of the allies dissolved in the postwar negotiations into the promotion of national self-interest, the German role in the massacres, as Turkey's principal ally in the war, seems safely to have disappeared in the punitive politics that drove Weimar Germany into unsustainable inflation and fascism. What is extraordinary is how few, if any—perhaps excepting Adolf Hitler himself—saw the direct relationship (or willingness to publicly acknowledge it) between the extermination of the Armenians and the yet-to-come eradication of European Jewry. Hitler early on recognized that large numbers of people could be exterminated and nothing would be done about it. In fact, it would be soon forgotten.[13] The real question of the genocide is whether Turkey's extermination policy was subsumed in the country's involvement in World War I.

What appears puzzling is why the Armenian elites, especially the political classes, had failed to analyze the current situation and grasp the import of conduct of their Young Turks contemporaries, with whom they had on occasion collaborated in bringing to realization a constitutional government. Even at the end, when Turks began disarming Armenians and organizing men into labor battalions, ostensibly for the war effort (but really for absolute slave labor), there was indication of the possibility of worse things to come, even though some writers have insisted that genocide was not linked to this policy of disarming. And yet Werfel's description of how the Musa Dagh villages managed to hide weapons in anticipation of a Turkish assault could have been done on a much wider scale in Anatolia.[14] Perhaps this is an unfair expectation and simply shows the extent to which the larger narratives concerning the war and genocide have eclipsed the true nature of the kind of society that existed at that time, which was principally still a precapitalist formation. After all, it was an empire at its end, precisely because it was mired in a form of Hegelian "standstill" that Marx and Friedrich Engels later loosely named the Asiatic Mode of Production. Societies like Ottoman Turkey, Persia, and perhaps India were closer to the more familiar image associated with the "Orient" than China, Japan, or the states of Southeast Asia. Regardless of this particular Marxian figuration, Ottoman Turkey had not fared well in the nineteenth century, even though it was technically part of Europe. It was not accidental that it was increasingly described as the sick man of Europe. Its economic and political unevenness was in fact a sign of this "sickness," and the Young Turks (also called the Committee of Union and Progress) represented themselves as deliverers of modernization and rationality. But the various narratives have given too much credence to the complexities and intricacies of their plans to transform an empire entering the last move of its endgame into a somewhat reduced territorial nation-state. The principal plan was to finally rid Turkey of its unwanted ethnic minorities, and the imminence of a world war converged with this program to provide the justification and cover required by so radical a transformation. In fact, ethnic purification was linked to an ideological fantasy calling for Pan-Turkish expansion into central Asia, an idea revived recently by an equally delusionary President Recep Tayyip Erdogan in a new incarnation called "neo-Ottomanism."

What too many historical narratives overlook in this account of the formation of a modern Turkish nation-state is the intimate and interactive relation between the nation-state and capital accumulation. The modern form of nation-state required, and was necessitated by, the availability of capital and of capital accumulation; neither could exist without the other, just as in time the nation came to serve as the placeholder for capitalism and capital, which, in turn, was seen as the basis of the nation's "natural political economy." Turkey certainly had grievances with the West, especially as the new nationalism, assisted by European powers, enabled the sprouting of independence movements in southeastern Europe that finally forced the Turks to withdraw from their European imperial territories back to Anatolia. The failures in the Balkans and the deportation of a population of nearly half a million Turkish residents back to Anatolia made one set of problems relating to resettlement, but this complexity was reduced to a form of integral nationalism, whereby the political nation-state form was to become ethnically homogeneous (or religiously homogeneous) and would, at the time, solve the equally complicated problem of economic modernization by dispossessing the minorities of property and wealth that would be transferred to Turkish coffers. Augmenting a process of capital accumulation necessitated the active dispossession and expropriation of the wealth of minority ethnicities and deprivation of their forms of production and subsistence. Original accumulation invariably brought the execution of policies of enclosure through coercion and violence that subsumed what was outside—the everyday lived by Armenians in Anatolia—to the demands of an inside.

As for a perspective capable of moving below (and I would say beyond) the national narrative, Franz Werfel offers a comparable model in *The Forty Days of Musa Dagh*, a book whose importance lies in starting from an everyday present in a specific locale and proceeding to show how the "Great Catastrophe" eventually arrived to force the villagers to abandon their time-tested rhythms and routines in order to defend themselves and survive. Most Armenian families urged their children to read Werfel's novel (or claimed to do so) and impressed upon them its value as a portrayal of the bravery of a fighting spirit of resistance rather than its absence in the midst of massive and systematic murders and forced deportations into the desert. Werfel was not on our reading list, and I am persuaded that our experience was atypical among Armenians, even though I know my mother read the novel. The novel became, I believe, a kind of national epic for the Armenians. (There is a statue of Werfel in Yerevan.) I had heard that it was to be made into a movie by MGM before the war, with Clark Gable playing the role of Gabriel Bagradian, but the project was stopped by the Turkish government exerting pressure on Washington. It is still unclear to me what pressure Turkey could have applied at that time before its membership in the North Atlantic Treaty Organization (NATO).

Werfel's narrative strategy begins with the everydayness of Armenian villages and shows they were converted into the everyday of death marches constituting the deportation convoys. By contrast to a perspective based on fragmentary memories and the form of collage, Werfel's approach of the account of everydayness is constrained within the form of the novel, which, like historical narrative, imposes the structure of a story line with beginning and end. It follows a different trajectory from the form of a montage or even collage, which are composed of splintered events and episodes comprised of partial lives that are put together with no discernible causal relationship between the time of a before and an after presented only as a construct of juxtapositions capable of opening up to any number of possible readings. Werfel clearly saw as his task not simply reconstructing lived accounts but rather recording what was seen and heard and proposing and recomposing a construction out of it. (His sources were starving refugee survivors of the death march to the desert whom he apparently interviewed in Syria.) Where he was able to fictionalize the drawing of full portraits of the characters of his novel, the evidence based on memories, by contrast, is limited to negative glimpses that do not add up to full portrayals. Because he resorted to a novelistic form, the account seemed to fuse the outline of reconstruction with imaginative fiction, possibly approaching the means employed in envisaging a historical novel. Today, a reading of *The Forty Days of Musa Dagh* resembles the form of a historical novel more than any other genre, even though it probably was not intended to do so.

This approach informs Werfel's epic novel and, in part, exemplifies the articulation of how the relationship of history and everydayness might proceed. It provides a different pathway guiding us to a confrontation between the relationship of the historical narrative detailing the Turkish involvement in the war and the occasion it supplied to inaugurate the massive genocidal removal of Armenians and extinguishing of Armenian daily life in Anatolia and how it was then transfigured into an everyday hell of deportation convoys to the desert. Despite the different routes taken by the novel and collage, they converge at the same point: genocide opened the way not only for telling the story of executing mass murder of the population but also its corollary narrative of the systematic implementation of massive appropriation, dispossession, and theft that reverses the everyday into its negative, a living hell of a necropolitics.

This observation means beginning the narrative not with the "Armenian Question," as such, which would have required starting with the Ottoman state and implying that it was one of the emergent problems the empire had to resolve, in order to prevent further diminution. Solving the Armenian Question promised to remove what was ailing the empire. In this regard it prefigured the later "Jewish Question" in Germany. In other words, the question was posed by Turks, not Armenians, just as later it was posed by Germans, not Jews.

World War I was simply the principal genocidal event in a sequence that had begun in continents like Africa decades before, where white European imperial powers decimated populations by the millions and went on to reduce their populations on a comparable scale. These imperializing spaces provided the ground for unlimited expropriation and theft and unaccountable violence in the act of accumulation. All forms of colonial and imperial expropriation are nothing more than extractions amounting to acts of original accumulation. In the Ottoman Empire, imperial depredations subsequently fused with Turkish efforts, assisted by German complicity, to eliminate the entirety of a population. The war itself was a form of mutual suicidal genocide. To situate the Armenian massacres within the explanatory context of World War I is merely another way of explaining it away as an effect of a pointless conflict between nation-states or as a form of collateral damage. But the question is, Collateral to what? And what kind of commentary did the so-called sideshow produce to illuminate the main act of war? In this regard, it recalls Turkey's successful socialization of several generations who do not have the faintest idea of what happened to a million and a half Armenians and other Christians (Greeks, Assyro-Chaldeans, etc.) within Anatolia, or insist on claiming so.

Reading Grigoris Balakian's long account of his escape from deportation and what he lived through and saw, and witnessed and heard from others along the route, is very difficult to sustain in long sittings. Yet this personal memoir of the genocidal years detailing the everydayness of deportation convoys and his own escape is still our best eyewitness. The indescribable savagery of each reported episode seems to compete with the next in a grotesque Grand-Guignol contest to determine which group of Turkish, Kurdish, and Circassian marauders managed to carry out the worst program of atrocities. In a recent article on the "undeclared" war against the Kurds in Diyarbakir, the reporter was apparently stunned by reports of destroyed Kurdish buildings and the discovery of nude women's bodies that showed the breasts had been cut off. Yet this outrage was a daily occurrence for thousands of Armenian women and girls in 1915 and 1916, when obscene crimes were committed by Kurdish security battalions and convicts put up to do precisely this job. What some Kurds got for performing this service was the right to seize empty houses and whatever else left by murdered and deported Armenians, and they received neither precious little land nor a nation-state.

Mikael Nichanian is one of the few historians who has directly considered the role played by "primitive accumulation." But even in his study, published in French and one of the very best in the current literature, Nichanian gets to the economic importance of theft as a demonstration of primitive accumulation only late in his account: "The destruction of the Armenian populations (and Greeks) and the confiscation of their goods were a determinate influence on the economic development of modern

Turkey after the war, notably by the primitive accumulation of capital, a necessary condition of the industrial revolution."[15] Attention to the subject late in the book suggests its importance but not necessarily the vital relationship between the decision to inaugurate the genocide and the material returns and benefits it offered. In fairness, Nichanian supplies a brief accounting, based on solid secondary works by Turkish scholars who have specifically examined the uncountable confiscation of wealth and property and the accompanying destruction of Armenian village sites.

An interesting contrast is provided by anecdotal accounts throughout Balakian's memoir of theft at the lowest levels, the mutilation of dead bodies to see if any jewelry has been consumed, the theft of clothes, the occupation of homes deserted by deportees, the murders, and extortion by the guards along the deportation routes. It is important to notice a number of things about violent theft, dispossession, and expropriation. Remember that in Marx's reading, primitive or original accumulation was not a one-time event but would continue to be carried out by developed, mature nation-states.[16] By the same token, there was the large quotient of the wealth of goods and property stolen from confiscating Armenian and Greek companies, many of which functioned in the capitalist sector, which would thus have represented the accumulation of capital. I would add to this the land and relics held by countless Armenian churches, whose ruined remains are today used in picturesque travel brochures advertising Turkey's long, multicultural heritage: tourism of the cultural ruins created by genocide as a new form of original accumulation since the churches and the relics were produced long before the onset of modern capitalism. What Turkey's extermination policy signified was eliminating the holders of different forms of wealth, capitalist and non- or precapitalist, "primitive," and what might be called originary accumulation. In other words, as a historical process, accumulation is rarely completely primitive, as might be exemplified in the "classic" English model, and more often mixed, pointing to the capacity of precapitalist and capitalist forms of accumulation to coexist under the command of a capitalist production agenda, and suggesting a continuation of earlier precapital modes of accumulating and exploitation, whereby noncapital is put to use in the capitalist process.

However, it was not merely theft and expropriation of Armenian goods and property. What invariably gets left out of the picture is the amount of slave labor Armenians were forced to perform. The disarmament of Armenian and Greek soldiers serving in the Ottoman army prefigured their forcible conversion into slave laborers. Disarming these troops was a fundamental condition of the ethnic cleansing that was to come. Even if the disarming was not directly linked to a genocidal politics, which is a doubtful assumption, the reorganization of these disarmed soldiers pressed into labor battalions provided the Ottomans with a large reservoir of labor power at little expense, especially in road repair and transport services. The concern for a link between the disarming of Armenian troops who were put to work as slave laborers and the genocide is a casuistic exercise: most of these slave laborers were killed. The same was true of those large numbers of men and women who were able to secure some immunity from the certain death promised by deportation convoys by escaping and securing employment as laborers in the German, Swiss, and Austrian companies contracted to construct the Constantinople/Baghdad Railway. This was particularly evident in the areas of the south, in the mountainous Taurus and Amanos regions of the line's tunnel construction, as vividly reported by Balakian, whose own escape from a convoy was enabled by Swiss and German engineers and employment in railroad construction. The tradeoff was obviously work for low wages, if any, and the prospect of surviving (which, apparently, was successful for a fairly large number). And, of course, there is the inestimable number of women and children either adopted by Muslim families or sold into slavery, which would still encompass an absolute appropriation of labor power and worse. Finally, there are unaccounted numbers of women, especially, who chose to convert to Islam in order to save their children, as Arlene Voski Avakian reported of her grandmother in her memoir of growing up in an Armenian American family in New York City and northern New Jersey.[17] Although Avakian confesses that when she was young she did not want to hear her grandmother's story of survival, it later became a constituent factor in her transition from wanting to be merely an American to evolving into an Armenian American identity.

Expropriation, theft, and dispossession must be first grasped as an ideological fantasy. The processes of deportation and the subsequent massacres included an economic dimension that had always been identified by all the parties, insofar as it represented a shared belief among Turkey's population that Armenians were rich. In the popular mythology of empire, even if small peasant landholders constituted three-quarters of the Armenian population, much of the wealth held by Armenians and Greeks was anchored in Constantinople, not in the countryside. But regardless of this concentration, the wealth generated by the various devised forms of violent primitive and original accumulation was enough to permit the state to underwrite the processes of deportation and even the exterminations. Moreover, monies recuperated by the state served the war effort by paying off a large portion of the Ottoman debt to the Germans, and even "dumping three tons of gold at the Reichsbank of Berlin, which probably represented a small fraction of gains obtained by the confiscation of Armenian goods."[18]

Whatever else the Ottoman Young Turks claimed they derived from a policy of ethnic cleansing, it all originated from the principal formula that sanctioned theft, the massive transfer of wealth—accumulation—in its different forms, and the necessary separation of Armenians and Greeks from what they owned through a policy of extermination that removed barriers to seizure of land and property. Theft and dispossession severed the Armenian population permanently and irretrievably from the one instrument that had provided it with a modicum of power and protection in an empire devoted to constantly squeezing its minorities by taxing expropriations. Ottoman Turkey was motivated by the will to remove Armenians and Greeks from the only footing on which they were still able to position themselves within the uncertain environment of empire, "the economic tools considered the basis of their supposed power."[19] It was the illusion of wealth that presupposed an imagined ratio of power they simply did not have. In this regard, it was easy to mobilize the population to participate in the criminal act of voluntarily exterminating Armenians for the promise of enriching themselves. The last segment of the equation was, in addition to lining the pockets of the elite few, its capacity to empower the ascendance of Mustafa Kemal (Ataturk), who was nothing more than a poorly disguised avatar of the discredited Young Turks like Ismail Enver (Pasa), Mehmet Talaat (Pasa), and others.

The reason for this neglect in overlooking the quantity of theft as a principal generative factor accompanying the genocide at this time and not earlier during the nineteenth century, when there were still pogroms, may have resulted from the conviction that the confiscation of wealth did not necessarily fit into the larger narrative occupied by World War I and Turkey's involvement. There is little doubt that the scale of death, destruction, and outright senseless slaughter of hundreds of thousands in World War I in Europe eclipsed all other considerations during the duration of the conflict. What seems clearer to me is that such concerns did not dissuade Turkey under cover of war from undertaking the massive accumulation carried out in 1915 and 1916, compared to the pillaging pogroms in the nineteenth century, which may well have already reflected the changes in global capitalism and how it was inflected in the errant empire. My father had no trouble in reporting the traces he witnessed during his time in the Armenian brigades of the massive dispossession of Armenian property and personal belongings and the ruination of whole villages, including his own, literally wiped out, leaving only the most mournful traces to signify its skeleton for the totality of calamitous destruction. Both Werfel and Balakian provide additional evidence. It is almost another mystery of the genocide why so many of the historical accounts have simply bypassed the magnitude and significance of expropriated wealth connected to the mass murder. While Armenian survivors in the genocide's aftermath stubbornly sought to press personal claims for their losses, without any success, Turkey's stance was supported by the reluctance of large European states and the United States to do more than look the other way. Nobody was listening. The question that still needs to be answered is, why not? In the post–World War II years, the apparent downplaying of the relationship of genocide to massive dispossession and murder may have had something to do with the lingering Cold War view that Turkey's membership in NATO, along with the U.S., and the establishment of American air bases along the Turkish–Soviet frontier made the country a trusted and valued ally. The attitude of the larger Western states was repeated during genocide years and now was probably reinforced by the desire to discourage the opening of a Pandora's box filled with Armenian demands for compensation for the material wealth they had lost. Peter Balakian's important memoir *Black Dog of Fate* (1997) reports how his grandmother relentlessly sought through legal means to secure compensatory restitution from the Turkish government for her family's losses.[20] While there have undoubtedly been several such attempts to legally compel the Turkish government to make good on what they have stolen, confiscated, and expropriated, without any success, it is evident how sensitive an issue the pursuit of reparations entails since any sign of relaxing policy by the Turkish government would automatically result in a clear acknowledgment of what it has always disavowed since 1916. I can recall my father speaking, late in life, not only of the disappearance of his large family but also of the material loss incurred with their vanishing. He never knew what had happened to them but guessed that the men like his father, grandfather, brothers, and cousins had been murdered, while the women were sent on the deportation death march. He was from a rural priestly family; though they were not wealthy, his family did own land and other property. This experience must have been replicated innumerable times and does not even include the moveable wealth taken in acts of murder and mutilation. As I grew older, this topic of conversation testifying to personal loss turned to become more prominent at Armenian-related social gatherings, which means I began to understand conversations that inevitably were concerned with death and material forfeiture.

Whatever else may have resulted from this seismic destruction of lives, wealth, and property was clearly reflected in the tight relationship between Turkey's World War I aims and the policy of extermination, and how each worked against the other, and especially how the latter actually contributed to undermining the conduct of the Ottoman military effort and campaigns. In addition, the expropriations would provide the necessary foundation for the forthcoming modern Turkish Republic, whose capitalism would still rely on squeezing its minorities and more recently employing tactical exercises of extortion of "allies" like the United States and the states of the EU that wish to rid themselves of Syrian and other ethnically marked refugees. The genocide of Armenians, Greeks, Assyro-Chaldeans, and other minorities was simply indistinguishable from a hunting "open season" that invited the Muslim population to participate in endless pillage, looting, murder, rape, and unspeakable mutilation in return for a delusionary offer of rewarding enrichment. We know the major proportions of theft went to government officials and functionaries, while those who actually carried out theft and murder received small handouts and tidbits.[21] Anatolia during World War I was nothing less than an immense killing field dedicated to ethnic purification and dispossession of Armenians as preparation for a new or putatively modern Turkish order, born out of defeat and the final destruction of the remnants of empire. In this regard, it might be said that the modern Turkish state was probably a mistake or an accident of history. It originated in the extermination of the Armenians with the untended or "collateral" effect of dismembering the empire the murders and theft were supposed to rescue.

Yet the role of original accumulation introduces the important consequences of capitalism as it penetrated and spread throughout Anatolia in the nineteenth century. While some scholarly accounts include discussions of the importance of capitalism in Anatolia in the complex politics of empire's end, few that I know of have emphasized the centrality of its role in the genocide as reflected in the process of actively promoting original accumulation. Accounts of primitive accumulation and the development of capitalism are not always the same thing. Both Ronald Grigor Suny, in his recently published and authoritative book on the genocide, *"They Can*

Live in the Desert but Nowhere Else": A History of the Armenian Genocide, and Taner Akçam, in *A Shameful Act: The Armenian Genocide and the Question of Turkish Responsibility*, briefly appeal to "primitive accumulation," even though Akçam describes the confiscations and expropriations without naming them as such in the making of the genocidal event.[22] Yet the role of original accumulation introduces the important figure of capitalism as it seeped into and spread throughout Anatolia in the nineteenth century, demanding its insertion and integration into the expansion of capital in the region and the larger context of historical circumstances constituting Armenian–Turkish relations.[23] Suny proposes that "the extermination of the Armenians had a catastrophic effect on the whole of Anatolian society and economy" and "while some Muslims benefited from the seizure of property and goods of Armenians—a most 'primitive accumulation of capital'—many others suffered from the removal of productive farmers and craftsmen, pharmacists, doctors, and merchants."[24] For his part, Akçam appeals to the more familiar explanation of the palpable wealth of Armenians. "Adana's Armenians," he writes, had openly supported earlier programs of modernization, eliciting attacks from the Muslim community for embracing economic and politically new ideas and projects. He explains, quoting from a few others along the way, "There was also an important economic factor. Local Armenians 'were the richest and most prosperous class in the region. In every field, they were ahead of the Turks.'"[25] Turkish policy toward the Greeks resulted in massive massacres (never, strangely, named as a genocide) and dispossession of property and goods, which set the terms of theft and robbery once the Armenian genocide began. A German military officer, assigned to the Special Organization, the body of former convicts and other miscreants released from prisons to prey on and pillage Armenian villages, observed that their main objective was dedicated to looting and committing criminal acts for the purpose of "'self-enrichment.'"[26] But "self-enrichment" was merely the lure to facilitating recruitment.

Suny is sensitive to capital's larger need to plow under existing social relations and its capacity to assimilate or even remove all impediments to its pursuit of surplus value. He is also correct to see in the development of capital the production of vast asymmetries of economic unevenness, between city and countryside, region and region, and, especially, between Muslim and non-Muslim constituencies. It is true that minorities like the Armenians, Greeks, and Jews (who greatly benefited from the expropriation of Armenian properties and goods)[27] inhabiting urban centers had seized the initiative of moving into economic areas of capitalist practice. Much of this was possible because of a long history of experience in merchant and commercial affairs and the strong links minority-operated businesses had been able to form with foreign traders. This is not to say that Turkey had no interest in traditional forms of commerce or even capitalist practices but only to suggest the advantage seized and possessed by minority houses. In large part, Turkey, like any number of Asian societies, remained officially committed to the idea of an agrarian-based "natural economy," the kind Vladimir Lenin described in his struggle with *narodniks* who, in the nineteenth century, embraced ancient Russian principles in their opposition to capitalist change as an uninvited Western export. The same conditions existed in Imperial China, feudal Japan, and Mughal India until the British showed up in the eighteenth century.

As Akçam proposed, the plan was to destroy a considerable and well-endowed Armenian middle class and replace it with a Turkish Muslim middle class. In this connection, it might be noted that interpreters like Michael Mann, in his well-researched book *The Dark Side of Democracy: Explaining Ethnic Cleansing*, puts forth the additional argument that organic nationalism was the principal impulse behind the genocide, even though economic rationality was an important factor.[28] But organic nationalism is merely the political means to achieve primitive accumulation and is not incompatible with the promotion of economic interests. To support this argument, Mann cites stray remarks by Interior Minister Mehmet Talaat who presumably recognized that despite the economic losses to Turkey incurred by destroying an Armenian middle class, the policy of deportation was worth it. A plan specifically designed to eliminate a whole population would of course be acknowledged to be worth the effort and sacrifice. Why do it if it was not? But it is difficult to take Talaat's disavowal of economic motives seriously, and it is always a more appealing explanation for the undertaking of extreme measures to employ the fulfillment of higher religious or political reasons. To acknowledge that Turkey was particularly interested in exterminating its minorities to seize land and property would have been an embarrassment for "enlightened" modernizers like Talaat. What Talaat was not reported to have said is that destroying an entire middle class is still not the same thing as expropriating its wealth and whatever else that could be extracted from the rest of the Armenian and Greek populations as Turkish troops and local inhabitants raked them over in the process of extinguishing their ethnic presence forever. Mann does not report U.S. ambassador Henry Morganthau's discussion with Talaat and his refusal to honor Talaat's request for assistance in securing from American insurance companies the benefits and payouts of Armenian policyholders now that they were dead.[29] Also overlooked is that the acquisition of this treasure was the accrued compensatory wealth accumulated through direct theft and dispossession that ultimately enabled the making of a Turkish Muslim middle class. More important, Mann, like many others, attributes primal agency to a form of organic nationalism in bringing about the genocide and neglects the possibility of considering the costs, privileging a political cause that seems to bracket the immense economic price and benefits that accompanied the event. It was mentioned earlier that Turkey forfeited classes of skilled artisans and technicians who, especially in the countryside, provided invaluable services to both Turkish and minority populations, from the most basic goods like the making of shoes to the most advanced forms related to increasing agricultural production, medicine, and other services. The failure derives from ignoring the crucial historical relationship between capital accumulation and the formation of the nation-state. Moreover, it makes the decision to embark on an expensive extermination policy without considering the economic benefits and costs accompanying it look like either a momentary act of sheer madness or the impulse to commit national suicide.

Franz Werfel provides a portrait of an Armenian merchant house that reflected a capitalist orientation through the character of his principal protagonist, Gabriel Bagradian (whose name unsurprisingly recalls the Bagratid Dynasty of medieval Armenia and Ani). Bagradian, along with his brother, runs a successful capitalist enterprise and is assimilated into Western life and culture, having been educated in France and married into a French family; he also speaks better French than Armenian. It is interesting to observe how Bagradian's experience in organizing villages in the defense of Musa Dagh gradually returns him to the culture of native ethnicity as his assimilated Western (French) demeanor slowly peels off and he becomes increasingly estranged from his French wife. Just as there was an immense distance between the lives of Armenian business and financial classes, who inhabited the Europeanized sector of Istanbul, and the peasants of Anatolia, this cleft was even wider between Armenians and Turks and their Kurdish coreligionists. Whatever advantage Armenians accumulated in business and finance, they shared with other peasant non-Muslim minorities the disadvantages of occupying the same status in the eyes of Islamic law: they remained subordinated and subject to the arbitrary conduct exercised by Muslims toward any minority group. This would have enormous consequences in Eastern Anatolia, where the competition for arable land between Armenians and Kurds and Turks was sharpened by recent migrations from the Balkans and became a fiercely contested flashpoint usually ending in violence and forced expropriations. In his yearlong journey as a deportee, the priest Balakian took notice of how villages and homes vacated by the genocide were being occupied by Turkish refugees from Europe and land once worked by Armenians had now fallen into the hands of Turkish cultivators. But one wonders how successful these new settler transplants were. My father's experience during his years with the Armenian brigades differs. The chronic conflict over the acquisition of land between Armenians and Turks and especially Kurds, the forcible seizure of it, and the law's constant privileging of Muslim over non-Muslim in the settlement of disputes fueled the antagonism between groups over strictly economic problems. Sparked by the gradual commercialization of agriculture, the conflict was translated into the idiom of ethnoreligious rivalry that inevitably worked against the Armenians since privatization by large landowners affected both Muslim and non-Muslim peasants. Moreover, the role played by officials in adjudicating disputes that favored Muslims was seen as a refraction of Ottoman policy directed at undermining the Christian populations. Despite putative reforms implemented by Sultan Abdülhamid II and later the Young Turks, presumably aimed at correcting or removing the more obvious sources of *ressentiment*—often in response to Armenian demands for fairer treatment, greater equality under the law, and the abrogation of the more oppressive practices and institutions founded on the inequality of non-Muslim peoples in the empire—such changes were seen by Turkish political leaders as weakening and undermining the traditional hierarchical relationships between Muslim and non-Muslim. It is thus interesting that the intention of such reforms leading to modernizing measures would have enhanced not simply minorities but also the development of capitalism. Yet they were seen as impediments to further progress, which meant eliminating minorities like the Armenians and Greeks rather than incorporating them into a new political and social edifice. Instead, the claims of the natural economic order always took precedence, which prompted Rosa Luxemburg to observe that the reforms lacked any discernable modern (capitalist) component and made Turkey look more medieval and "Oriental" than before.[30] Its proximity to Europe and the flourishing of the capitalist mode of production made the comparison even more extreme than it might have been and the prospect for successful capitalist modernization in the empire more urgent and impossible to conceive of under the existing ethnoreligious constraints. What lay at the heart of this traditional hierarchical social and political order was still the persistence of the fictional natural economy and the arbitrary use of state violence—reflected in heavy taxation and coercion—pledged to keeping those who occupied an inferior status in their rightful place. In the struggle, Armenians who lost out in their effort to acquire land drifted to the cities for work and even emigrated abroad. Real emigration to countries like the U.S. began in earnest in the early twentieth century, with Armenians signing up for contract labor and sending monies back to their families—manifesting another form of original accumulation. My father was among this army of emigrants who left their villages, possibly because of the loss of land—in his case, it may have been prompted as well by the desire for independence and adventure or because he was one of the younger sons of a priestly family and did not stand to inherit family lands. Emigration saved him from the fate suffered by his family.

The principal thrust of Balakian's long narrative of survival and escape is to show how normal village everydayness was inverted into and dominated by a "deportee" everyday, composed of those forcibly embarked on a journey punctuated at every step by looting, pillage, rape, and murder. Balakian, it should be pointed out, expressed no illusions concerning the nature of the everyday lived by Armenians, representing it as some sort of golden age. Above all else, he was an urbanized intellectual who had studied abroad but appeared aware of both the solidarity of Armenian rural communities and the difficulties they faced daily, owing to their status as Christians and as a minority. In the replacement of that rhythm with an everyday dominated by the arrhythmic necropolitics of the deportations, there was no apparent transition. It is along the paths of deportation to a desert destination and death that the fusion of primitive accumulation and the daily "slaughter of the innocents" became the principal guiding logic of what Balakian renamed the "Armenian Golgotha." Rounding up first deportees meant forfeiting everything; the journey would do the rest. The transformation seemed to occur virtually overnight.

What attended this everyday terror of imminent death was the anticipation that it would occur at the next bend of the road or bridge crossing. If this sense of dread captures the psychology of a lived dailyness, it was made even worse by the incessant preoccupation with securing water, food, and rest. But the recurring intuition that violence would strike the deportees at any moment must have been a form of torture unparalleled in the empire more urgent and impossible to conceive of under the existing ethnoreligious constraints. What lay at the heart of this traditional hierarchical social and political order was still the persistence of the fictional natural economy and the arbitrary use of state violence—reflected in heavy taxation and coercion—pledged to keeping those who occupied an inferior status in their rightful place. In the struggle, Armenians who lost out in their effort to acquire land drifted to the cities for work and even emigrated abroad. Real emigration to countries like the U.S. began in earnest in the early twentieth century, with Armenians signing up for contract labor and sending monies back to their families—manifesting another form of original accumulation. My father was among this army of emigrants who left their villages, possibly because of the loss of land—in his case, it may have been prompted as well by the desire for independence and adventure or because he was one of the younger sons of a priestly family and did not stand to inherit family lands. Emigration saved him from the fate suffered by his family.

The principal thrust of Balakian's long narrative of survival and escape is to show how normal village everydayness was inverted into and dominated by a "deportee" everyday, composed of those forcibly embarked on a journey punctuated at every step by looting, pillage, rape, and murder. Balakian, it should be pointed out, expressed no illusions concerning the nature of the everyday lived by Armenians, representing it as some sort of golden age. Above all else, he was an urbanized intellectual who had studied abroad but appeared aware of both the solidarity of Armenian rural communities and the difficulties they faced daily, owing to their status as Christians and as a minority. In the replacement of that rhythm with an everyday dominated by the arrhythmic necropolitics of the deportations, there was no apparent transition. It is along the paths of deportation to a desert destination and death that the fusion of primitive accumulation and the daily "slaughter of the innocents" became the principal guiding logic of what Balakian renamed the "Armenian Golgotha." Rounding up first deportees meant forfeiting everything; the journey would do the rest. The transformation seemed to occur virtually overnight.

What attended this everyday terror of imminent death was the anticipation that it would occur at the next bend of the road or bridge crossing. If this sense of dread captures the psychology of a lived dailyness, it was made even worse by the incessant preoccupation with securing water, food, and rest. But the recurring intuition that violence would strike the deportees at any moment must have been a form of torture unparalleled in the historical annals of collective fear; knowing at the same time that they were being forced to march to their deaths in the desert created an underlying temporal arrhythmia disrupting any possibility for establishing a routinized pace. Balakian's memoir, especially, provides excruciating detail of the ceaseless psychological distress among survivors that defined the deportation as it moved toward its desert destiny. In many instances, mass deaths occurred long before reaching the fateful destination. The marching deportees often encountered the remains of bodies from prior ambushes along the route. The plundering of wealth of Armenians designated for deportation made it impossible to bring much, if anything, of necessities: little more than whatever money they might carry for bribes and bread. It is impossible to imagine this brutally abrupt refiguration of the everyday into its darkened negative of terror charged with uncertainty and expectancy. This was particularly true as the temporality of the deportation lengthened from days into weeks into months, only to arrive at a place where the certainty of death could no longer be deferred. The everyday became the space-time site of a fearful, unrelenting daily labor of murder and mutilation. I have tried to grasp the particular psychology implicated in genocidal decisions and what enduring the daily fear of imminent death must have been like, and I explain to myself the motivating encouragement that drove its perpetrators to employ the cruelest forms of sadism to adorn a policy already committed to exterminating an ethnic group. I cannot improve on Balakian's witness, apart from saying I heard fragments of comparable accounts, not from my parents but from older folks at Armenian socials who often broke down in involuntary spasms of tears, reporting what they had heard and seen.

If there may be ways to explain certain forms of violent behavior sanctioned by crudely articulated practices of protofascism, the mass murderers among Turkish and Kurdish populaces, and convicts and other opportunists, resist easy reduction to such explanations based on given conceptions of a modern modal social and political personality. Anatolia was still more a precapitalist social order than modern, despite the shards of capital unevenly manifest in economic life and its social effects that were beginning to appear in Istanbul and other urban areas. While I have no doubt that participants in mutilation and murder enjoyed what they were doing, it derived not from the experience of modern warfare but from historical grievances stoked and animated over centuries. It was religiously and racially articulated and motivated by origins in a long history of oppressing minority populations in the empire whose expendability would have finally removed any claim to the territory made by those who had been settled in Anatolia long before the arrival of the Ottoman Turks and whose presence was a constant reminder of such a scandal. It took the Ottomans nearly five hundred years to devise a final solution and only after they had lost their possessions in southern Europe and seen the deportation of their own population back to Anatolia.

This return to Anatolia, which probably counted as a return to Asia for the Turks, undoubtedly contributed to finding a way to rid the territory of undesirable minorities who were, what is more, Christian, as if they belonged someplace else. However, the deportation of Armenians was not conceived to send them back to their ancestral home, as had been the case of the Turks in southeastern Europe, but to a desert inferno. The Armenians already occupied their historic homeland and had done so for centuries, long before the Turkic migrations out of the steppe.

The labor of killing was done largely by the military, ordinary peasants, convicts, and opportunists, often assisted by local villagers in vicinities the deportations were moving through; and this meant that it was not simply limited to males but frequently involved women and children as well. Moreover, Turks and Kurds were killing people with whom they had been in close contact for a long time, people whose lives were interwoven with theirs as peasants. Balakian provides ample evidence of how he and members in his convoy were constantly fearful of such attacks by local villagers and reports the aftermath of numerous such raids along the route; in some instances, when he had money, he would use it for bribing guards to secure advance knowledge of waiting ambushes and even protection. According to him, it was clear that guards watching over the convoy would in fact inform villages or gangs of marauding convicts of their arrival. But we have no sure way of penetrating the psychology of people inhabiting precapitalist and premodern social formations to explain their behavior and can only offer a guess at the socialization processes. My father was never at ease when referring to the Turkish and Kurdish populace, more often than not at a loss for words when unequivocally dismissing them as "barbarians" and "savages," suggesting some form of preliterate socialization. I do not know if he ever had Turkish or Kurdish friends; if he did, he never mentioned them. He undoubtedly had neighbors with whom he must have had some interaction but he never mentioned such instances and would have included them in his general denunciation. But what we know of "barbarians" as a type does not adequately describe the inhuman nature of such behavior. As willing agents of the executions, they must have also undergone some sort of profound transformation. Certainly the act of arbitrary killing and murder must have been individually transforming. Or perhaps it was simply the resentment of those at the economic bottom of a highly structured social hierarchy of status rungs, a resentment fueled by recognizing that members of a Christian minority seemed to enjoy a better life than they, who were members of the Islamic majority, what Slavoj Žižek years ago explained as an expression of "surplus enjoyment" and "pleasure theft" or enjoyment by the other.[31] We know that the Unionist attempt to recruit popular support for its policy wisely called attention to exaggerated accounts of Armenian wealth and the promise of rewards that came with active participation in the processes of dispossession and extermination, to take back what the other had been enjoying.

Grigoris Balakian's firsthand account of his experience in the deportation march and subsequent escape provides a virtual inventory of the petty theft and its relationship to murder committed at the lowest local level on individuals, dead and alive. He seems to have possessed total recall and forgot nothing. In one episode he recounts that he encountered a tent with three men lying on rags. He discovers one of them is a wealthy Armenian Catholic from Ankara and inquires into the details of what had happened to him, since he knew that Catholics had been granted exemption from the deportations: "His story was the same heart-wrenching one I had seen and heard a thousand times. After his goats, houses, vineyards, stores, wagons, and horses—worth tens of thousands of gold pounds—were seized, he had been sent on foot on the road from Ankara, together with his fellow Armenian Catholics."[32] He escaped and found refuge along the route of a railway construction, after bribing the officials holding him captive and ultimately rescued by the director of the railroad. Throughout his account there is a steady identification of murder, mutilation, and theft, as if it were a natural mantra that Turkish and Kurdish raiders were obliged to satisfy and put into practice every time they encountered Armenians. In some instances, there seemed to be a competition between officials and local scavengers who, after murdering Armenian victims, set about to pick over the mutilated bodies. "Meanwhile hundreds of greedy Turkish officials," Grigoris Balakian reports, "like hungry wolves set upon (the) abandoned goods. High-level officials came to the site of plunder with carriages, carts, and porters to cart away the valuables by the trunk load. More than the civilians, it was the military that engaged in the looting. They left the crumbs of these rich spoils to the poor Muslim people as their rightful share."[33] What is important about such reports is that they occurred all the time and the amount of wealth that had been stolen must not only have been considerable but its scale virtually incalculable because it included everything but the bones of the dead.

Historians such as Mikael Nichanian have asked, "The Armenian genocide, like Shoah, thus poses a singular question to the historian: at what moment did total hatred tip toward genocidal hatred and what are the factors that favored the passage into the act?"[34] The question is pertinent since Armenians in the empire, like Jews in Central Europe, were already socialized to observing the laws, language, and culture of their respective oppressors. They were not like outside enemies. Yet it is also possible to propose that recurrent racial hatred is always "tipped" toward violence. It has its own dynamic driving it to spill over into acts of aggression, as contemporary white animosity toward African Americans and immigrants in contemporary America shows daily. Nichanian's interpretation is persuasive, inasmuch as he seeks to attribute irrationality to the general outburst, ignited by conjuring a phantasmagoric enemy that had to be destroyed at the risk of being destroyed by it. Europe was resolved to destroy the empire but went about it in a simple and unsatisfactory and incomplete way. In this script, it was assumed that Armenians, owing to their Christianity, were closely allied with European powers and served as their surrogate agents in Anatolia, an advance guard working to undermine Ottomanism. The myth of the Armenian menace was thus superimposed on another "founding" myth, which was the conviction that Europe was determined to destroy the Ottoman Empire. It is difficult to ascertain whether this latter myth was credible, but even if it possessed a shred of truth, it would not have led to using Armenians as an advance guard of agent provocateurs bent on undermining the Ottoman Empire for Europeans. What is certain is that it was overdetermined.

The problem of the empire, as with most imperial structures, was an unreflexive self-satisfaction of empire itself, an archaic system from a remote time of conquest, indeed a conquest empire dedicated to the timeless eternality of conquered space, now trying to adjust itself to new historical circumstances and increasingly reassigning its place to the zone of stagnant anachrony. Turkish tribes that left the steppe centuries earlier had finally settled in Anatolia and Southern Europe for the past five hundred years to remain suspended in the spatial figure of a conquest empire devoted only to military subjugation and occupation on the basis of a "natural economy" committed to agricultural cultivation and expropriation, structurally hierarchic, employing Islam's concept of holy war in the form of jihad to provide the religious sanction for murder, mutilation, and theft.[35] In this respect, Turkish ambitions were probably closer to the aspiration of Christian crusades of earlier centuries and their appeal to self-righteous pieties to justify conquest and dispossession. But the similarity ends here since the two instances of dispossession and theft served two different economic systems.

The Ottoman Empire became hostage to its own spatial history and incapable of adapting to the demands of capitalist modernization—much like other empires such as the Qing in China or Mughals of India—a task left to its republican successor. In a striking way, the duration of the Ottomans seemed only to delay what appeared as the fateful repetition of all conquering dynasties that swept out of the steppe and subsequently disappeared. In this regard, there may have been a parallelism between the figure of this fearful historical destiny at the core of the Turkish political unconscious and the vanishing of Ani that would agitate the worst dreams of Armenians. But it is important to keep in mind the other side of the symmetry that Turkey, by having resolved the Armenian Question, had nothing left to remember, whereas Armenians were left with only unanswered questions that could never be forgotten.

Early in 2016 we (my spouse and I) took a trip down to the Mille Vaches region of France and stopped over for a few days in a small town named Eymoutier. The surprise was the town's museum, basically dedicated to housing and exhibiting the work of a locally born artist, Paul Rebeyrolle.[36] It seems that Rebeyrolle's wife had been a model for Henri Matisse and was of Armenian descent. In tribute to his wife and her mother, who apparently had escaped the genocide, the artist composed a number of paintings dramatizing this episode in her life. The theme that caught me appeared in a few large paintings of a series: "Le Sac de Madame Tellikdjian" [The purse of Madame Tellikdjian], portraying the theft of the purse; "Au pied du barrage" [At the foot of the dam], the attempt to retain the purse; and "Le Voleur" [The thief], the purse carried away. Both the first and second paintings portrayed a woman losing her purse, the theft of it in one painting and her desperate attempt at the foot of a dam to grab it, before it was carried off by a torrent of water in the third painting. The theme is clear enough: Madame Telikdjian, Rebeyrolle's mother-in-law, had lost everything in her effort to escape and survive the massacres but her purse, containing all her belongings, tenaciously clutching it because it was her life. In a sense, it was her life, all she had, the price of survival, which was her history. In "The Thief," the painting distilled for me the massive theft carried out by a mobilized Turkish populace bent on destroying Armenians in Anatolia but not before ransacking their homes and bodies for what they could take; in the second painting I saw the frenzied effort to hold on to one last thing when everything else and everybody have been swept away in a surging tsunami. Madame Telikdjian, Rebeyrolle's mother-in-law, like most Armenians, had lost everything in the vortex of genocidal fury in her effort to escape and survive the massacres but her purse, which constituted all her belongings and represented her history as an Armenian. In effect, the paintings struck a forceful resonance that reminded me of what my parents had lost, everything but a fragile grasp of history and their frantic attempt to hang on to it in the diminished life of the diaspora before that too was taken from them or carried off, stolen or swept away in a great surge of water. It was evident that Rebeyrolle had captured in condensed form the crucial and fundamental meaning of the genocide and its relationship to "primitive accumulation." Surviving signified saving the heritage of Armenian history or what the survivors thought it was for them, like the contents of a purse—it was all any of the victims who were able to escape had left to them. I would like to think that Vehanush valued the history, that it was worth hanging on to as a guarantee against complete diminishment, as Rebeyrolle's paintings dramatize, but I am not at all sure she did. Ohannes certainly did. He fought and risked his life for it.

FIVE. HOUSE OF STRANGERS/DIMINISHED LIVES

After World War II, it became apparent that the basic difference between our mother and father was that Ohannes appeared more drawn out than Vehanush to speaking about Anatolian life, as if he delighted in breaking an agreement dedicated to silence. He especially liked telling stories, as suggested earlier, from and about the "old country," as he often put it, and his years of adolescence, but not beyond. Perhaps this loquacity was encouraged by the fact that we were all getting older and were in a position to understand or that he in turn was aging and involuntarily returning to more distant memories of childhood. They were usually tales, sometimes repetitions, many he may have made up, or older ones told to him that he reconfigured and were often funny but also provided a concrete texture of peasant life in a premodern setting. He often referred to one of his favorite Armenian adages of "a man who could fool a dog." In time it became obvious to me that he was that man, even though we had no dog. He had a sense of humor, and liked having a good time and an occasional drink, an activity usually limited to the weekends and consigned to the basement, unless it was a special occasion with guests. But this restraint may have been the result of the earlier period of economic depression when apparently he drank to excess.

Our mother was mostly humorless. What few things I recall when she spoke of her days in the missionary orphanage/school referred to pleasurable moments, but she was not a woman who seemed to have ever had much fun when growing up or even after, apart from going to the movies. And she seemed to be on guard against levity surfacing in the household. I remember her once singing the Christmas carol "Christmas Tree" in German, and she apparently had reported something of her time in Greece to my sisters. I think her pleasures were limited to the movies twice a week; a few favorite radio programs such as "One Man's Family," "Fibber McGee and Molly," and some quiz shows; a reward of a sweet to herself after the week's schedule had been realized; and time with a few women friends. I also recall that she was enthusiastic about Christmas, which must have been a product of the missionary school since Armenians were traditionally prone to celebrate Epiphany in January rather than Christmas in December. But the Christmas she celebrated was increasingly Americanized and became, for her, a sign of being an American. I was never convinced that being around small children brought her much joy, and she reminded me on more than one occasion that she would not be interested in taking care of mine. In a sense I admired her for redefining the role of grandmother, perhaps recuperating the role played by her mother toward us.

Vehanush's chronology has proved to be more difficult to determine than my father's. In his accounting there were verifiable episodes that were datable, such as his story of traveling from Russia to Liverpool, where supposedly he was slated to board the *Lusitania* but apparently missed it and traveled to the U.S. on the *Mauritania*. In any event, the *Mauritania* was just as susceptible to German U-boats as the *Lusitania*. The story itself may have been untrue, for all I know, but it gives an idea of where he was and when. Vehanush's early life seemed shorn of verifiable, datable markers. I have not been able to nail down dates or times of any of the significant moments in her life in Anatolia and subsequent voyage to France. In fact, her marriage to Ohannes is the first datable event in her life I have and that was 1920.

Our parents were involved in not simply a second start. Even more so, a new beginning was brutally forced upon them that resulted from an abruptly interrupted youth, bending them in ways they could never have explained or even anticipated. We might wonder what their lives might have become had they not been dislocated so suddenly by the threat of cataclysmic events. The diaspora's existence was the price paid for continuing to lead what seemed like diminished lives, where tremendous energies were expended to secure the sparest results. Our father, unlike Vehanush, embroidered moments of his past as a boy and teenager, a fantasy he must have in large part conjured and that he relayed to his children, who would envision a society filled with the daily contacts and conflicts with brothers, sisters, aunts, uncles, cousins, and grandparents situated in a larger community composed of kin and friends; that is, its principal theme was normalcy. Some of that was true. But Vehanush was deprived of a comparable experience during her early childhood. Arlene Voski Avakian's memoir of family life in an Armenian American household presented details dramatically different from what we had known, experienced, and remembered. Her early family life was filled with relatives who came and left, a grandmother who had survived the genocide, and parents who had made their way to the United States but still had relatives in Persia (Iran). And, by comparison, her family was economically far better off than ours since her father and his brothers ran an Oriental carpet business.[1] But, like her, I felt the same ambition to become an American, only in my case it was more of a vocation since I really had no other aspiration when growing up. There seemed to be no compelling imperative to retain a sense of Armenianness since my associations, apart from life in our family, were with non-Armenians. This may have derived from an inflected stage of self-loathing I suspect many children of first-generation migrants pass through. But even the family environment changed when the three of us entered public schools and our culture of reference gradually shifted to a world outside the household. In those days, I began to think about a society and its educational institutions that virtually implanted through programmatic socialization such a singular goal informed by an ahistorical model into its second-generation migrant sons and daughters, insisting they pour their energies into becoming something they were not and could never be, completely displacing the pursuit of other possibilities, discouraging both bilinguality and bicultural life. Years later, it still occurred to me that the apparent alchemical magic devised by public schools to transmogrify the children of plural ethnicities into the singular figure of an Americanness was an experiment that had not only failed but inflicted unforeseen consequences on its subjects or victims.

Armenian everyday life embodied a conception of the social held together by religion and extended families or clans. The diaspora lives of the survivors were an imperfect or incomplete replication of the traditional model. Owing to the circumstances demanded by the necessity to run for one's life and the massive elimination of relatives and friends who could not get out in time, the reconstitution of the diasporic social was more of a bricolage than a reproduction. And, as I have suggested, the role of the church was diminished in the new environment. Avakian presents a picture of social reproduction that is closer to the traditional model, especially in her description of how relatives seemed to be always coming and going. But it is her grandmother who had experienced and survived the genocide by consenting to convert to Islam in order to save her children. It is her story told to Avakian when she was young that she did not want to hear; this story is retrieved in adulthood to reinforce her identity as a woman and an Armenian. "Why would I," she writes, "want to know about people who were unknown to most of the world, who were hated so much when they were recognized that they were forced to leave their homes and to give up their religion, who were even killed. . . . I was sorry that I had asked her [grandmother] to tell it to me. I didn't want to know it. It was bad enough to be unknown, strange, and different from everyone else, but it was unbearable to be despised. I would forget it."[2] When I was her age I cannot claim to have acquired such insightful understanding of what it meant to be an Armenian, the diminished status accorded to unknown people who were remembered largely for the reminder of their starving children used to induce American kids to clean off their dinner plates. But I understand what she means when she refers to how different I was often made to feel from my WASP classmates or even neighborhood Irish Catholic kids, who belonged to the same working class as us, were just as unknowing and uncaring. Avakian is right to propose that the story simply worked to make her more "determined to deny my difference from everyone else."[3] Unlike Avakian, I had neither the imagination nor inclination to change our customary ways of living and found most of my energy poured into the futile exercise of trying to become the American I observed in school and the movies.

Avakian provides a translation of the transcript taken from her grandmother that conveys both the fierceness and the bravery of her struggle to retrieve one of her sons from a Turkish official in a language that accurately captures the larger historicity of the genocidal event and time. I was reminded of what I had missed and lost in not raising questions when I had the opportunity to have done so. What such testimonials as Avakian's grandmother's and Balakian's provide is, in fact, that everyday life during the genocide years converted into the repetition of terror and the fear that each day might be your last. For my generation, who never experienced the genocide's redefinition of the everyday as a repetitive death sentence, the testimonies allow us to momentarily reimagine the ways our own relatives—in my case, grandparents, great-grandparents, uncles, aunts, and so on—perished, providing a brief glimpse of how they may have confronted their executioners and thinking the thoughts that must have passed through them in their last moments. Both of these texts not only supply the forbidding factual details of what was taking place in the killing fields of Anatolia, personalizing the mass quantity of nameless deaths that would soon be forgotten and could not be tallied until the end, but also make of us, who came after, their witnesses.[4] As suggested earlier, the statistical data is all we have of such murderous episodes, but the surviving witnesses provide us with the valuable knowledge of how those whose names we never knew and relatives whose presence would forever remain unapproachably absent and beyond our experience were still our kin who had led lives of individual quality and died as unknown numbers with their names and personal histories.

In the U.S. we had none of this kind of contact with relatives (apart from exaggerated tales about the good life in Istanbul), though our parents did their best to accomplish some measure of normalcy while we were growing up in the late years of the Depression. But what kind of normalcy is possible when so much has been lost and there is so much to learn in a new environment, when you have to make your way by trial and error and the margin of error can be disastrously narrow? Their idea of normalcy was simply to shut out any reference to their early pasts, unlike Avakian's grandmother, who insisted on recounting the story of her survival to her granddaughter since she must have believed it was as much of who she would become as it was of herself. But bracketing their pasts to achieve some sort of normalcy to shield their children contributed to the diminishment of both their lives and ours. I often thought, when I was older, that we were a house of strangers rather than a family, and as I look back on those years I am not persuaded that I was completely wrong. Our mother lived with somebody else's name that I did not know until I began writing this memoir. My sister Victoria left the family after she graduated from high school and married young; I left a few years later never really to return, apart from short visits; and only my sister Sena continued to live with Vehanush and Ohannes until they passed away. There seemed to be an absence of any lasting bond of solidarity to our family unit, nothing to hold it together but the void we all were made to occupy and live out. The question that seemed to ask itself was who was Vehanush when she was a Kupalian and whom did she become when she adopted the name Bedrosian? And did Kupalian remain in the recesses of Bedrosian's memories or were they banished?

The thought of leading diminished lives has bothered me since youth. Part of the reason for this preoccupation with diminishment was the youthful experience of living through episodes of exclusion for reasons I only began to understand as I moved into my teens; small instances and incidents gradually aggregated under the sign of exclusion, being left out. Perhaps this was more the case for migrants who came with the first wave of workers to the U.S. For me, "diminish" refers to what immigrants, such as my parents, had to settle for by coming to the U.S. at that time and by extension what we had to carry with us for having different skin tones and unpronounceable names and for failing to look like some figure modeled by the Hollywood dream machine. I am explicitly referring to the experience of the genocide that robbed them of whatever future they might have normally expected in Anatolia and then lives mediated by the diaspora existence, which merged with the economic depression in Detroit to inflict on them a second form of diminishment. I am not suggesting that their life in Anatolia would have been better off but only that they would have had there an already defined place for themselves; they would have belonged and have had the facility to make of it what they could have. I had earlier expressed the belief that our parents clearly recognized they had no future in the U.S. but only the prospect of the sparest existence in an unending present. In some respects, this sense of a diminished life affected us (my sisters and me) as well, not simply as a family but as children who entered the wider society provided by public schools. My own early experience in schools made me daily aware of my immigrant status that separated us from those who were not the children of immigrant families. It also began to pull me away from the difference I was forced to live as an Armenian, or at least away from the prospect of remaining connected to it. I remember an incident in grade school when I was recruited to be a special friend and helper of a German Jewish immigrant boy whose family had just arrived in America. On afterthought it occurred to me that I was designated to help him make his way because it was supposed I had the requisite experience. Years later, in my teens, I was told by the father of a friend of mine that "they didn't want my kind in the neighborhood." It was a coercive moment, tinged with threat and violence. The problem was that I did not know what kind I was supposed to represent since I had already been socialized to internalize the abstract figure of the good American, whatever that meant. The incident was useful in one regard: it showed the bankruptcy of the image of the modular American peddled in civics classes and how in society different people had their own idea of what it meant to be a real American. But I did recognize I was not allowed to be like him or his daughter and that a racial divide permanently separated us. In graduate school, I worked as a dishwasher in a boarding house; the woman who ran it regularly had trouble with my name and repetitively wanted to know when I came to this country. She was usually drunk by that time of the day when the dinner meal was served and cleanup began. My doctoral advisor never had anything substantive to say about my dissertation, apart from expressing an anxious concern that I should fix the "split infinitives" in the manuscript, which from the beginning defined our non-relationship and which seemed to be his principal and only preoccupation. In the course of time, I began to think that this response inflected his own distrust that I had not yet acquired a full command of native English because of my foreignness. I knew he had never encountered an Armenian or entertained the idea of one. This curious absence of offering substantive criticism and comment also reflected his own incapacity to actually think critically, which apparently he was never trained to do in the Ivy League institution that granted him his doctoral degree. In those days, critical thinking did not appear to be a necessity in the training of young men and women in those institutions. Why learn the necessity of thinking critically when you're made to believe you're at the center of the world? I always had the feeling that most of my graduate instructors had trouble seeing me as simply another student, like others, through their WASP-like prism. I think the roadblock or psychological astigmatism was caused by the name.

But beyond that, most of us from migrant families were simply targeted for vocational education programs. Even though I was older than Arlene Voski Avakian, her experience in the public schools corresponds uncannily close to sentiments I would have expressed in my own inarticulate feelings in high school, and especially resembles what she was made to endure when her family moved from Manhattan to a "white bread" community in north New Jersey and attended Ridgewood High School: "I felt like an outcast . . . , not only around students but teachers as well. . . . I felt as if my teachers expected very little from me."[5] While Detroit was no white-bread community, Ann Arbor was, as was the university the town housed. In high school Avakian's teacher believed she "was part of the very small group of students who would not go on to college."[6] In the high school I attended (Highland Park) there was a larger quotient of migrant girls and boys and African Americans (whose parents worked in local factories) that formed a categorical group that simply was not slated to go to college, as if it was a law of nature (excepting the class valedictorian, who was an Armenian). In this environment, I learned that there was a very narrow definition of what being an American meant that did not always fully include people like us. What I was able to glean early from the experience, without having the capacity to quite express it, taught me that I was not simply average but less than average, that I had no idea whatsoever what I would do if I graduated, and that the only friends I had came from the same migrant pool. That is to say, I learned how race was used to reinforce and even disguise class and presumptions of ethnic superiority that substituted for class advantage, lessons that were missing in our civics class where the work of ideological socialization was carried out. The early years were thus marked by exclusions because of my difference, and it is interesting to see how in a generation's time, difference itself became the primary principle of inclusion. It was almost as if it was the working through of a law of historical repetition, with difference.

There is, of course, a contrast between those who specifically migrate to this country for a better life, who come because the U.S. is mythologized as the future, and those caught between the prospect of imminent death and imminent poverty to feel lucky to be alive and who have either found their future in the immediate present or have indefinitely deferred it. Yet in America people were not supposed to be simply alive. Being simply alive in an endless present is a form of diminishment. It lessens what one is, one's importance, outlook, and hope without a future to look toward, and reduces the notation of one's difference to smallness and unworthiness. Moreover, it represents a diminishing of prospects not only because the status runs counter to expectations offered by the ideological promise associated with American life (even though people like our parents did not come for that) but because one's own experience in this country resulted in finding no real place in it—as I said, living somebody else's history but not really being of it. Raised in a meager environment, it was for this reason we were taught to expect no more than what we had.

Vehanush's move to the West, as I have suggested, is more difficult to nail down than Ohannes's trajectory. I do not know if she was accompanied by the other girls or whether the group had been broken up and dispersed—another question that went unanswered in an already crowded inventory of unanswered questions signifying only the negative lapses of an uncompleted life. It is possible she and the school group left Marash later than the time I have imagined and remained in Turkey throughout the genocidal period, under the protection of the German missionaries. They then could have left later, under the general amnesty ending the war in 1918, which means three years or more of voluntary internment in the orphanage's precincts within the crucible of massacre. This experience would likely explain her later silence and complete rejection of the "old country." She must have heard and seen things she did not want to remember.

Starting over again for my parents did not mean that their prior lives would remain fixed and comfortably dormant in a distant past that eventually would be interred in a sealed but forgotten memory. Rather, I felt that the iron discipline of silence, their refusal to really share their earlier experiences and talk about their respective lives and survivals, would continue to trouble them in their new beginning. Beginning a family in a new and alienating environment was a little like a work in progress: Vehanush brought little experience of family life to this challenge; Ohannes was, perhaps, hobbled by too much experience that was no longer useful or adaptable to the demands of not only a new and different environment but a vastly different kind of society that historically, politically, economically, and culturally resembled nothing of what both had once known. What could they teach us of American life, which they were in the process of trying to understand? Learning it through another language risks losing something in translation. I still find myself expressing certain things I learned when younger in Armenian words. My mother substituted her lack of a deep experience of living in a family with the discipline she learned from German missionaries. She organized the week on the basis of daily chores that had to be done on that day alone, between Monday and Friday, without deviation. These were chores she assigned to herself, but everybody else in the household had to observe them as well: Monday washday, Tuesday ironing, Wednesday and/or Thursday house cleaning, and Friday grocery shopping, with little allowable room for play or divergence. On Fridays, as mentioned earlier, she sometimes set aside time to reward herself with a sweet, usually ice cream or something like that—a compensatory gesture signaling youthful deprivations? Cooking dinners was also her task and quite late in life, as I noted earlier, she learned how to prepare Armenian dishes. She would go to the movies (where she eventually learned English) twice a week, on "dish night," to add to her collection, when she dragged either one of my sisters or me, and again on Sunday. In those days just before World War II and immediately after, neighborhood movie houses had two changes a week and a double bill on weeknights, which invariably were classified as B movies, apparently of lesser quality and inexpensively produced, now many ranked as classic film noirs; on the weekends were top-rated feature films. In almost every way, she left her imprint on the household.

My father spent most of the weekdays at work, but Vehanush made sure dinner was ready by 5:30 p.m. Evenings were spent listening to radio programs (until TV arrived and discovered Groucho Marx); both parents went to bed comparatively early since my father usually had to get up early for day shifts in some car plant, especially when he landed a secure job at the outset of the war, and my mother would have his lunch prepared as well as his breakfast. She never slept past 5:00 a.m., a habit undoubtedly acquired in the missionary school. When Ohannes was home on the weekends, it was time for visiting friends or attending some Armenian function. Both would regularly go to an Armenian grocery on Woodrow Wilson Avenue, within walking distance of our flat, run by a tall man who was also their friend and whom everybody called Haji (some people mistranslated it into Archie) but whose real name was Hovaness. Only later I discovered that it was some sort of Turkish term of respect and signified people who made a trip to a holy city, which in this case was a Christian site like Jerusalem or Bethlehem, indicated by a tattooed cross on one's hand. The last time I saw Haji was on his one hundredth birthday or close enough to it, still erect, in command of clear thinking and expression. I should add that it was usual practice in the Armenian community to use services run by Armenians like groceries, cleaners, medical doctors, dentists, cleaners, and others. When we were smaller, I remember our father taking us to a local park on the weekends during the summer. But as we all grew older, he would spend Saturdays and sometimes Sunday afternoons at the Azadamard Club, where he played pinochle and backgammon and talked of current politics within the larger Armenian diaspora community. I was never privy to these conversations but I suspect that in time they morphed into stories quite remote from the way things had been. He was a regular subscriber to an Armenian newspaper (*Hairenik*), reading it from cover to cover and often singing the praises of the written language, distantly echoing the Soviet poet Osip Mandelstam's own discovery of Armenian and his confident observation of "the stone like hardness of articulate speech" whose "boots are stone," preserved in this ancient language. The newspaper came out of Boston until 1970 and reflected the political views of the ARF or Dashnaks. For such a small community, the Armenians seemed to be riven with far too many political factions, many of them inflecting political positions of certain church dioceses. This meant that if you were sympathetic to the ARF, you would go to the church associated with that political ideology and participate in its social functions; if you were involved in an opposing political view, you would choose another. What appeared noticeable to me was that these political lines were like borders that rarely were, if ever, crossed. The problem of politics and religion in the Armenian community was complicated and the close identification with religion often spilled over into political acts of violence. It is likely that diaspora, itself a condensation of the heterology of Anatolian life, reinforced the sharpening of religiopolitical commitments that would have been once more diffuse and now bolstered greater antagonisms exploding into violence. I was never sure of how Vehanush felt about these diverse political factions, since she clearly had no or little affiliation with the Armenian Apostolic Church when she was a child and her encounter with German Protestantism in the missionary school must have contributed to separating her further from the older church. But I had the feeling that she was somewhat indifferent, if not dismissive toward their various political positions, primarily seeing in some of the auxiliary organizations the offer of the sociality of women. Part of this antipathy for the politics embraced by the Armenian Church derived from her profound disaffection from the Armenian Apostolic Church, which, she knew, was usually at the core of most of the political conflict within the community. It was also greatly strengthened by what she must have learned in the mission school, which inevitably identified the native churches with backwardness and a barrier to progress. With Ohannes it was a lifelong commitment, even though his ardor began to wane the older he became. His enthusiasm for the prospect of an independent Armenia, what he and his age cohort had fought for, was vanishing. I remember a conversation we had a few years before he went to Fresno. We discussed an incident related to an elder Armenian gentleman who, I believe, lived in Fresno and who persuaded a Turkish official from the consulate in San Francisco to come down on the promise to show him a rare Oriental rug. There may have been the suggestion of a donation. I am not sure. When the official showed up, the elder Armenian shot and killed him. My father's response to this was to approve of it, declaring that he would have done the same thing. He might have done so when he was younger but not any longer at his age at the time. Yet I do not think that this announcement was merely the empty bravado of an old man but rather was consistent with the political program of the Dashnaks after World War I that Ohannes had always extolled and their determined mission to send agents wherever Young Turks officials had fled, especially to Germany, to assassinate those responsible for the genocide. I always had the feeling that his sympathies for this activity betrayed a more personal commitment to its program. But at the same time he remained adamantly silent on any concrete information concerning his Dashnak affiliations, apart from his time in the brigades and his membership. But his unwavering approval exceeded the satisfaction of revenge for having lost his whole family and the nature of his commitment to the cause.

Part of the complication of politics and religion is explainable by the particular nature of the church itself. It was called the Armenian Apostolic Church and represented, along with the Coptic Church, perhaps the earliest schism within Christendom. Organized in the fourth century, it drew authority presumably from a claimed relation to one of the Apostles, and was from the very beginning a national or better yet ethnically based Christian Church. Its rites and rituals resemble those belonging to the Greek Orthodox faith, inasmuch as the liturgy was in the native tongue, not Latin; it also differed in its theology as a result of participating in numerous historic synods in the early history of Christianity, especially those that tried to fix the nature of the trinity and resolve what were Christological controversies that usually ended up splintering other groups along ethnic lines like the Nestorians.[7] With Armenians of my father's generation there was the additional problem of the location of the church's supreme authority figure, the Catholicos, whose seat—Etchmiadzin—was located in Soviet Armenia. For the ARF, there was no possibility of reconciliation, and if memory serves me correctly, I believe Dashnak agents in New York City assassinated an archbishop of the church in 1933 for having been a vocal supporter of the Soviet regime in Armenia. Such were the politics of the diaspora. Third-generation Armenians, principally from France, continued this program after World War II.

While Ohannes expressed support of such acts, he was no longer a follower of the faith, despite his own family's priestly heritage. Vehanush, as I mentioned earlier, had no religious affiliation, as such, nor interest in the Armenian Church. The world she created in the household reflected what she had learned in the missionary school and how to order the everyday into routines consisting of worthwhile tasks and pursuits. In many ways, this quality probably goes a long way toward explaining her capacity to survive in both environments. But it resulted in some significant absences. In my memory, there were few expressions of affection and there was no atmosphere of excessive warmth in our household. This is not to say that our parents were indifferent to the three of us. But they tended to our needs as part of the contract; we were always fed regularly, had clean clothes and were cared for, but as if we were part of the regular routines of the domestic political economy. In a sense, this conforms to the view of my sister Victoria, who observed that our parents were not necessarily a compatible couple. And I observed something of this incompatibility as they grew older but am willing to attribute it to aging as another probable explanation. Ohannes would often acknowledge to me how he was lost after Vehanush died. This probably had to do with the structured life she had put into place in the household and its disappearance after she died. My response to Victoria was to agree with her and think that this must have reflected the general condition of arranged marriages, which did not necessarily develop into affective or deeply emotional relationships but rather resembled more the fulfilling of long-standing terms of a contract. It explains the nature of our relationships with both parents. It may have been different with my sisters, but I think Victoria's evaluation really speaks to the experience of all three of us. Sena would not have agreed. I am not accusing our parents of depriving us of a loving environment, marked by warmth and affection—they gave what they could. Escaping to the United States saved their lives but forced them to face yet another challenge of survival that would take a severe and immense toll on lives already irreparably damaged and disabled. In a sense, they, like most first-generation immigrants, paid a price by indemnifying their lives in such a way as to ensure that their offspring might have not simply a better future but rather a future itself.

Genocide survivors, like Armenians, who were able to flee to a new shore to save their lives were initially less preoccupied with the enormous task of making a living that awaited them, since the journey was lived on a day-to-day basis, even though the question of finding economic security would loom as a principal fixation. For those who migrate for economic reasons, they appear to be fixed on little else since it is precisely this problem and how to go about resolving it that has commanded their attention. In the equation between the two kinds of migrants, the former explains a progressively diminished existence while the latter points to the possibility of realizing a new and better kind of life from the one that had been left behind. In this regard, it is important to observe how the meaning of diaspora has changed: when before it was usually associated with people running for their lives, now it is principally identified with people looking for a better quality of life, even though there are still instances, as the recent Syrian migrations have shown, of people running from the certain promise of death and destruction. Sometimes it can be both at the same time, which has been more characteristic of our post–World War II present. I always thought that our parents knew they would face a futureless life in this land once they reached it. Their prospect of a future had vanished with the countless victims of the genocide. What actually was eradicated was a history that might have been, one permanently interrupted, which would have disclosed the future present they might have lived and shared. But under such circumstances they probably would not have met each other. All that seemed left was the blank seriality of unfulfilled empty time, of getting through an everyday marked by the expectation of chronic economic insecurity and permanent disappointment. The ordeal they withstood and the burden that weighed on them all their lives perhaps explains why parents like ours remained silent on what had befallen so many and speaks directly to their unexplainable sense of unspoken guilt for not having perished, as they should have. It was not that the genocide or indeed any genocidal event is capable of defying our capacity for representation, as Adorno once proposed with regard to the production of poetry itself.[8] It was, I believe, the conviction that the massacres and attending obligatory mutilation constituted an obscene and senseless offense to human memory and experience, an indecent interruption unworthy of any effort to represent its evident rage and depravity, even though it was always representable. It has even destroyed the names of those who were a part of us. What good is it to remember or, worse, quibble over whether there is enough evidence to authenticate its reality? While I respect more recent efforts of Armenian historians and others to uncover documentary materials attesting to the incidence of massacres in specific and diverse regions of Anatolia, such as Van, the problem of genocide is never reducible to the identification of adequate documentation, which plays to the interests of deniers and is invariably as indeterminate an exercise as trying to calculate how many swallows make a summer. The only question that needs be asked of any genocide is, Where did all those people go? Genocidal events are never a matter of historical judgment but rather a matter for the dead. The nameless tell us what happened and that is all the evidence we need. Let historians argue over what happens to the future when there is no more history being made, instead of counting documents as if a magical quantity will light up the sky, like the lucky winning numbers of a lottery. Why dignify Turkish silence, whose entire modern history has been spent in disavowing complicity in committing such an obscenity imprinted on its origin? Who would admit to it? At the same time, there is the struggle of migrant life, the threadbare remains of a whole way of life and its people, which, in its own way, proved to consume time and energy throughout a lifetime that daily appeared permanent and demanding by contrast to the shorter duration of the genocidal moment receding into the background of the new life. This may well contribute to explaining the decision to continue a determined silence on the past when the present required the expenditure of such supreme effort.

Perhaps any year is as good as 2015, the one hundredth anniversary of the genocide, when I actually made the effort to compose this memoir, to praise all those nameless victims—men and women—who perished in the century's inaugural genocidal episode, which would become a vocation successively leading to even greater systematic massacres of whole populations to become the twentieth century's principal signature and brand trademark. The importance of the Turkish genocidal rage against Armenians is manifest also in what it represents in the register of world history. While the genocide's program of dispossession—theft—and expropriation began earlier, it became policy by 1915 and continued in different forms after the massacres and deportations and well into modern Turkey's history. Armenian, Assyrian, and Greek churches were systematically confiscated well into the decades between the two wars and even after; Grigoris Balakian reports that in his journey to the desert, he observed Armenian churches in irreparable ruin, wrecked by cannon shells while others were being used to house animals and military barracks—ironically the same churches that now appear in glossy and colored contemporary travel guides and posters designed to advertise the rich traces of diverse but nameless civilizations in Anatolia. Anatolia is filled with these ruined churches, emptied of their relics and now often abandoned after they had been abused to house soldiers and animals. As already noted, the ones selected for travel brochures attesting to Turkey's collection of diverse cultures comprise a shameless displacement from the tradition of ruin inaugurated by Ani, still signifying the continuing Turkish impulse to expropriate the property of its minorities for capital accumulation.

Moreover, it is important to recognize that these minority populations were excessively taxed on all fixed assets and wealth and required to make payments by a deadline, which resulted in destroying the remaining non-Muslim merchant class. Those who were unable to pay the tax were sent to labor camps, resulting in unaccounted deaths. If the earlier massacres in the nineteenth century under Abdülhamid II aimed to reduce agitation from minority populations, the later genocide was a technique harnessed to the modernizing makeover of the Young Turks. In both instances, the purpose amounted to primitive accumulation, and the only difference between the two episodes is that the earlier massacres were unsystematic. The deportations of Armenians in 1915 into the Syrian Desert were clearly devised to eliminate a whole population and suggest an interesting analogue to the later Nazi death camps and their reliance on more advanced technology to accelerate the killing of a whole population. The difference between bullets, swords, knives, other household and farm implements, and an uninhabitable desert as weapons of murder employed by a mobilized peasantry and gas chambers is really the difference between a precapitalist society and capitalist modernization. One hundred years later, the priest Grigoris Balakian's great-nephew Peter Balakian revisited the desert site recorded in his book of poetry, *Ozone Journal*.

> At the caves,
> M. is obsessed with light flickering down—
> affect of the punctum:
> while remaining a detail, the space fills up the whole picture.
>
> M. *Were thousands of Armenians stuffed in here?*
> B. *Fisk called them primitive gas chambers.*
>
> M. drops the boom mic into darkness; sand floats through
>   light-chipped space.
>
> If you try to imagine death here, the detail is not the whole—
>   the whole disappears.
> The cave is a black gullet swallowing itself—[9]

For his part, the priest, who was among the deportees heading for the desert but managed to escape, saw this wasteland as a vast, open-air grave without tombstones, whose bones and skulls were covered by the sands of Mesopotamia, waiting to be consecrated as the sacred place of martyrdom. Today it is the site of an interminable struggle. Conceivably, it would have been this vision that was transmitted to the survivors to accompany them on their frantic journeys to new lands promising safe refuge that became the silent principle binding diasporic life.

This relationship of Turkish and German styles of mass murder was more than analogic since German scholarship in recent years has acknowledged the German role in the earlier mass murders, a role that had been consistently denied despite Germany's wartime alliance with the Ottomans. Since Ambassador Morgenthau published his diary, in which the last chapter is devoted to detailing German complicity, the German role in the Armenian genocide has been an open secret and a long symphony of denial, laying the blame on World War I. But among important German policy makers and military officials, those who opposed the genocide are far outnumbered by those who supported it. We know from Franz Werfel's prescient novel, banned in Nazi Germany, that German missionaries in Istanbul and elsewhere pleaded with Turkish and German diplomatic officials to stop the policy. Missionaries, especially, provided testimony that attested to the broad influence the German military genuinely commanded over the shaping of Ottoman policy and that they could easily have intervened in the mass murders before they began. Grigoris Balakian is unequivocal in his conviction that Germans, and especially the military, were directly involved in augmenting and providing continuing support to Turkey's deportation policy, knowing that deportation meant murder.[10] While supplying ample evidence of German complicity, Balakian, like others, also proposed that German anti-Semitism was easily mobilized to include the Armenians as reviled targets of elimination.[11] Recently unearthed evidence of more direct German involvement clearly suggests a form of dress rehearsal for the later genocidal event. This willful complicity was particularly active among German military officials during World War I and there is abundant testimony showing how high-ranking officials expressed contempt for the Armenians and actually compared them to the Jews, as "a deracinated parasite sucking the marrow of countries that have received them."[12] In this regard, the writer and poet Aimé Césaire was only partially correct when he attributed the highest heap of corpses to European depredations in Africa.[13] Turkey was a way station on the direct route of genocide to Europe and Germany, which harnessed technology to this deadly vocation. Between Africa and Anatolia, the genealogy of later genocidal acts in Europe was already in place. Behind it was capital's imperial impulse, for acquisitions or the preservation of imperial space for capital.

In more recent contemporary reports, Germany has been reported to have provided the Ottoman Empire with modern weapons to carry out the mass murders. Another account has declared that German officers were deeply implicated in formulating the "ideological foundations" informing the genocidal scenario. But the material assistance was undoubtedly more important than mere ideology, which the Young Turks perpetrators had already devised. German manufacturers like Mausser (or Mauser), maker of small arms, furnished the Ottoman army with millions of rifles and handguns that were directly put to use in carrying out the genocidal murders, with the active cooperation of German officers. The Turkish army was also supplied with hundreds of cannons produced by Krupp that were used to bomb civilian homes in Urfa (October 1915), killing those inside and others who tried to escape the bombardment by fleeing to the church. According to this report, German officers actually took part in the murders by firing on civilian Armenians in the Urfa region.[14]

As earlier suggested, it is not the Armenian Question that explains the historical event but rather the Turkish Question, an uncontrolled explosion of an unnamed irrational impulse demanding mutilation that made the crime scene a human abattoir. If the persistence of genocidal memory has been consistently kept alive by generations of diasporic Armenians, to suggest the grip of one kind of obsessive commemoration of a collectivity, surely its opposite manifestly appears in the unrelenting denial qualifying as another form of a persisting cultural consciousness that has preoccupied Turkey since the defining event and with which it has had to live without understanding or knowing why. That it is a recognition they cannot face or articulate makes it their question since, in many ways, Armenians can talk about it and, sometimes, nothing else. The formation of modern Turkey has been a historical fiction, weighted down by what can only be described as genocidal seizure, the price of shirking off the atrophied husk of a dying empire for the realization of a modern nation-state and society through ethnic cleansing. To imagine that modern states required ethnic purification, as a form of a rite of passage on their way to realizing nationhood, was itself an immense misrecognition bordering on mass delusion.

One of the more indecent expressions of this pathological denial has been the concealment of the identities of those Armenian children who were rescued and saved by Kurdish and Turkish families and who only discovered what they were years later in adulthood or well into succeeding generations. In some instances, this was linked to the ongoing abuse of Armenians who survived in Turkey and stayed on not simply as second-class citizens, a status enjoyed by immigrants in the U.S., but as genuine subhumans, even though the intended result is the concealment of a child's true identity. In contemporary Turkey, the genre of captivity narratives has begun to surface with increasing regularity. What this makes manifest is the sign of the uninterrupted desire of Turkey to show the world that it had actually saved children from the worst of the genocide's determined depredations, signaling acts of human kindness. What has not been said is how many of them had been exploited for their labor. Regardless of their subsequent fate in Turkish households, these children had the birthright to be told who they were and how and where they came from, as well as what had happened to their parents. At the same time this declaration of acts disclosing the kindness of strangers must be balanced against another unintended admission pointing to how the rescue mission of Armenian children testifies to an indirect acknowledgment that the massacres did take place, which works to undermine the official genocidal denial. While they have been criticized and even maligned for mistreating these captive children, modern Turkish society has managed to turn around the relationship between victimizer and victim to achieve a classic example of how the former seeks to reconfigure itself into the latter.

Moreover, the year 2015 was also as good a time as any to praise not only the nameless victims but the nameless survivors whose many individual stories of escape, survival, and endurance of ordeals caused by the upheavals and disruption of diaspora residency in foreign lands are still as unknown as their identities. In the final analysis, the problem is further compounded by the Genocide Convention, which has sought to provide a legal basis for determining whether mass murder qualifies as "genocide" and has ultimately concluded that the qualifying criterion is the intention to accomplish complete extermination, a view that reflects the German determination to eliminate Europe's Jewish population. Such a judgment seems to claim precedence over the principle of primitive accumulation and contributes to showing how fascist ideology was made to finesse the realities of economic desire and policy. The irony of placing primary emphasis on the declared intention of a fascist ideology that formulated the program dedicated to exterminating a whole ethnic group is that it gradually opened the way for the refashioning of a counterideology of victimhood, whereby the survivors now reinforce the rarity granted to the event to supply its privilege with entitlement and exclusive exceptionality. This paradoxical convergence is capable of fostering the formation of views dedicated to discounting and rejecting the claims of others who experienced mass murder, the imminent threat of ethnic extinction, and the denial of entry into a pantheon reserved for candidates meriting genocidal recognition capable of fulfilling what, after all, is the outcome of an arbitrary definition. The problem appears to be the privilege accorded to conceptions of culture and civilization as criteria for constructing such a classification system that in the nineteenth century was first put into place to justify and explain imperialism and colonialism. In this regard, the Holocaust unfortunately is too often made to be the stand-in for all mass murders and its continuing memory machinery has inadvertently contributed to the myth of Europe's exceptionalism—a kind of return of the repressed of the West's unity and its familiar racial associations. In fact, consideration of how the present must reckon with its past has too often singularly relied on the Holocaust as the basic template with which to grasp an understanding of all genocides. A cursory look at the killings in Africa or Anatolia immediately suggests important differences despite the shared common ground of mass murder. What this intimates is that the respective killing fields of Europe thus look as if they trump all other claimants, even though what started on its periphery by Europeans—in the empires and among their oppressed captive peoples—made its way to the center. (This is an interesting negative reversal of Hegel's "history of freedom," moving, more or less, in the same direction.) What lies at the heart of this murderous impulse is the makeover demanded by capitalist modernization—that is, the attention it requires to understand its history or the meaning of its historicity. One of the principal ironies of Turkey's quest for modernization is the way the very terms of the historical experience enabling it were obliterated with the Armenians, who apparently were seen to stand in its way. But this particular consequence is how capitalism everywhere behaves to remove or disguise its historical antecedents, what lies behind it, or to disclose its capacious talent for refiguring historical time according to its own necessity of establishing an eternal present. Just as capitalism has effectively "forgotten" the horrors of a process of primitive accumulation that has accounted for its origins and subsequent success, so nations remove the embarrassing stigmas of their more immediate origins for a new narrative that projects the idea that the nation has always existed, since time immemorial—a presumed "fact," on which slick travel brochures constantly remind us.

In this way, the Kemalist Revolution presents itself as a bourgeois revolution that removed its origins in the more recent past, resituating it in a more remote and indeterminate duration of time that left the custodianship of its real history to the diaspora survivors as memory anchoring their new and uncertain lives. Establishing a commission to determine what constitutes a "real" genocide is not only a useless verbal exercise but in fact contributes to displacing what can thus be named as such by making its real history invisible. This takes us back to Steedman's numbers and quantities authorizing Auslander's "passport" to enter history.

My father rarely talked about the journey that first took him to the U.S. several times before World War I. It is astonishing, as I look back now, how I developed a disciplined lack of curiosity that bordered on indifference. Here, I would agree with Avakian's question that asks, Why bother with people who are seen as different and despised and that nobody knows or cares for? It never occurred to me that Ohannes's journey involved great distances and complex negotiations. My own indifference must have been encouraged by his unyielding silence; in my case it was also hastened by a desire to become American, like everybody else, I thought at the time. Over the years, I learned that people like us in the U.S. could not be exactly like everybody else, even if it was an imaginable achievement. If, as Avakian proposed, being an Armenian was difficult, becoming an American was almost impossible. As I suggested, my generation of immigrant children was cast into playing the unsought role of hybridity, but not the romanticized version dreamed up by postcolonial theorists, which would skillfully enable the subaltern to navigate his or her way through "negotiation," thus proving the viability and presumed equal status of one's own subject position to one's colonial masters. The hybridity we were consigned to live worked to veil differences that would never disappear in the blending promised by melting pot assimilation into American life. If decolonization brought relief to the colonized oppressed, our lives, while not subjected to colonial oppression, as such, resulted in a kind of colonized subjugation of the mind or personality leading to permanent inequality demanded by the status of second-class citizenship. All of this was made achievable by civics programs directed at socializing the young but acting more effectively as body snatchers and molding them into what we are today. If this imperative to be like everyone else was fueled by entering the broader society provided by public schools, it was, I believe, fortified by my mother's own desire to see her children adapt to the new environment, as she would, and find a permanent place in it. (She was no Parent Teacher Association enthusiast, nor Avakian's Episcopalian, a familiar path taken by most migrant parents, for obvious reasons.) Years later this called to mind a recognition that, as she was convinced, this was the best parents could do for their children. As for themselves, their lives were committed to ensuring our collective survival in a harsh land filled with the constant threat of uncertainty produced by the world depression. My father's wave of immigrant workers was, as I earlier said, the generation scheduled for entering the Depression to reveal to those who came to the United States as a refuge that America was an immensely imperfect society. It is hard to exaggerate the fears cast by this experience of surviving. It was only World War II that rescued our family from an everyday driven by the struggle to find work, usually through the agency of the WPA, and secure some permanence in the auto factories promised by the formation of unionization and its violent struggle with both management and the state to acquire a foothold in capitalism's constrained system of income distribution and habit of enriching the rich. My father was active in this struggle, especially the effort to unionize the Ford River Rouge plant. I was just old enough to see and remember to this day his return home one evening with a bloodied face.

In the end, I was convinced that Ohannes, as a result of his experience with Armenian brigades in eastern Anatolia, was persuaded that the cause of independence had failed, perhaps for the time being, and that the best course was for him to return to the United States and join up with the American army to secure citizenship. Upon joining, he apparently was sent quickly to France in the last years of the Great War, as part of an army of immigrants granted citizenship if they survived the horrors of trench warfare, a frontline phalanx used as cannon fodder, not much different from those armies of Chinese laborers brought to France to dig trenches. His time there was short. He survived a gas attack that disabled him and sent him back to a hospital behind the lines, where he was eventually discharged in 1919. His chronology of the immediate postwar years is less clear to my sisters and me. He must have returned to the U.S., where he did work in East Pullman. My mother and father finally found a way to the United States from France, after a brief duration in Marseilles, and in time settled in Detroit, where he found employment in automobile factories and sweatshops, joining another frontline phalanx that served as an industrial reserve army sacrificed to the Depression. Here, the life he lived was driven by fractured memories and some nostalgia, leavened by recollecting what once had been and had been brutally taken from him and a nameless generation of Armenian men and women who were needlessly erased along with their history and forgotten, to be forfeited to the birth of a modern Turkish state and its capitalist aspirations. But I did promise him I would take him to Armenia (then the Soviet Republic) once he retired. Vehanush would not have accepted the offer. But before making this trip, my mother died, and Ohannes wanted to resettle in Fresno, where he met up with old friends he had not seen in more than fifty years and where the climate and landscape reminded him of his youthful home. In this regard, Fresno became a momentary surrogate of what he had lost decades earlier. He died before we could make the trip to Armenia.

Ohannes always wanted to visit California and specifically Fresno. I thought it might have the attraction of an elephant graveyard for aging Armenians but only in the sense that its topography provided a facsimile of Anatolia. To get a sense of the world he and my mother came from in the effort to visualize it, without ethnographic corroboration, Fresno and its environs in the central valley provided an oblique glimpse. Or so he thought. I knew a lot of Armenians had settled there and it was where the writer William Saroyan (1908–1981) came from. Somebody once told me that pop singer and actress Cher was also from there. Saroyan wrote of the life of migrant Armenians in Fresno and second-generation descendants like himself, recording what it was like growing up in an ethnic community. He was always a little too optimistic and upbeat for me. I remember, when younger, reading *My Name Is Aram* (first published in 1937), his collection of interrelated short stories about Armenians in Fresno. But my favorite was especially "The Theological Student," where he defined what distinguished a number of ethnic groups and then the Armenians.

> "Well, I'll give you the answer, to save him the trouble. You are going to ask him what he means by getting into complications of all sorts every other Friday, and I will answer from him that he doesn't mean anything at all by it.... A few ... like myself and this boy, my nephew Aram Garoghlanian come in to this world asleep, and then one fair Friday wake up and look around and notice what we are."
>
> "What are we?" the Old Man asked politely.
>
> "Armenians," my uncle Khosrove said quickly. "Could anything be more ridiculous? The Englishman has an empire to govern. The Frenchman has art to guide and measure. The German has an army to train and test. The Russian has a revolution to start. The Swiss have hotels to manage, the Mexicans mandolins to play, the Spaniards bulls to fight, the Austrians waltzes to dance, and so on and so forth, but what have WE?"
>
> "Loud mouths to shut up?" the Old Man suggested.
>
> "And the Irish," my uncle Khosrove went on. "The Irish have a whole island in which to be poverty-stricken; the Arabs a thousand tribes to bring together in the desert; the Jews child prodigies to send on concert tours; the Gypsies wagons and fortune-telling cards; the Americans CHRONIC NERVOUSNESS WHICH THEY CALL FREEDOM, but what have the Armenians?"
>
> "Since you insist, tell me," said the Old Man. "What have the Armenians?
>
> "Manners," my uncle Khosrove said.
>
> "Are you mad?" the Old Man said. "NOTHING IS SO UNNATURAL AS A POLITE ARMENIAN."

"I did not say GOOD manners," my uncle Khosrove said. "I said manners. The good or bad of it I leave to others. Manners is what we have, and very little of anything else. You are going to ask this boy what he means by getting into complications of all sorts every other Friday. Your asking is manners. Well, go ahead and ask him. I'm going to the Arax Coffee House for a couple of hours of tavli (backgammon). My going is more manners."[15]

Ohannes had heard of the existence of a residential hotel, apparently run by Armenians, where he could stay on a long-term residential basis and even take his meals, which were prepared by an Armenian chef. His reports back were always filled with satisfaction and a happiness bordering on a longing for the world from which he was forcibly separated. The reason for this was because of his identification of the region around Fresno and its climate with his natal village. He loved the hot and even humid weather of the Central Valley, apparently similar to what he remembered of his village and its environs, and confessed that the mountains in the distance (the Sierras) reminded him of the rugged topography of his southeastern Anatolia. He reconnected with people he had not seen in a lifetime and renewed acquaintances with some that in his last days strengthened his impression that he had been momentarily transported back in an act of reversible time to his youthful village years. One of the people with whom he formed a close relationship owned a vineyard, where he spent a good deal of his time helping out and recovering a moment of the agrarian rootedness that never quite left him, despite all those years he spent working in Detroit's airless automobile factories. When he and his friends were not trading stories and embellishing their personal memories, he regularly played pinochle. It occurred to me that the playing of pinochle, which he enjoyed (my mother played on occasion but drew no pleasure from it, as I remember), consisted of moments, as well, to repetitively go over the old ground of experience and memory, either of the places people came from (the regionalism in these precapitalist societies resembles an ontological grounding) or those lost to the genocidal murders and memories of the flight. It became clear that it was in such situations that men and even women spoke about their lives and experiences and exchanged their stories. It bonded them closer together, wherever Armenians met one another, even if they had met for the first time. All that was necessary was to ask whether the person was an Armenian and spoke the language. By the same measure, it appeared as a kind of secret code that validated their membership in a society, which we would never acquire. These were stories rarely, if ever, shared by our parents with us.

The decision to not share these memories and experiences with the children is still a mystery. It could have been the enormity of experiences, its virtual unbelievability, a negative fable from the *Tales of the Arabian Nights*, putting into question the credibility of occurrences that exceeded the capability of children and anything they might be able to grasp. This is a problem of all great natural and historical catastrophic events. The exchanging of stories and memories of the genocidal years and before was a way of sharing a sense of sociality and solidarity with people one might not know—all you needed to know is that they were Armenian and spoke the language. That these stories remained mainly repressed yet at the heart of the Armenian diaspora communities in the United States to comprise the cement that held them together is not surprising. What is surprising is that most Americans would never know of these stories and experiences but only hear of the genocide as a distantly remote event that took place in some indeterminate and indefinite time and place, echoed in the hackneyed phrase used to admonish children to eat everything on their plates because of the "starving Armenians."

My father died in Fresno in his sleep and missed an appointment for a game of pinochle—his "Armenian manner," scheduled the morning after—which is how his friends discovered he had passed away. It may well have been the way he would have chosen to leave the scene—missing an appointment to play cards. I do not know what he thought about in the time he lived in Fresno, apart from sharing his observations that he felt, at times, that he was reminded of his "home." I wondered if he thought about his children and his departed wife. After Vehanush died, he rarely mentioned her, not out of indifference, nor the fact that he would have known she would not have wanted to accompany him to Fresno had she lived. When he mentioned her, he would always confess how lost he felt. I think the phrase had several meanings that did not always refer to Vehanush. He once told me that he had an opportunity for work in Oakland but Vehanush did not want to leave Detroit for California, even though she must have known how much Ohannes would have liked to make the change of place. What appeared as an interesting symmetry is that while in Fresno he was no longer with our mother, a place that resembled his youthful home, and when he was reminded of his home, it was both a time and a place before he actually knew and married her. When she died, and was being interred, I remember him solemnly but audibly wishing her good luck.

Our parents thus joined a new nameless generation of immigrants who had found their way to the U.S. to become the base of a reserve industrial working class but who had no access to political or historical visibility in the representations of America's history, other than playing the unwanted role of willing participants in the foolishly mythic and dangerous ideology of becoming part of a great "melting pot." Ironically, the price paid for escaping the horrors of genocide and nameless deaths was to become nameless, dead labor among the living, unnoticed and diminished lives in a land that valorized recognition above all else. It was a melting pot that apparently sought to dissolve both class and ethnicity yet used both to maintain a political and economic hierarchy controlled by others with prior claims. It is laughable now to recall a moment in American history when immigration was exalted as an experience, literally offering the prospect of a new life when for most migrants it demanded unspeakable deprivation and endless insecurity. And of course it was the condition of creating a society where its diversities were presumably melted into a solidary unity. What was overlooked was the ideology that actually concealed the countless ways American society preserved and even reproduced ethnic and class differentiation, sometimes perilously bordering on caste, in order to maintain a particular social division of labor, whereby historical scholarship willingly committed its resources to certifying a foolishly cruel and tragic hoax. We are now witness to the historical swing from exclusion to inclusion—and as hybrids we are forced to live both.

With my father, the political choice was the turn to union formation in the interwar period and diaspora politics supporting the ARF, which in exile became less committed to socialism and more dedicated to the politics of ethnic exceptionalism, as it struggled to win over adherents to its cause in the increasingly fractious political environment of the Armenian immigrant community in the U.S. I could not help thinking that for my father, the Dashnaks in diaspora, dreaming of a return to an independent nation-state, had become hostage to a revolution that never happened. For him, his few distant relatives and friends and comrades supplied a sociality for its failed politics. I remember a particular incident when still in my teens. As a member of the Armenian Youth Federation (AYF), I wrote an article in an ongoing debate in the AYF newspaper arguing that there was no way to tell the difference between Armenian or Turkish music at festive gatherings, apart from the language it was sung in, or differences in food, apart from slightly different names and pronunciations. (I was probably wrong on the former assertion but less so on the latter.) What the episode taught me was that the Armenian community always got around to emphasizing the difference between Armenians and Turks and the capacious centrality of the genocide to define the distinctiveness of Armenian everyday life everywhere there was a diaspora community. The article and comments about it made their way to the local ARF headquarters, where my father usually played cards, whereupon he was pointedly asked if he was related to the author of the article. He told me later that he denied we were related but I knew he was joking. I left the organization soon after and virtually turned away from the activities of the Armenian community and its frozen political vocation. My time in the AYF was neither long nor intense. It was a brief moment in my late teens when I had turned back to trying to figure out the nature of my Armenian heritage, as my father, but not my mother, repetitively encouraged me to pursue and make its meaning part of some lived reality. Membership in the AYF involved meetings, attending social gatherings and conferences, connecting and associating with Armenians in my age cohort, making a stab at learning how to read and write Armenian, and dating Armenian girls. In the end, none of this activity took or seemed to have much meaning once I collided with the diaspora ideology, which, I believed, discouraged the prospect of criticism bordering on censorship and prompted the decision to leave the organization. Looking back, I probably overreacted and exaggerated my thoughtless response as a cover of a more basic impulse pulling me in an opposite direction, demanded by having been formed by a hybrid structure.

My father once asked why I did not utilize the languages I knew and specialize in a historical experience closer to home or more accessible, and I answered that I did not want to get caught in the ethnic box, especially one that would have required spending a lifetime curating an aborted national history that would make me into a patriot of a nation that did not exist. I did not want the genocide to define my life, even though it had already done so without my clearly recognizing it until much later. I also knew I could not forget the unspoken memories never directly experienced but would be daily reminded of them if only through the silence of our parents. It gradually became apparent that whatever else I did, the genocide would remain imprinted as an adverse but unseen stigma, permanently part of our collective heritage. What remained unrecognizable then was that any choice made would have led to the same end and perhaps it was better to be a patriot of a history closer to home, however unrealized, than one that belonged to others. At the time it was hard to see a separation between the study of Armenian history or its broader placement in the Middle East and the narrow political concerns of the diaspora community. It was difficult as well to imagine a career devoted to criticism of a community's pieties and desires when I knew they derived from a traumatic experience of jarring national loss in which its painful past ended by yielding no future but to keeping the aspirations of survivors on the run in an endless present.

In a *New York Times* article, Meline Toumani reported how she was attacked by Armenian groups and denounced as a "self-hating Armenian" even before her book, *There Was and There Was Not: A Journey through Hate and Possibility in Turkey, Armenia, and Beyond*, was issued.[16] Her critical perspective no more expresses Armenian self-hatred than my decision to disallow the genocide to define my life. In fact, it was precisely this kind of unknowing and mindless secondhand patriotism nurtured by a politically diminished ARF I was trying to avoid when I explained to my father the reasons why I chose a different career path. But since history is bonded to the nation-state and thus preoccupied with filling in details of an official national narrative, the choice of any country invariably leads historians into the narrow path of becoming involuntary patriots of countries other than their own; I felt then, as I do today, that it is pointless to redefine the vocation of a whole ethnic group to indefinitely and solely dedicate itself to the immanent presence of the genocide to the exclusion of other considerations. This is still far from advising some sort of effort at reconciliation or optimistic life affirmation, even though it seems to be moving in this direction. But such understanding is an all-too-common reflex leading simply to forgetting or to impulses to bury the injustices of the past. Dedication to centering genocide reflects a fear that the slightest disciplinary laxness will risk permanent forgetfulness. In this respect, there is an unwanted symmetry between the Armenian obsession to never forget and the Turkish endeavor to never remember. I think all these genocidal experiences invariably lead to this kind of repetitive memoration, which offers no promise of reconciliation but only endless remembering of what we already know. Unintentionally, the symmetry between Armenians and Turks appears in the following way: if Armenians are squeezed in the embrace of a repetitive memory of virtually total extinction, Turks are imprisoned in collective forgetfulness. For both, each day is like *Groundhog Day*. What is worse? The former remembers too much, while the latter forgets everything.

The real question is how the scale of human destruction can be forgotten. But, along the way, do we require sacrificing the way future generations devote their lives to its remembrance? In this regard, the Armenians are no different from the Jews, inasmuch as both are committed to endless remembering. The difference comes from the German willingness to acknowledge everything and constantly remind us of their guilt and remorse—not all Germans but certainly those raised in the Western sector. Yet must we go as far as Toumani to suggest the possibility of some sort of reunion with Turkey? As for myself, probably not. The problem, as it appears today, is that the event has produced two claims to victimhood: the Armenians of Anatolia who lost two-thirds of their brothers and sisters in the most savagely systematic effort to obliterate a whole population until Hitler exceeded the Turkish record, and the Turkish perpetrators who since that time have embraced an overdetermined forgetfulness to spare them of worldly embarrassment of making a full accounting of what they did and a willingness to assume responsibility for it.

When both sides of any conflict claim victimization, there is no chance of a possible reconciliation. In this ongoing scenario, both sides are closely identified with the status of victim and abandonment of this position after nearly a century's commitment to it would mean sacrifice, the loss of identity, and admission of some sort of responsibility. Of course, this narrative really adds up to an absurdity: the Armenians lost nearly everything while Turkey gained a new nation-state, land, and treasure. Under these conditions, it is hardly convincing to sympathize with Turkish claims of victimization, and any expectation to elicit support on such grounds can only attest to the collective pathology that apparently has gripped the Turkish population in its embrace since the time of the event. In fact, it is precisely this social and psychological pathology that fuels Turkish nationalism to periodically explode in wanton acts of senseless murder, as in the assassination on January 19, 2007, of Hrant Dink, the courageous editor who had devoted his life to speaking for the Armenians in Turkey and finding a way out of the long-standing historical dilemma. Despite the outpouring of sympathy, nothing has been gained by the call declaring "we are all Hrant Dink." If, as Toumani asserts, citing the Soviet writer Vasily Grossman (1962), Armenians lack any self-confidence, owing to constant vigil dictated by the genocide demanding its complete embodiment and living in an indeterminate space-time zone indefinitely prolonged by the failure to win recognition of responsibility from Turkey, Turkey, by the same measure, suffers equally from a form of self-loathing bereft of self-confidence in its incapacity to contemplate such a move, without fearing the worst psychological consequences and threat of the whole population rising up in anger against both its leaders and its minorities who have deceived and betrayed its people for so long.[17] I have often wondered about the effects the murders and mutilations had on those who committed them. But Grossman should have first consulted his countryman Osip Mandelstam's *Journey to Armenia* (1930) before making his easy dismissal of Armenian self-confidence. Armenia fortified Mandelstam and brought him back from a hiatus to compose poetry: "I have cultivated a sixth sense," an "'Ararat' sense: the sense of attraction. Now, no matter where I might be carried, it is already speculative and will abide with me."[18] And in one of his poems, he writes, "How dear to me in its strenuous life, / Reckoning as a century a year, / This breeding, sleeping, brawling, / Earth-rooted people."[19] Armenia, for Mandelstam, was thus "a State of bawling stones," "summoning the hoarse hills to arms," first in the defense of Christianity and then the repetitious and rapacious invading waves of Tatar hordes from the East: "Muffling your mouth, like a moist rose, / Holding in your hands the eight-sided honeycombs, / All the morning of the days on the borders of the world / You stayed, swallowing tears. / And turned away in shame and grief / from the bearded cities of the East."[20] This is not lacking confidence but rather signifies a long, exhausting lament over the struggle waged against a history that eventually threatened to finally overcome and make the Armenians extinct, into an archaeological trace to be excavated like the ancient city of Ani, dusted off and put in a museum's glass case or losing its historical identity in allegory that refers only to itself.

What interests me is the psychological state of obsessional behavior concentrated on the Armenian. For the Turks whose elimination of the Armenians would resolve everything, from the collapsing imperial structure of a bankrupt political, social, and economic order (the true meaning of the apt title "the chaos of empire") and its territorial shrinkage, to the unsuccessful promotion of an illusory Pan-Turkish (a transformation of an older Pan-Turanist) movement that would unify Muslims throughout Central and South Asia against Russia and revivify the caliphate to resolving problems inherited from a distant past in a present that has actually created them. This overdetermination of divergent causes and grievances was momentarily unified by the figure of the Armenian, who was made to embody and personify the source of everything ailing Turkey. As one of the three principal Unionist leaders Ahmed Cemel (pasa) explained, Turkey's woes could be ameliorated by "rescu[ing] the homeland from the blemish of this accursed nation (i.e., the Armenians)" and "wash[ing] our hands of the responsibility for this stain that has been smeared across Ottoman history."[21] The "stain," a reverse but negative rune, marked the moment the oppressed became the oppressor in a spectacular role reversal. In this statement, the inversion is complete and the victimizer is converted into victim; the dominant majority must finally free itself from those whom it had dominated before it is itself extinguished. This is also the logic of the irrational, a strange whining concession of self-defeat and self-loathing. Even though its main purpose is to enhance an ideology directing the population to take up arms against the hated minorities, there is a strange, involuntary confession of victimization, whereby Hegel's slave now rules the master.

Taner Akçam has thus proposed that when defeat in the war seemed inevitable, the Armenian presence had to be immediately resolved and mass deportation was the answer. But when did this occur? In 1915? It seems like an early moment to already decide the war will be lost. Rather, it appears likely that panic and hysteria and the fear among the leadership of failure meant they had to link their fate to the elimination of the Armenians, the continuation of their rule to the disappearance of the Armenians. The strategy may have looked to them as a win-win plan. This program was neither rational nor grounded in any discernable strategy, other than hallucinatory anxiety and the promise of a quick fix. In other words, the psychological pathology of the leadership, which subsequently became the basis of a socializing ideological campaign to reeducate the republic's population, lay behind the decision and planning of the genocide. How else to explain the implementation of mass deportations of such a large population so quickly, or to understand the releasing from prisons of a murderous and psychologically unstable criminal population, which was subsequently organized as gangs assigned to attack Armenian villages, rape women and children, kill its male inhabitants, and pillage what was left as payment? Is it any wonder that Turkish leaders and the population want to forget and deny their complicity? Denial is a necessity to conceal the cracks of a premodern ferocity that the sheen of modernization still has trouble suppressing. Is it any puzzle that Turkey's "modernizing" would want to refuse acknowledging such a descent into depravity? Only a fool would accept such a fairy tale.[22] Subsequent Turkish writers and politicians have valorized the foresight of these instigators of mass murder for having saved the "future of the homeland," which, it seems, was reason enough to hereafter forget about the event itself. Save it from what? Behind the occasion supplied by war was the opportunity to dispossess and expropriate the vast properties of the Greeks in the West and Armenians in the East. The whole campaign for Turkification, as it was called, was a thinly veiled explanation for theft and murder, primitive accumulation, that would transform the Turks overnight into a bourgeoisie, the CUP into a bourgeois rulership, and Armenians into the forgotten rubble of everyday Ani. What happened to the criminal thugs and Kurds who became the advance guard of this carnage is never reported, but it is hard not to think at least that some form of criminality became the basis of modern Turkish leadership. We have no reluctance to refer to German leadership in the war as criminal and the Nazi state as an example of what Franz Neumann described as dedicated to racketeering, colossal systemic corruption, and shakedown.[23] In the end, Kurds won nothing in the long run and were subject to large-scale military action and deaths in the interwar period down to our present. The problem is the corrosive control exerted by the memory machine, which seemingly relies on repetition to maintain its demanding domination. As for the Turks, the more compelling question was the absence of any concern for history, as such, and what lay behind this indifference. Moreover, what kind of history instruction did people receive after the language reforms? If it is the fear of arousing a whole population into rising up against their leaders in the event of an actual acknowledgment of genocide as a historical occurrence, we have a clue to the kind of history lessons that were taught to the general population once it was made literate. Akçam supplies an all-too-brief but important explanation: "In general, Turkish society is disinclined to consider its past. In the prevailing culture, not only the Armenian genocide but much of Turkey's recent history is consigned to silence, the Kurdish question and the role of the military being but two examples. The Alphabet Reform of 1928, which changed Turkish script from Arabic to Latin letters, served to compound the problem. With the stroke of a pen, the Turkish people lost their connection to written history."[24] Akçam continues by reminding us that in Turkey people cannot read their own newspapers, letters, and diaries if written before 1928. The pre-1928 past thus appears as a historically blank sheet and the production of history seems to have fallen into the hands of the state, which defines its form and content. But this loss of an "honest history" apparently stems also from the "trauma" of the political leadership in the late nineteenth and early twentieth centuries and from the shrinking and collapse of the empire.[25] The problem with this account is that Akçam, at one level, is describing the familiar historical phenomenon of transition, experienced by many other societies—the immense consequences of the transformations of precapitalist political orders into the world of capitalism. Such transformations have invariably been accompanied by consequentially violent breaks from long-standing pasts anchored in traditional social relationships and principles of a natural economy. Turkey, in this respect, was no exception, and we know from the experiences of societies like Japan, China, and India that while languages are changed and standardized to meet the demands of mass societies, access to the past is not forfeited in its entirety since components from prior practices inevitably are retained in new political and economic configurations through the process of uneven and combined developments. The question not asked or answered is, What happened to the reservoir consisting of memories of the hordes of people who actually participated in the implementation of the massacres and the military whose active role is well authenticated?

I did not know these things or even think about them when I was growing up, and I make no claims to having possessed any sign of youthful prescience. My life in Detroit was ordinary and often relentlessly American and completely aimless. My high school educational performance earned me the nickname *tutuom khaluckh*—"pumpkin head"—from both parents. This may have been the lot of immigrant children who were rigidly classified and socialized into the pious principles of the melting pot through courses on civics, shop, home economics, and personal sanitation, while at the same time becoming the major occupants of vocational tracks designed to make of them useful worker-citizens and in their proper place rather than attending the coveted "college preparatory" track to professional careers. I always felt that the socialization we were submitted to led only to a provisional assimilation into American life, never completed—the route to an unwanted hybridity—which meant orderly and useful but not fully integrated into the fabric of normative American society. Even at that time, I was subjected, together with others from similar backgrounds, to exposure to the message of a process of Americanization whose content seemed distant from lived experience, as if it came from another planet. To be exposed to a mythic and ideologically constructed history and persuaded to identify with an archaic eighteenth-century system and constitution envisioned in a wilderness surrounded by an agrarian order that had made no room for the vast diversity and deeply classed and ethnic society of urban America that would characterize the twentieth century could have been the product of the most misguided or cynical. Imagine what it meant when confronted by references to "our founding fathers," transplanted white, Anglo-Saxon Englishmen, many of whom were landowners and slaveholders who had made their fortunes in a colonial environment and for whom "freedom" signified greater access to the wealth the land offered, without sharing it with a distant home country and its ruling class or indeed anyone else. This was the unstated history behind the content of civic courses, designed to implant some sense of lasting national allegiance in us, children of migrant families who could see no further than the streets of our crowded neighborhoods, or measure time beyond the moments of our everyday lives.

Perhaps this was one of the saving graces of America's imperfection. In fact, it seemed like a technique to systematically hold back large numbers of immigrants from and out of the spectrum of rewards allegedly offered by the "American Dream" machine. For most of us, the options were not great: we could go to the car factories, like our fathers before us; or enter a trade, if one was lucky enough to have the connections of a sponsor; or join up with the military since the United States had enthusiastically embarked upon a new national vocation of waging continuous warfare to continue the economic boost inadvertently provided by World War II (to end the Depression). Or we could prolong the agony of defining our uncertain life direction by attending the local junior college (now called community college), which was free. This is the pathway I chose, with the urging of my father (who presented the flawless logical argument, "Why work like a jackass the rest of your life?" Regardless, I ended up working like the proverbial jackass) and Sena, and much to my surprise, it worked by giving me a course to follow. I have often wondered, more today than earlier, whether this represented some sort of cosmic gift of compensation for the enormity of my parents' loss or other women and men like them. If it did, the offer bypassed my sisters, and the compensatory value of the gift could never come close to making up for the extent of the loss they incurred. But Sena was probably more right than wrong when she said I was lucky, without explaining that it was because I was a male and I came later and because public education in the U.S. was still free. Even though I worked through both undergraduate and graduate years, none of this would have been possible had not the schools been free or tuition affordable. My sisters were both incredibly good students (one a salutatorian in a large high school class) and should have gone to college, but at that time the opportunities for girls from immigrant families were limited to either some sort of stenographic work or early marriage. I was simply the beneficiary of our parents' second struggle to survive the terror of uneasily trying to live in somebody else's history and only narrowly evaded the purpose of reproducing a socialization designated to keep us in our place.

EPILOGUE. **RETURNING TO ANI**

It should be recalled that when the first news of the massacres reached the West and Russia in May 1915, the joint declaration of protest, signed by Great Britain, France, and Russia, charged the Ottoman government with sole responsibility for committing a "crime against humanity and civilization." This meant nothing since it displaced the necessity for some sort of concerted action that was never forthcoming. The grim labor of killing Armenians was carried out by a large portion of Kurds, who apparently believed they would inherit the lands of the emptied-out provinces in southeastern Anatolia, only to later realize that their reward came in being selected to replace the eliminated Armenians as a roadblock to Turkey's modernist aspirations. The subsequent leader of the new Turkish republic General Mustafa Kemal's (Ataturk) conception of a modern Turkish nation-state was premised on the conviction that the country was ethnically homogenous, something that mandated the convenience of suppressing the multiethnic heritage of the Ottoman Empire. It should be pointed out that Kemal was both responsible for the Greek and Armenian massacres in Smyrna (Izmir) after World War I (1922) and the founder of and first president of the nation and author of the official narrative of modern Turkey's origin, which excluded reference to both the fate of the Armenians and the role played by the Kurds. If it was secular, it was the reserved habitat for non-Muslim Turks. In a sense this deliberate policy of historical amnesia undoubtedly signified the combined trauma of losing the war and territory and nearly eliminated its largest minority population. The erased historicity of the empire's plural ethnic groups also meant peoples who had inhabited the region long before the invasion of the Ottomans reflected in theory a broader program of secularization predicated on separating religion from state.

In Ataturk's jumbled conception of modernization, strangely emulative of Japan's prior progress and the force attributed to a single ethnic identity, the modern nation form required a commitment to a nationalism founded on the presumption of racial purity and homogeneity. Yet it was immensely convenient since it separated the "new" present from a baneful and destructive immediate past, skipping over it for an indeterminately long duration reaching back to the formation of human communities in Anatolia. The Kemalist Republic was always misrecognized in the West as "democratic," just as the current regime of Erdogan has continued to be seen as its successor, a hopeful democratic order given entry to NATO. The sleight of hand enabled by this form of banishment of the more recent past opened the pathway to collective forgetting as the foundation of the new nation's ideology of Turkishness that functioned to sustain the realization of claims to modern rationality and the achievement of civilization. It was a rather delayed implementation of the enlightened ideals said to have nourished the Young Turks but still clinging to the contradictory recurrence of a mythic dream of an archaic imperial imaginary calling for the Turkic unification of Central Asia.

Although the problem of denial still remains for the Turks at the level of history and the apparent need to acquire supporting evidence in the face of a surplus of facticity, the exercise is both endless and purposeless. A few of the leading Young Turks were tried; some, like Talaat, fled to Europe, especially to Germany, where he was assassinated; others were tracked down in the Caucuses region and killed, while most of them secured a new lease on life in the new Kemalist Republic. The Turkish response to the question of genocide has been to repetitively call for joint historical commissions to further study the problem, paradoxically repeating a faith in history it has steadfastly disavowed, even though it is never clear how history will resolve itself into a satisfactory consensus or induce the Turks to finally accept the authority of history. The constant search for and the unearthing of documents that purportedly reveal the "smoking gun" demonstrate only that those who believe history will solve the problem share a kinship with the active deniers.

Here, it seems, Turkey's leaders shared a common ground with those deniers of the Holocaust who claim that there are no eyewitnesses to the actual extermination of Jews in gas chambers, even though there is no way to account for the piles of bodies that have been found nor for the disappearance of millions of people. Unfortunately for Turkey, there were too many eyewitnesses and of course there were the dispersed diaspora survivors, who embodied the memory of the event and transmitted it to succeeding generations. Turkey's most cooperative ally, the Germans, left a long paper trail, complete with photographs that would easily incriminate Turkey and at the same time serve as a sure guide to Germany's future objective to implement an even greater genocide to eradicate the Jews. And then there were the bones of deportees found in the Syrian Desert, waiting to be dug up, still anticipating Grigoris Balakian's hope for some form of consecration to remind the future of the meaning of their presence. According to Taner Akçam, not only was there expressed systematic intent, but the scale of operation, like the magnitude later implemented by Germany against the Jews, is itself monumental evidence that attests to the complicity involving the Ottoman government at its highest levels of policy making. Acknowledging a planned intention to carry out the annihilation of a whole population would open the door to claims for compensation for expropriated property and financial settlements for other material losses.[1] The obduracy of insistent denial among the "founders of the republic" has effectively closed all discussion. But I think this problem of historical amnesia is connected to the greater anxiety over the risk of recognizing "some of Turkey's founders as war criminals," which would result in the additional effect of "call[ing] into question the state's very identity."[2] In this light and perhaps more significant is that the articulation of any accusation of barbaric behavior inevitably ends up acknowledging that the founders are all murderers and thieves. Even more important, the "Unionists" (Young Turks who planned and executed the mass murders) were in fact the same people who subsequently brought down the empire and opened the way to establishing the Turkish Republic. Like Germans implicated in the Nazi movement and Japan's war criminals, they ended up in positions of responsibility in the postwar, post-empire states after World Wars I and II.

The real question of history lies in the obvious fact that the republic's origins derived from the policy conceived and directed at the annihilation of the Armenians; the perpetrators of the great catastrophe, as Armenians have called it, are the same people who were valorized as founders and heroes of the new republic. Any admission of the genocide would run the gamble of unraveling the shaky foundations of the republic and probably lead to dissolving the thin screen of civilized modernity that sought to conceal the horrors of such an ambitious undertaking to eliminate a whole ethnic population in order to achieve homogenization. It could have been said that these heroic founders, down to the current president, Erdogan, are all liars as well, or self-deluding fascistic fantasists. We have here the leitmotif of the narrative of denial, underlying all the declarations of repudiation, demands for historical evidence, and expressions of the anxious fears risking charges and accusations of having committed uncivilized and less-than-human behavior: the recurring dread that any expression of official acknowledgment will automatically invite insistent requests for reparations to compensate for the vast amounts of land expropriated, property stolen, and lives extinguished before their time.

In the trip I took to Istanbul a few years ago, it was pointed out to me, as if it were an indoor sport for amusement of tourists, the grand homes lining the Bosphorus once owned and occupied by Armenians and now inhabited by Turks.[3] The Turkish author Orhan Pamuk, in his novel *Snow*, has his protagonist travel to Erzerum, in eastern Anatolia (Kars), where he sees the darkened and vacated houses of Armenian merchants, standing erect, mourning the absence of any other recognition.[4] Yet Pamuk could also have imagined, in the trip to the east, a countryside littered with ruined Armenian churches dating back one thousand years or more, and the ghostly intimation of hundreds of villages once occupied by their peasant parishioners that no longer exist. Even in his sentimental tribute to growing up in Istanbul, Pamuk seems to have overlooked that he was contemporary to killings that took place in his city in the 1950s![5] In any case, it is difficult to know what the reference to empty homes once owned by Armenians means to him, other than recalling a dead past and setting a mood for the reader, who in some instances would not have known its real meaning was found in the rapidity with which the Ottoman state sought to shift property vacated by Armenians sent on the death marches to Muslims before survivors returned to claim ownership.

April 24 is now designated as the day to commemorate the 1915 genocide. The choice of date, undoubtedly agreed upon by multiple Armenian groups, refers to the first incident that would disclose the broader plan of genocidal extermination, which was when approximately two hundred Armenian professional men, intellectuals, and educators were rounded up in Istanbul, imprisoned, and executed. Since 2015 was the one hundredth anniversary, the day undoubtedly yielded more than expected of the usual commemorative activities. But for Armenians every day is April 24, a day of commemoration. The anniversary was met by announcements from the Barack Obama White House that the president believes a genocide had taken place but he was reluctant to call it by its name, even though he had no qualms in acknowledging the genocidal dimensions of the event when he was running for president during the earlier campaign and was virtually aggressive about his desire to side with the Armenians. Now, of course, he would, like his predecessors and dubious successor, oppose any official congressional action on recognizing the status of genocide, in order to avoid bruising Turkish feelings. All this seems transparently purposeless. Turkey, after all, is a member of NATO. Now Turkey, under Erdogan, has reconstituted itself into a fascism, which raises the question of its membership in NATO, for which one of the principal qualifications of membership is supposedly a democratic social order.

I have never cared for official commemorations, which are often no more than empty pursuits in search of the traumas of memory. It is possible that the idea of commemoratives prompted me in the first place to take up this improbable project. I had a little help from a billboard in New Jersey, close to the turnpike, announcing to passing drivers that one and a half million Armenians were killed. Commemoratives inevitably remove the necessity of commemoration as a living remembrance in the conduct of everyday life. Genocides like the Armenian catastrophe are of such a nature that for those of us who have lived its fractured memory, there is the obligation to commemorate every day—a day has not passed when I have not thought about it, or tried to envision its enormous impact on each of my parents as they must have thought and felt and how they escaped Turkish and Kurdish death squads and lived the rest of their lives involuntarily recalling to themselves what they and we had lost. America is an environment that banished memory and, in its own way, was as harsh and relentlessly uncertain and insecure (in an economic and social sense) as what they had faced in Anatolia. I would think it has been no different now for Jews, or indeed any ethnic group that has had the misfortune of experiencing near extinction at the hands of another. Nothing is gained by citing April 24 as a special day of remembrance and observance. The Armenian massacres in modern times began in the nineteenth century under the Ottoman sultan Abdülhamid II and were periodically reenacted until the beginning of World War I. Turkish alibis point to the war as the enabling circumstances in which both sides killed the other's subjects, when in fact killing Armenians and other minorities had become a habitually repetitive routine by World War I. After all the charge must take into consideration that the Turks disarmed the Armenians, not the other way around.

The large numbers of Armenians murdered before the events of 1915 were neither inconsiderable nor separate from the main event and led up to its scorching epicenter in deportations that represented the Turkish equivalent of the "Final Solution."

Perhaps we have grown numb to the scale of more recent genocidal events after the German annihilation of the Jews: the Indian and Pakistani massacres at the time of partition (1946), the Cambodian Khmer Rouge destruction of a large percentage of its population (1975–79), Indonesian massacres of Chinese (1965–66), and the ravages in Rwanda (1994). And let us not forget the Belgians in Central Africa in the late nineteenth century. History, like laughing gas, manages to temporarily anesthetize us to the actual horror of its pain. Then it kills us. But the real issue is the scale of the operation and the kind of planning and state coordination it would necessitate, in most cases, to carry out such an undertaking, the actual labor of genocide. In this regard, genocides are already world historical events even before the staging of the killing fields. I have often wondered about historians seized by the compulsion to arbitrarily divide time in order, I suppose, to enforce a sense of different causation but more important to show, in this instance, that there was no relationship between the eventfulness of earlier massacres and the main event. Can time actually be divided, cut up, sliced? Is the slicing capable of yielding more than a before and an after? This kind of historian's game is played too often with chronology, often resembling musical chairs, which allows them to maintain one story line without going through the trouble of finding another or even others. Actually it stamps the fear of totalizing. But what it really accomplishes is the fulfillment of a presupposition that proposes that while the present always evolves from its immediate past, the present is free from the past's lingering traces. What an event like the Armenian genocide shows is the reverse—that the lines differentiating pasts from presents are always indefinite and blurred and that presents, whatever else distinguishes their temporal accent, are invariably filled with residues of pasts demanding recognition. Any attempt to suggest that life was better for Armenians in the nineteenth century is merely a historical delusion based on what came later, even though these people had been constrained to already live a prefigured ending.

I cannot say, as did Mandelstam, that I had found my sixth "Ararat sense" that accounts for my decision to write this memoir. Nor have the various days announcing the times of commemoration and remembrance—chronological markers in an official history—prompted me in doing so. I would like to think that the construction of this memoir discloses an index of both my historical moment and my identification with one of the Armenian generations whose parents survived the genocidal death sentence to secure their future, however stunted and blocked, which made possible ours. My placement was in an unexceptional second generation, which, as I have tried to explain, was composed of hybrids compelled to negotiate a difficult comparative terrain in what increasingly became evident, in contrast to the images we were taught, was a distant and imperfect America. It was not a place for hybrids, even though to this day it has prided itself as such a place. Most of my contemporaries I grew up with went into factories, low-level jobs, the military and early death, and even prison, and a few benefited from the postwar largesse of expanded educational opportunities in free public colleges and universities filled with returning veterans from military conflict who were given a GI Bill that enabled them to pursue careers they would not have had the opportunity to achieve before the war. This was what my sister meant when she said I was lucky. It was also the American recognition of its own imperfection and the attempt to make up for it.

At the same time I realized that by not inquiring into our parents' lives, I really did not know much about myself. This may have been my principal purpose. There are, it seems to me, a few factors that might explain what I have done, without necessarily clarifying what it is I have done. I think in part the impulse to try writing a memoir of parents I did not know was related to the kind of work I have done most of my professional career as a historian. I have spent most of my life actually writing about another people's history, and I believe that the desire to write an account of parents who escaped a cataclysmic genocide only to endure the economic and social uncertainties in a new environment was a compelling reason that actually brought me closer to a history that I partially lived. There has been an interesting irony in this switchover of the object of inquiry from another's history to one closer to home: while the former has always been accompanied by an abundance of sources and materials, the latter has been based on trying to make sense of silences. An unfamiliar history that has been remote from my personal experience has become more familiar to me owing to the availability of historical sources, while the apparently familiar one has been made more inaccessible by the silence of my parents. If the absences of even the most unreadable shred of documentary accounts aspire to contributing to some sort of reconstruction, memoirs are constrained to rely on experience and memory that classify them as unreliable constructions. But that difference is crucial since the form of a construction has allowed me to draw from my experiences and memories that a reconstruction of other people's history would neither permit nor find relevant.

In my work, I have long been interested in how the past continually reappears in and constantly impinges on the present, to suggest that it really does not go away. Frantz Fanon named this process the "zone of occult instability," and entry into its dangerous ground entails a difficult journey since we confront an entangled labyrinth of mixed temporalities. Fanon observed that the contest is invariably between a normative social time produced by capitalism and those distinct expressions embedded in the lived experience of particular everydays they have entered. Hence, the "zone of instability" meant not simply "getting back to the people in the past out of which they have already emerged," rescuing archaic forms in the present, but rather "join[ing] them in that fluctuating movement which they are just giving shape to, and which . . . will be the signal for everything to be called into question."[6] This has been true of events like genocide, which do not pass into pasts but remain within each present as constituent components. An outgrowth of this particular interest has been to identify the various ways older political discourses and experiences manage to appear in different presents from which they originated and often in altered and reconfigured forms to press their demands in a different historical time. Sometimes this leads to sentiments of nostalgia and at other times to extreme political seizures of power like fascism that seek to reinstate the lost, pure ideas of a society's tradition. In both instances, these appeals to the primacy of pasts and their attempted recovery comprise what the Russian writer Svetlana Alexievich has named "secondhand time."[7] It is precisely the articulation of these fraudulent old values as timeless and their temporal recall in the present, though in reality secondhand, that informs the political refiguration of American political society and its reliance on a form of organic nationalism that is currently being reenacted.

Despite the uneasiness immigrants felt in finding their way into American society, and the resulting experience of diminishment, these migrants were still allowed entry. But the contemporary closing down of immigration and of specific ethnic and religious exclusions strangely recalls Japan's seventeenth-century seclusion policies, which barred foreigners and foreign missionaries entry into Japan on pain of death and prohibited Japanese from entering the world at large. While the Japanese seclusion policy was based on the fear of foreign invasion (as of this writing Trump seems to believe the U.S. is about to be invaded by migrants from Mexico), it was simply a strategy that bolstered the authority of the leading feudal domain. The logic of these forms of exclusion was inevitably positioned to lead to genocide, as dramatically exemplified by Andrew Jackson's implementation of the removal of Native Americans in the 1830s, such as the Cherokee, and what came to be called the "Trail of Tears" in order to expropriate lands wanted by white settlers for cotton production. In this regard, it was the United States as it moved west that provided the model for the equation of expropriation and dispossession, a form of internal colonization, resulting in deportation marches and ultimately genocide in the service of primitive accumulation. Subsequent efforts to push Native Americans from their lands, to the reaches of less hospitable regions and ultimately into reservations, and the coercive violence used to carry out these seizures of land brought the relationship between theft and dispossession and primitive accumulation closer to home. Genocide is never far from the occurrence of primitive accumulation.

It is likely I will never revisit Anatolia or return to what had once been Armenia. It has never been a place I fantasized or could even envision, apart from my errant youthful dreams of an Ani I never saw. Ani will remain what it has been, a pile of ruins long emptied of its history. Mandelstam's great *Journey to Armenia* and his enthusiastic description of what he saw ended a long time ago but will have to serve in its place. But the Armenia he visited in 1930, whose ambience reenergized his poetic vocation, was not the land in which my parents had lived and fled. Mandelstam's Armenia was the land dominated by the presence of Mount Ararat, the postage-stamp-size former Soviet republic cobbled together from the bad faith resulting from the remains and residues of the genocide, and a disappointed history of European and American deception and indifference that ultimately failed to make good on its promise to create an independent territorial state of eastern Armenia and some of the provinces of western Anatolia. Although the Soviet Republic of Armenia embodied the "heritage" of genocide and was dedicated to remembering it in the place that had been at the core of the people's long history and civilization, it was not the Armenia of my parents, the killing fields whose memories reside in the soil, trees, and abandoned empty churches, lying in ruins after serving villagers for so many centuries. Not even Ararat and Ani remain in Armenia but are now on the Turkish side of the border. Armenia's empty stone churches and their relics, remnants, and rubble have become like Georg Simmel's "ruin," not even a rune of another life, no longer in the foreground but moved into the background, engaged in their slow passage of reincorporation back into nature.[8] "I was blind-sided by the sign—30 kilometers ANI," Peter Balakian spotted in *Ozone Journal,*

> where the border slid into Turkey and the open plain was bleached—
> a few boulders, some cattle, and beyond the tenth-century city of Ani
> was a mislabeled ruin cordoned off by barbed wire, a river, and Turkish guards.[9]

In Balakian's poem, Ani never manages to fulfill the aspiration of even becoming an allegory. Once it has lost its historical identity, all that is left is a "mislabeled ruin" that has become the faint trace of an archaic presence now cohabiting a space with rocks, cattle, barbed wire, and Turkish soldiers.[10] Underlying the heap of strewn rocks constituting the vague silhouette of former forms appears what Benjamin named the "bleak confusion of Golgotha." But the condition of becoming an allegory is its "secularization," the moment its historical existence disappears, when it becomes a ruin and history passes into the surrounding landscape. In the ruin, nature and history fuse into a single figure.[11] The historical events associated with Ani have "shriveled up," absorbed in narratives. History now assumes the countenance of "irresistible decay" and the allegory appears in the shape of a "fragment" and a "remnant," eliciting an ambiguous mix of polarized opposites simultaneously sanctioning imminence and transcendence that defy resolution and resist unity of meaning.[12] Under such circumstances, as Benjamin noted of the profane's dominium, "it is characterized as a world in which the detail is of no great importance." While allegory has the power to "sanctify" profane things, it can also "devalue" them.[13] It is only in this double sense that both Ani and the genocidal "Great Catastrophe" share a common fate in the form of a ruin, now a fragment or a residue, that belongs neither to history nor nature but ambiguously to both and to the untimely revenants who appear from "the realm of mourning."[14]

For Mandelstam, the trip to Armenia was a reawakening of what in him had lain dormant for so long. And it was a discovery: "The Armenians' fullness of life, their rough tenderness, their noble inclination for hard work, their inexplicable aversion to any kind of metaphysics, and their splendid intimacy with the world of real things—all this said to me: you're awake, don't be afraid of your own time, don't be sly."[15] It was thus the place that exemplified for him poetry's vocation of performing the labor of "the plow that turns up time so that deep layers of time, the black soil, appear on top."[16] Upon his arrival to an island in Lake Sevan and throughout his stay in the new Soviet Republic of Armenia, Mandelstam was constantly attracted to the copresence of remainders from the remote past and signs of the new, a "Young Armenia" surrounded by thick reminders of different pasts. "Wasn't this, " he asks, "because I found myself among people, renowned for their teeming activity, who nevertheless told time not by the railroad station or the office clock, but by the sundial, such as the one I saw among the ruins of Zvartnots in the form of a zodiac or of a rose inscribed in the stone?"[17] The persisting and unmoving untimeliness of the past and the present's distracted but time-bound "teeming activity" combine to form the lasting emblems of the modern. If this was not the Armenia of my parents, it was still a fleeting glance of what might have been a future they had been forced to forfeit.

When I was in Istanbul, a few Turkish anthropologists volunteered to take me to the region my father came from to see if we could locate any documentary records pertaining to his family. I thought it was improbable such records would still be extant much less exist for people who disappeared one hundred years ago. I kept this thought to myself, but I did respond by asking them what such documentation would tell me. I may have been wrong about not making such a trip. But my reason for not wanting to visit the regions of my parents is because neither they nor the land they occupied any longer exist; they are the empty spaces of their memories. These were the scenes of killing fields traversed by the deportation convoys of countless numbers to their death in a blazing desert mausoleum, if they managed to survive until that last instance, now hallowed and consecrated in the blood of those who perished, giving all they had to a land that gave nothing in return, neither momentary remorse nor apology, only disavowal and the blank nothingness of historical amnesia. The homeland of our parents had long ago moved to the realm of mourning and silence. After all these years, I still grieve their passing but now for the lives they might have had. Mandelstam said it best when he asked: "What tense do you live in? 'I want to live in the imperative of the future passive participle,' in the what ought to be."[18]

NOTES

One. The Unrealized Everyday

1. Mikael Nichanian, *Détruire les Arméniens: Histoire d'un génocide* (Paris: Presses Universitaires de France, 2015), 7. All translations are mine unless otherwise noted.

2. Osip Mandelstam, *Journey to Armenia*, translated by Sidney Monas (London: Notting Hill Editions, 2011), 71.

3. The phrase *inventory of traces* is from Antonio Gramsci, *Selections from the Prison Notebooks*, ed. and trans. by Quintin Hoare and Geoffrey Nowell Smith (New York: International Publishers, 1971), 324. See also Aijaz Ahmad, *In Theory: Classes, Nations, Literatures* (London: Verso, 1994), 162; Edward Said, *Orientalism* (New York: Pantheon, 1978), 25.

4. Edward Said, *Orientalism* (New York: Vintage, 1979), 26, 353–54.

5. The full passage appears in Said, *Orientalism*, 354n16. *Quaderni del Carcere*, vol. 2, ed. Valentino Gerrtana (Turin: Einaudi Editore, 1975), 1363.

6. I have found useful J. M. Coetzee's own views on this problem, even though it occurred to me that psychotherapist and novelist were talking past each other. See J. M. Coetzee and Arabella Kurtz, *The Good Story: Exchanges on Truth, Fiction and Psychotherapy* (New York: Penguin, 2015). My thanks to Nancy Armstrong for alerting me to this study.

7. Kristin Ross, *Communal Luxury: The Political Imaginary of the Paris Commune* (London: Verso, 2015), 1–9.

8. The observations in this paragraph are from Professor Rey Chow, personal correspondence, June 15, 2017.

9. Maurice Blanchot, "Everyday Speech," translated by Susan Hanson, in "Everyday Life," ed. Alice J. Kaplan and Kristin Ross, special issue, *Yale French Studies*, no. 73 (1987): 12–15.

10. Fernando Pessoa, *The Book of Disquietude*, trans. Richard Zenith (Riverdale-on-Hudson, NY: Sheep Meadow Press, 1996), 9–20.

11. Henri Lefebvre, "The Everyday and Everydayness," in "Everyday Life," ed. Alice Kaplan and Kristin Ross, *Yale French Studies* 73 (1987): 10; see also Henri Lefebvre, *Critique of Everyday Life: Foundations for a Sociology of the Everyday*, vol. 2, trans. by John Moore (London: Verso, 2002), 41–63.

12. Blanchot, "Everyday Speech," 19–20, in "The Everyday," ed. Kaplan and Ross, *Yale French Studies* 73 (1987): 19–20.

13. Etienne Copeaux, "Turkish Nationalism and the Invention of History," Part 2, in *Repair: Armeno-Turkish Platform* (October 2016), http://repairfuture.net/index.php/en/contact, no pagination.

14. Eelco Runia, *Moved by the Past: Discontinuity and Historical Mutation* (New York: Columbia University Press, 2015).

15. See Pierre Bourdieu, "The Biographical Illusion," trans. Yves Winkin and Wendy Leeds-Hurwitz, in *Identity: A Reader*, ed. Paul du Gay, Jessica Evans, and Peter Redman (London: SAGE, 2004), 297–303; as well as Jean-Paul Sartre, *The Search for a Method*, trans. Hazel Barnes (New York: Vintage, 1960), where Sartre puts into question biography as an instance of the "genetic fallacy."

16. Sartre, *The Search for a Method*, 140–66.

17. Karl Marx, *Capital*, vol. 1, trans. Ben Fowkes (London: Penguin, 1990), 873–74.

18. Silvia Federici, *Caliban and the Witch: Women, the Body and Primitive Accumulation* (Brooklyn, NY: Autonomedia, 2009), 62.

Two. Unnoticed Lives/Unanswered Questions

1. Carolyn Kay Steedman, *Landscape for a Good Woman: A Story of Two Lives* (New Brunswick, NJ: Rutgers University Press, 1987).

2. Helen McCready Kearney, "American Images of the Middle East, 1824–1924: A Century of Apathy" (PhD diss., University of Rochester, 1975), 1–30.

3. Theodor Adorno, *Minima Moralia: Reflections from Damaged Life*, trans. E. F. N. Jephcott (London: Verso, 1974), 103.

4. Svetlana Boym, *Common Places: Mythologies of Everyday Life in Russia* (Cambridge, MA: Harvard University Press, 1994).

5. Paul Ricoeur, *Memory, History, Forgetting*, trans. Kathleen Blamey and David Pellauer (Chicago: University of Chicago Press, 2004), 141–45.

6. Enzo Traverso, *Le passé, modes d'emploi: Histoire, mémoire, politique* (Paris: La Fabrique, 2005), 21.

7. Traverso, *Le passé*, 21.

8. Marie-Aude Baronian has also seen representations of the Armenian genocide in the figure of the photomontage form. See Marie-Aude Baronian, *Mémoire et image: Regards sur la catastrophe arménienne* (Lausanne: L'Âge d'Homme, 2013).

9. Grigoris Balakian, *Armenian Golgotha: A Memoir of the Armenian Genocide, 1915–1918*, trans. Peter Balakian with Aris Sevag (New York: Vintage, 2010), 352.

10. Balakian, *Armenian Golgotha*, 352.

11. Gerard J. Libaridian, "What Was Revolutionary about Armenian Revolutionary Parties in the Ottoman Empire?," in *A Question of Genocide: Armenians and Turks at the End of the Ottoman Empire*, ed. Ronald Grigor Suny, Fatma Müge Göçek, and Norman M. Naimark (Oxford: Oxford University Press, 2011), 94.

12. Balakian, *Armenian Golgotha*, 353.

13. Stephen H. Astourian, "The Silence of the Land: Agrarian Relations, Ethnicity, and Power," in *A Question of Genocide: Armenians and Turks at the End of the Ottoman Empire*, ed. Ronald Grigor Suny, Fatma Müge Göçek, and Norman M. Naimark (Oxford: Oxford University Press, 2011), 51–81.

14. Etienne Copeaux, "Turkish Nationalism and the Invention of History—Part 2," *Repair: Armeno-Turkish Platform* (October 2016), https://repairfuture.net/index.php/en/identity-other-standpoint/turkish-nationalism-and-the-invention-of-history-part-2.

15. Carolyn Steedman, *An Everyday Life of the English Working Class* (Cambridge: Cambridge University Press, 2013), Kindle version, preface.

16. Steedman, "Prologue," in *An Everyday Life of the English Working Class*, fn11, Kindle version.

17. Steedman, "Prologue," in *An Everyday Life of the English Working Class*, fn11, Kindle version.

18. For Walter Benjamin on the nameless, see his "Paralipomena to 'On the Concept of History,'" in *Selected Writings, 1938–1940*, vol. 4, trans. Edmund Jephcott and others, ed. Howard Eiland and Michael W. Jennings (Cambridge, MA: Harvard University Press, 2003), 406–7; for Ernst Bloch's input, which Benjamin equated with "awakening," see Walter Benjamin, *The Arcades Project*, trans. Howard Eiland and Kevin McLaughlin, prepared on the basis of the German volume edited by Rolf Tiedemann (Cambridge, MA: Harvard University Press, 1999), 389.

19. The term *dialectic of enlightenment* was popularized by the great book of the 1940s, authored by Max Horkheimer and Theodor Adorno, *Dialectic of Enlightenment*, ed. Gunzelin Noerr, trans. Edmund Jephcott (Stanford, CA: Stanford University Press, 2002.

Three. Traces of a Vanished Everyday

1. Libaridian, "What Was Revolutionary," 94.

2. Franz Werfel, *The Forty Days of Musa Dagh*, trans. Geoffrey Dunlop and James Reidel (New York: Penguin, 2017). The opening scene of Chris Bohjalian's novel *The Sandcastle Girls* (New York: Vintage, 2012) provides a grimly memo-

rable and heartbreaking description of emaciated women survivors of the deportations, often unclothed, who had reached Aleppo in Syria on their way to the desert and declared themselves as the "unkillable." Bohjalian, *The Sandcastle Girls*, 17.

3. Werfel's books were burned in Nazi Germany and the remaining copies of *The Forty Days of Musa Dagh* were confiscated and destroyed by the Nazis in 1934, a year after the novel was published. Werfel apparently equated his fate with the Armenians and the Young Turks with Nazis. He is said to have remarked at the time that he now stood in his own ruins.

4. Denis Echard, private correspondence, January 21, 2017.

5. Nichanian, *Détruire les Arméniens*, 253.

6. Thomas De Waal, *Great Catastrophe: Armenians and Turks in the Shadow of Genocide* (New York: Oxford University Press, 2015), 92.

7. De Waal, *Great Catastrophe*, 93.

8. Ronald Grigor Suny, *"They Can Live in the Desert but Nowhere Else": A History of the Armenian Genocide* (Princeton, NJ: Princeton University Press, 2015), 363.

9. Pierre Bourdieu, *An Outline of a Theory of Practice*, trans. Richard Nice (Cambridge: Cambridge University Press, 1977), 18, 80, 167.

10. Walter Benjamin, *The Origin of German Tragic Drama*, trans. John Osborne (London: New Left Books, 1977), 224.

Four. History's Interruption

1. Marx, *Capital*, 1:873–940, 875.

2. The idea of dispossession has been recently popularized in David Harvey, *The New Imperialism* (Oxford: Oxford University Press, 2003), 137–44. The actual idea goes back to Rosa Luxemburg and ultimately Marx himself. What Harvey accomplishes is an updating of Marx's concept of original accumulation and Luxemburg's proposal that the accumulation is "organically" linked to an outside of capitalism, its methods starting with colonial policy and war: "Force, fraud, oppression, looting are openly displayed without any attempt at concealment." Harvey approvingly quotes from Luxemburg (137) and renames the event "accumulation by dispossession" (144). See Rosa Luxemburg, "The Accumulation of Capital," in *The Complete Works*, vol. 2, ed. Peter Hudis and Paul LeBlanc, trans. Nicholas Gray and George Shriver, 265–305 (London: Verso, 2015).

3. Federici, *Caliban and the Witch*, 61–131.

4. Federici, *Caliban and the Witch*, 62.

5. See Harry Harootunian, *Marx after Marx: History and Time in the Expansion of Capitalism* (New York: Columbia University Press, 2015), especially 21–72, for a critique of stagist Marxism of the vulgate version and an explanation of how Marx actually conceived of prolonged temporal processes—a virtual

mode of production—in which capitalism and noncapitalism coexisted, whereby the latter reinforced the former in the new political economy.

6. Marx, *Capital*, 1:400, n19. Marx was referring to Mexico in this note but expressing precisely the same idea in his discussions on formal subsumption, which he saw as a rule of all capitalist development and which pointed to the appropriation of prior practices by capitalism.

7. See Michael Perelman, *The Invention of Capitalism: Classical Political Economy and the Secret History of Accumulation* (Durham, NC: Duke University Press, 2000), 27.

8. Perelman, *The Invention of Capitalism*, 37.

9. Massimiliano Tomba, *Marx's Temporalities*, trans. Peter D. Thomas and Sara R. Farris (Leiden: Brill, 2013), 67.

10. Luxemburg, *The Accumulation of Capital*, 424.

11. Some writers, such as Alexander Anieves and Kerman Nisancioglue in *How the West Came to Rule* (London: Pluto Books, 2015), have seen the Mongol invasion as a prefiguration of accumulation exemplifying nomadic societies and their formation into world historical empires. In this regard, they propose that the "expansion of the Mongolian empire was a crucial 'vector' of uneven and combined development which contributed to the making of capitalist modernity over the *long duree*" (66).

12. One exception was the German missionary Dr. Johannes Lepsius. For a dramatic account of his attempted intervention, see Werfel, *The Forty Days of Musa Dagh*, 129–56.

13. On Hitler and Armenians, see the informative article by Margaret Livinia Anderson, "Who Still Talked about the Extermination of the Armenians? German Talk and German Silences," in *A Question of Genocide: Armenians and Turks at the End of the Ottoman Empire*, ed. Ronald Grigor Suny, Fatma Müge Goçek, and Norman M. Naimark (Oxford: Oxford University Press, 2011), 199–217.

14. Werfel, *The Forty Days of Musa Dagh*, 177–79.

15. Nichanian, *Détruire les Arméniens*, 173.

16. Marx, *Capital*, 1:921.

17. Arlene Voski Avakian, *Lion Woman's Legacy: An Armenian-American Memoir* (New York: Feminist Press at the City University of New York, 1991), 30–32.

18. Nichanian, *Détruire les Arméniens*, 172.

19. Nichanian, *Détruire les Arméniens*, 172.

20. Peter Balakian, a prize-winning poet and translator and author of a number of books on the genocide and Armenian-related subjects, is also the great nephew of the priest Grigoris Balakian, whose memoir of a year in the deportation *Armenian Golgotha* I have extensively consulted.

21. Nichanian, *Détruire les Arméniens*, 172–73.

22. Taner Akçam, *A Shameful Act: The Armenian Genocide and the Question of Turkish Responsibility*, trans. Paul Bessemer (New York: Metropolitan Books, 2006), 10.

23. Suny, "They Can Live in the Desert but Nowhere Else"; Akçam, *A Shameful Act*.

24. Suny, "They Can Live in the Desert but Nowhere Else," 316–17.

25. Akçam, *A Shameful Act*, 69. See Stephan H. Astourian, "The Silence of the Land: Agrarian Relations, Ethnicity and Power" (who quotes from a Turkish memoir of Damar Ankoglu), in *A Question of Genocide: Armenians and Turks at the End of the Ottoman Empire*, edited by Ronald Grigor Suny, Fatma Müge Göçek, and Norman M. Naimark, 77–78 (Oxford: Oxford University Press, 2011).

26. Akçam, *A Shameful Act*, 138. Akçam also supplies evidence to show how dispossession of Armenian property and goods was supposedly to be used to underwrite the deportations (184–93). But since the deportees received nothing from the Turkish authorities, and were themselves the constant target of looting and murder by marauding gangs associated with the Special Organization, one wonders why Akçam clings so tightly to the official documents that he appears to be diverted from going beyond considering the extent to which and how this money was used, apart from reproducing official documents attesting to the intention to reimburse Armenians and underwriting the deportations. The former was never realized while the latter is difficult to accept because the disbursements are never specified. Despite his best impulses, Akçam is principally engaged in providing documentation for the political origins, which makes his account appear authoritative in the literature until it is recognized that he rarely strays beyond this narrow preoccupation and is unable to move past his own bracketing of the larger processes and its consequences.

27. Akçam, *A Shameful Act*, 274: "One foreign consular report notes that 'not only have members of the committee [of Union and Progress] and Jews become rich by purchasing properties left behind by the Armenians at ridiculously low prices but state institutions [are also] taking material advantage from the mass deportation of the Armenians.' As a result, 'with the Armenian properties acquired for a song, a group of nouveau riche have now sprung up, while those who had been wealthy before were able to increase their assets.'"

28. Michael Mann, *The Dark Side of Democracy: Explaining Ethnic Cleansing* (Cambridge: Cambridge University Press, 2004), 155.

29. The episode is recounted from Henry Morgenthau, *Ambassador Morgenthau's Story* (Garden City, NY: Doubleday, Page, 1918), 335, 339, in Peter Balakian, *The Burning Tigris: The Armenian Genocide and America's Response* (New York: HarperCollins, 2003), 260–61.

30. Rosa Luxemburg, "Social Democracy and the National Struggles in Turkey," *Revolutionary History* 8, no. 3, *The Balkan Socialist Tradition and the Balkan Federation, 1871–1915* (2003): 37–46, cited in Neil Davidson, *How Revolutionary Were the Bourgeois Revolutions?* (Chicago: Haymarket Books, 2012), 292.

31. On "surplus enjoyment," see Slavoj Žižek, *For They Know Not What They Do: Enjoyment as a Political Factor* (London: Verso, 1991), especially 229–73. See also Slavoj Žižek, *The Sublime Object of Ideology* (London: Verso, 1989), 11–53.

32. G. Balakian, *Armenian Golgotha*, 274.

33. G. Balakian, *Armenian Golgotha*, 333.

34. Nichanian, *Détruire les Arméniens*, 10.

35. G. Balakian, *Armenian Golgotha*, 283.

36. The works of Paul Rebeyrolle (1926–2005) are displayed in Espace Paul Rebeyrolle, a museum devoted to his art in Eymoutier, thirty miles east of Limoges.

Five. House of Strangers/Diminished Lives

1. Avakian, *Lion Woman's Legacy*, 1–45.

2. Avakian, *Lion Woman's Legacy*, 32.

3. Avakian, *Lion Woman's Legacy*, 33.

4. Avakian, *Lion Woman's Legacy*, 265–80. This transcript stands as an important general reflection of how the event was daily lived by surviving witnesses, its imminent power to destroy, and the resulting sadness of loss. It parallels Grigoris Balakian's graphic descriptions of episodes he witnessed on the deportation march.

5. Avakian, *Lion Woman's Legacy*, 43.

6. Avakian, *Lion Woman's Legacy*, 43.

7. These early church synods preoccupied with questions of theological meaning used the form of Christological discourse and controversy to resolve political differences that invariably and predictably led to the breaking away from a unitary Catholic or universal church and the establishment of protonational churches like the Armenians, Nestorians, Copts, and even the Greeks centered on the importance of reciting the liturgy in a native language other than Latin. It seems necessary to mention this bit of history here to emphasize the way the relationship between politics and religion was articulated to become a principal tradition in the present.

8. Theodor Adorno, "Cultural Criticism and Society," in *Prisms*, trans. Samuel and Shierry Weber (Cambridge, MA: MIT Press, 1981), 34.

9. Peter Balakian, *Ozone Journal* (Chicago: University of Chicago Press, 2015), 50–51.

10. G. Balakian, *Armenian Golgotha*, 290.

11. G. Balakian, *Armenian Golgotha*, 281.

12. Nichanian, *Détruire les Arméniens*, 256.

13. Aimé Césaire, *Colonialism*, trans. by Joan Pinkham, new introduction by Robin D. G. Kelley, 44–45 (New York: Monthly Review Press, 2002).

14. Ben Knight, "New Report Details Germany's Role in Armenian Geno-

cide," *Deutsche Welle*, May 4, 2018, https://www.dw.com/en/new-report-details-germanys-role-in-armenian-genocide/a-43268266.

15. William Saroyan, *My Name Is Saroyan*, ed. James H. Tashjian (San Diego: Harcourt Brace Jovanovich, 1984).

16. Meline Toumani, "Armenians Shouldn't Let Genocide Define Us," *New York Times*, April 19, 2015, op-ed, SR6.

17. Vasily Grossman, *An Armenian Sketchbook*, ed. and trans. by Robert Chandler (New York: New York Review of Books Classics, 2013).

18. Mandelstam, *Journey to Armenia*, 91.

19. Mandelstam, *Journey to Armenia*, 15.

20. Mandelstam, *Journey to Armenia*, 15.

21. Quoted in Akçam, *A Shameful Act*, 129.

22. For such a fairy tale and the scholars who compose them, see Dankwart A. Rustow and Robert E. Ward, *Modernization in Japan and Turkey* (Princeton, NJ: Princeton University Press, 1964). There is no mention of the Armenian genocide in this book.

23. Franz Neumann, *Behemoth: The Structure and Practice of National Socialism, 1933–1944* (New York: Octagon, 1963).

24. Akçam, *A Shameful Act*, 10.

25. Akçam, *A Shameful Act*, 11.

Epilogue. Returning to Ani

1. Akçam, *A Shameful Act*, 10.

2. Akçam, *A Shameful Act*, 11.

3. See Yigit Akin, *When the War Came Home: The Ottomans' Great War and the Devastation of an Empire* (Stanford, CA: Stanford University Press, 2018), 178, for an account of the redistribution of Armenian homes in the aftermath of the genocide.

4. Orhan Pamuk, *Snow*, trans. Maureen Freely (London: Faber and Faber, 2004).

5. Orhan Pamuk, *Istanbul: Memories and the City*, trans. Maureen Freely (New York: Knopf, 2006).

6. Frantz Fanon, *The Wretched of the Earth*, trans. Constance Farrington, preface by Jean-Paul Sartre (New York: Grove Press, 1963), 227.

7. Svetlana Alexievich, *Secondhand Time*, trans. Bela Shayevich (New York: Random House, 2013).

8. Georg Simmel, "The Ruin," in *Georg Simmel, 1858–1918: Essays on Sociology, Philosophy and Aesthetics*, ed. Kurt H. Wolff (New York: Harper and Row, 1965), 259–66.

9. P. Balakian, *Ozone Journal*, 71.

10. See Benjamin, *The Origin of German Tragic Drama*, 176–78.

11. Benjamin, *The Origin of German Tragic Drama*, 177.

12. Benjamin, *The Origin of German Tragic Drama*, 179.
13. Benjamin, *The Origin of German Tragic Drama*, 175.
14. Benjamin, *The Origin of German Tragic Drama*, 193.
15. Mandelstam, *Journey to Armenia*, 53.
16. Mandelstam, *Journey to Armenia*, 36.
17. Mandelstam, *Journey to Armenia*, 54. Zvartnots was a seventh-century cathedral, near the present-day capital of Yerevan, that collapsed in the tenth century. A copy was constructed in Ani and the original ruin was excavated in the early twentieth century.
18. Mandelstam, *Journey to Armenia*, 94.

BIBLIOGRAPHY

Adorno, Theodor W. "Cultural Criticism and Society." In *Prisms*, translated by Samuel Weber and Shierry Weber, 17–34. Cambridge, MA: MIT Press, 1981.

Adorno, Theodor. *Minima Moralia: Reflections from Damaged Life*. Translated by E. F. N. Jephcott. London: Verso, 1974.

Ahmad, Aijaz. *In Theory: Classes, Nations, Literatures*. London: Verso, 1994.

Akçam, Taner. *A Shameful Act: The Armenian Genocide and the Question of Turkish Responsibility*. Translated by Paul Bessemer. New York: Metropolitan Books, 2006.

Akin, Yigit. *When the War Came Home: The Ottomans' Great War and the Devastation of an Empire*. Stanford, CA: Stanford University Press, 2018.

Alexievich, Svetlana. *Secondhand Time: The Last of the Soviets*. Translated by Bela Shayevich. New York: Random House, 2013.

Anderson, Margaret Livinia. "Who Still Talked about the Extermination of the Armenians? German Talk and German Silences." In *A Question of Genocide: Armenians and Turks at the End of the Ottoman Empire*, edited by Ronald Grigor Suny, Fatma Müge Goçek, and Norman M. Naimark, 199–217. Oxford: Oxford University Press, 2011.

Anieves, Alexander, and Kerman Nisancioglue. *How the West Came to Rule*. London: Pluto Books, 2015.

Astourian, Stephan H. "The Silence of the Land: Agrarian Relations, Ethnicity, and Power." In *A Question of Genocide: Armenians and Turks at the End of the Ottoman Empire*, edited by Ronald Grigor Suny, Fatma Müge Goçek, and Norman M. Naimark, 51–81. Oxford: Oxford University Press, 2011.

Avakian, Arlene Voski. *Lion Woman's Legacy: An Armenian-American Memoir*. New York: Feminist Press at the City University of New York, 1991.

Balakian, Grigoris. *Armenian Golgotha: A Memoir of the Armenian Genocide,*

1915–1918. Translated by Peter Balakian with Aris Sevag. New York: Vintage, 2010.

Balakian, Peter. *Black Dog of Fate: A Memoir; An American Son Discovers His Armenian Past*. New York: Basic Books, 1997.

Balakian, Peter. *The Burning Tigris: The Armenian Genocide and America's Response*. New York: HarperCollins, 2003.

Balakian, Peter. *Ozone Journal*. Chicago: University of Chicago Press, 2015.

Baronian, Marie-Aude. *Mémoire et image: Regards sur la catastrophe arménienne*. Lausanne: L'Âge d'Homme, 2013.

Benjamin, Walter. *The Arcades Project*. Translated by Howard Eiland and Kevin McLaughlin. Prepared on the basis of the German volume edited by Rolf Tiedemann. Cambridge, MA: Harvard University Press, 1999.

Benjamin, Walter. *The Origin of German Tragic Drama*. Translated by John Osborne. London: New Left Books, 1977.

Benjamin, Walter. "Paralipomena to 'On the Concept of History.'" In *Selected Writings, 1938–1940*, vol. 4, translated by Edmund Jephcott and others, edited by Howard Eiland and Michael W. Jennings, 406–7. Cambridge, MA: Harvard University Press, 2003.

Blanchot, Maurice. "Everyday Speech." Translated by Susan Hanson. In "Everyday Life," edited by Alice J. Kaplan and Kristin Ross, special issue. *Yale French Studies*, no. 71 (1987): 12–15.

Bohjalian, Chris. *The Sandcastle Girls*. New York: Vintage, 2012.

Bourdieu, Pierre. "The Biographical Illusion." Translated by Yves Winkin and Wendy Leeds-Hurwitz. In *Identity: A Reader*, edited by Paul du Gay, Jessica Evans, and Peter Redman, 297–303. London: SAGE, 2004.

Bourdieu, Pierre. *An Outline of a Theory of Practice*. Translated by Richard Nice. Cambridge: Cambridge University Press, 1977.

Boym, Svetlana. *Common Places: Mythologies of Everyday Life in Russia*. Cambridge, MA: Harvard University Press, 1994.

Césaire, Aimé. *Colonialism*. Translated by Joan Pinkham. New introduction by Robin D. G. Kelley. New York: Monthly Review Press, 2002.

Coetzee, J. M., and Arabella Kurtz. *The Good Story: Exchanges on Truth, Fiction and Psychotherapy*. New York: Penguin, 2015.

Copeaux, Etienne. "Turkish Nationalism and the Invention of History—Part 2." *Repair: Armeno-Turkish Platform* (October 2016). https://repairfuture.net/index.php/en/identity-other-standpoint/turkish-nationalism-and-the-invention-of-history-part-2.

Davidson, Neil. *How Revolutionary Were the Bourgeois Revolutions?* Chicago: Haymarket Books, 2012.

De Waal, Thomas. *Great Catastrophe: Armenians and Turks in the Shadow of Genocide*. New York: Oxford University Press, 2015.

Fanon, Frantz. *The Wretched of the Earth*. Translated by Constance Farrington. Preface by Jean-Paul Sartre. New York: Grove Press, 1963.

Federici, Silvia. *Caliban and the Witch: Women, the Body and Primitive Accumulation.* Brooklyn, NY: Autonomedia, 2009.

Gramsci, Antonio. *Prison Notebooks.* Translated and edited by Quintin Hoare and Geoffrey Nowell Smith. New York: International Publishers, 1971.

Grossman, Vasily. *An Armenian Sketchbook.* Edited and translated by Robert Chandler. New York: New York Review of Books Classics, 2013.

Harootunian, Harry. *Marx after Marx: History and Time in the Expansion of Capitalism.* New York: Columbia University Press, 2015.

Harvey, David. *The New Imperialism.* Oxford: Oxford University Press, 2003.

Horkheimer, Max, and Theodore Adorno. *Dialectic of Enlightenment*, edited by Gunzelin Noerr, and translated by Edmund Jephcott. Stanford, CA: Stanford University Press, 2002.

Kaplan, Alice, and Kristin Ross, eds. "Everyday Life," special issue. *Yale French Studies*, no. 73 (1987).

Kearney, Helen McCready. "American Images of the Middle East, 1824–1924: A Century of Apathy." PhD diss., University of Rochester, 1975.

Knight, Ben. "New Report Details Germany's Role in Armenian Genocide." *Deutsche Welle*, April 5, 2018. https://www.dw.com/en/new-report-details-germanys-role-in-armenian-genocide/a-43268266.

LeFebvre, Henri. *Critique of Everyday Life, Vol. 2: Foundations for a Sociology of Everyday Life.* Translated by John Moore. London: Verso, 2002.

Lefebvre, Henri. "The Everyday and Everydayness." In "Everyday Life," edited by Alice J. Kaplan and Kristin Ross. *Yale French Studies*, no. 73 (1987): 7–11.

Libaridian, Gerard J. "What Was Revolutionary about Armenian Revolutionary Parties in the Ottoman Empire?" In *A Question of Genocide: Armenians and Turks at the End of the Ottoman Empire*, edited by Ronald Grigor Suny, Fatma Müge Göçek, and Norman M. Naimark. Oxford: Oxford University Press, 2011.

Luxemburg, Rosa. *The Accumulation of Capital.* Translated by Agnes Schwarzschild. London: Routledge, 2003.

Luxemburg, Rosa. "Social Democracy and the National Struggles in Turkey." *Revolutionary History* 8, no. 3, *The Balkan Socialist Tradition and the Balkan Federation, 1871–1915* (2003): 37–46.

Mandelstam, Osip. *Journey to Armenia.* Translated by Sidney Monas. London: Notting Hill Editions, 2011.

Mann, Michael. *The Dark Side of Democracy: Explaining Ethnic Cleansing.* Cambridge: Cambridge University Press, 2004.

Marx, Karl. *Capital.* Vol. 1. Translated by Ben Fowkes. London: Penguin, 1990.

Marx, Karl. *Grundrisse, Foundations of the Critique of Political Economy* (Rough Draft). Translated by Martin Nicholas. London: Penguin, 1973.

Morgenthau, Henry. *Ambassador Morgenthau's Story.* Garden City, NY: Doubleday, Page, 1918.

Neumann, Franz. *Behemoth: The Structure and Practice of National Socialism, 1933–1944.* New York: Octagon, 1963.

Nichanian, Mikael. *Détruire les Arméniens: Histoire d'un génocide*. Paris: Presses Universitaires de France, 2015.

Pamuk, Orhan. *Istanbul: Memories and the City*. Translated by Maureen Freely. New York: Alfred A. Knopf, 2006.

Pamuk, Orhan. *Snow*. Translated by Maureen Freely. London: Faber and Faber, 2004.

Perelman, Michael. *The Invention of Capitalism: Classical Political Economy and the Secret History of Accumulation*. Durham, NC: Duke University Press, 2000.

Pessoa, Fernando. *The Book of Disquietude*. Translated by Richard Zenith. Riverdale-on-Hudson, NY: Sheep Meadow Press, 1996.

Ricoeur, Paul. *Memory, History, Forgetting*. Translated by Kathleen Blamey and David Pellauer. Chicago: University of Chicago Press, 2004.

Ross, Kristin. *Communal Luxury: The Political Imaginary of the Paris Commune*. London: Verso, 2015.

Runia, Eelco. *Moved by the Past: Discontinuity and Historical Mutation*. New York: Columbia University Press, 2015.

Rustow, Dankwart A., and Robert E. Ward. *Modernization in Japan and Turkey*. Princeton, NJ: Princeton University Press, 1964.

Said, Edward. *Orientalism*. New York: Vintage, 1979.

Saroyan, William. *My Name Is Saroyan/William Saroyan*. Edited by James H. Tashjian. San Diego: Harcourt Brace Jovanovich, 1984.

Sartre, Jean-Paul. *The Search for a Method*. Translated by Hazel Barnes. New York: Vintage, 1960.

Simmel, Georg. "The Ruin." In *Georg Simmel, 1858–1918: Essays on Sociology, Philosophy and Aesthetics*, edited by Kurt H. Wolff, 259–66. New York: Harper and Row, 1965.

Steedman, Carolyn. Prologue to *An Everyday Life of the English Working Class*. Cambridge: Cambridge University Press, 2013.

Steedman, Carolyn Kay. *Landscape for a Good Woman: A Story of Two Lives*. New Brunswick, NJ: Rutgers University Press, 1987.

Suny, Ronald Grigor. *"They Can Live in the Desert but Nowhere Else": A History of the Armenian Genocide*. Princeton, NJ: Princeton University Press, 2015.

Tomba, Massimiliano. *Marx's Temporalities*. Translated by Peter D. Thomas and Sara R. Farris. Leiden: Brill, 2013.

Toumani, Meline. *There Was and There Was Not: A Journey through Hate and Possibility in Turkey, Armenia and Beyond*. New York, Picador: 2014.

Traverso, Enzo. *Le passé, modes d'emploi: Histoire, mémoire, politique*. Paris: La Fabrique, 2005.

Werfel, Franz. *The Forty Days of Musa Dagh*. Translated by Geoffrey Dunlop and James Reidel. New York: Penguin, 2017.

Žižek, Slavoj. *For They Know Not What They Do: Enjoyment as a Political Factor*. London: Verso, 1991.

Žižek, Slavoj. *The Sublime Object of Ideology*. London: Verso, 1989.

INDEX

Abdulhamid II, Sultan, 22, 30, 51, 92, 106
Adana, 29, 92
Adorno, Theodore, 20, 127
Akçam, Taner, 102, 103, 104, 144–56, 151
Alexievich, Svetlana, 156
American Expeditionary Forces (AEF), 45
Anatolia, 1–9, 12, 22, 27, 38, 61–62, 65, 68, 70–73, 75, 81–84, 90–91, 93–94, 96–97, 102–3, 105, 108–9, 111, 113, 117, 119, 127–28, 130, 133, 135, 137, 142, 153, 157; eastern, 44, 48, 56–57; southwestern, 42–43; village, 24–25
Ani, 44, 71, 90–91, 105, 112, 125–26, 145, 157
Antranik Ozanyan (or Andranik) (Armenian general), 77
Arabs, 38
Armenia, state of, 45–46; Soviet Armenia, 57, 61, 157, 159
Armenian Apostolic Church, 41, 65, 67, 124–25
Armenian bourgeoisie, 30
Armenian clans: village yearly cycle, 39
Armenian diaspora, 5–6
Armenian General Benevolent Union, 67
Armenian genocide, 1–4, 9, 24, 26–27, 71, 73, 84, 90–91, 93–96, 98, 102, 113, 117, 126–30, 132, 137, 140–41, 145, 151–54, 157; affect, 8; experience of, 6–7; flight from, 49; historical repetition of, 34; marriage of, 31; world historical event, 34
Armenian identity, 17–18; "starving Armenians," image of, 18–19, 138
Armenian Question, 96, 112
Armenian Revolutionary Federation (ARF): Brigades, 44–46, 72, 75, 78, 123–25, 135; Dashnak, 23, 43, 68–69, 139, 141
Armenian Youth Federation (AYF), 139–40
Asiatic mode of production, 94
assimilation, 17, 84
Assyrian, 18
Auslander, Leora, 31–32, 133
Avakian, Arlene Voski, 99, 111–18, 133–34
Azadamard Club (Freeman's Club), 66

Bagratid, 105; kingdom, 105
Balakian, Grigoris, 14–15, 28–29, 39, 97–99, 101, 106–10, 117, 128, 130, 151

Balakian, Peter, 101, 129, 158
Balkans, 40; wars, 38
Bedrosian, 49–50, 54, 59, 80; farm, 50
Beirut, 47, 51–54, 58, 79–80
Benjamin, Walter, 32–33, 85, 158
Blanchot, Maurice, 10–11
Bohjalian, Chris (*The Sandcastle Girls*), 51
Bourdieu, Pierre, 13, 77
Boym, Svetlana, 21
Brest-Litovsk, Treaty of, 78

California, state of (Central Valley), 18
Cambodia, 91
capital, 88, 89
capitalism, 87–89, 91, 102–4
capitalist mode of production, 15
Cemel, Ahmed (pasa), 144
Central Powers, 2, 24
Césaire, Aimé, 130
Chaldo-Assyrian, 2
Circassian, 11, 30, 35; resettlement of refugees, 40. *See also* Turkey: Muslim minorities
class (U.S.), 17, 19, 20
"collateral damage" (also "sideshow"), 13, 30
colonization (Irish), 39, 90
Committee of Union and Progress (CUP, Ittihadist Party), 2. *See also* Young Turks
Constantinople, 99
Copeaux, Étienne, 11

De Gaulle, President Charles, 52
deportations, 39, 48, 51–52, 95, 97, 107–8
Der Zor (Desert Death March), 22. *See also* deportations; Syrian Desert
Detroit, 2, 8, 19, 20, 21, 48–49, 52–53, 57, 60, 66, 68, 70, 73–75, 119–20, 135, 138, 146
De Waal, Thomas, 64

diaspora, 4, 23, 40–41, 61, 63, 70–71, 73, 115–16, 123, 128, 138–40
Dink, Hrant, 142

Easter, 40
Engels, Friedrich, 94
England, 45–46, 78, 88–89. *See also* Great Britain
Erdogan, Recep Tayyip, 94, 152–53
ethnicity, 17–19, 20, 34–35, 62, 84, 91
everyday, 9–12, 16, 26, 38, 90–91, 96, 116; lives, 7

Fanon, Frantz, 156
Ford auto plants, 2; River Rouge, 135
France, 45–46, 70, 78, 91, 112, 125, 135, 149
Fresno, CA, 69, 124, 135–38

Genocide Convention, 132
Georgia, nation of, 44
Germany, 91, 93, 96, 100, 129, 131–32, 142, 150–51; military, 2; missionary, 89; Nazis, 130; school, 22, 37, 53, 65, 121–22
Gramsci, Antonio, 4, 10, 14
Great Britain, 91, 95, 158; "Great Catastrophe" (*Medz Yeghern*), 149. *See also* Armenian genocide; deportations
Great Depression, 19, 82, 84
Greece, 48–49, 65, 90, 103, 115; Greeks, 2, 12, 18, 74, 99–100, 145
Grossman, Vasily, 142
Grundrisse, 15

Harootunian, Ohannes, 6, 8, 21, 24, 37, 40–43, 45–46, 48–50, 53–56, 60, 63, 65, 69, 72–73, 76–78, 80–82, 85, 113–15, 118, 122–25, 133, 135, 137; Sena, 4, 8, 21, 49–50, 52, 56, 58, 76, 80, 118, 126, 147; Vehanush, 6, 8, 22, 24, 37, 41, 43, 46–49; as Bedrosian, 51–60, 63,

65, 73, 76–77, 79–81, 113, 115–16, 118, 121–22, 124–25, 135, 138
Harput, city of, 12, 22, 77
Hegel, Georg Wilhelm Friedrich, 26, 133, 144
Highland Park, city of, 2, 42, 74, 120
Hitler, Adolph, 93, 142
Hoare and Smith, 4
Holocaust, 31–32, 137, 150

Indonesia, 91
Ismail, Enver (pasa), 100
Istanbul, 12, 45, 74–75, 108, 152, 159

Japan, 51, 150–51, 156
Jewish Question, 96
Jews, 62, 74, 89, 93, 103, 111, 130, 132, 150–51
Jihad, 90
Johnson Immigration Act of 1924, 18
Julian Calendar, 40

Kearney, Helen McCready, 19
Kemal (pasa), Mustafa (Ataturk), 62, 100, 133, 149
Kurds, 11, 26, 30, 35, 40, 45. *See also* Turkey: Muslim minorities

Lefebvre, Henri, 10
Lenin, Vladmir Illyich, 104
Libaridian, Gerald J., 29
Luxemburg, Rosa, 90, 106

Mandelstam, Osip (*Journey to Armenia*), xi, 4, 13, 123, 143, 154, 157–59
Mann, Michael (*Dark of Democracy*), 104–5
Marash (Maraş), 21–22, 46–49, 51–52, 60, 80
Marseille, 45, 48
Marx, Karl, 15, 87, 94, 97

melting pot, 20
memory, 4, 26, 27
Middle East, 18–19
millet system, 10, 21, 29, 30, 41
Mongols, 1, 90
Morganthau, Henry, 104, 129

nameless, 7, 32, 63–65
names, 7, 85–86
NATO, 95, 153
neo-Orientalism, 94
Nestorians, 125
Neumann, Franz, 145, 168n23
Nichanian, Mikael, 97–98, 111

Obama, Barack, 153
"Orientals," 18
Ottoman Empire, 2–3, 10, 13, 18, 39, 45, 83, 89, 92, 111–12, 130, 149; state, 24

Pamuk, Orhan, 152
Pedersen, Victoria, 4, 8, 48, 52, 56, 76, 118, 126–27
Persia (Iran), 44
Pessoa, Fernando, 10
Petrosian, 49
precapitalist, 108–9. *See also* premodern
premodern, 9–10
primitive (or original) accumulation, 32, 87–90, 95–98, 102, 113, 145, 157

railway, Constantinople–Baghdad, 99
Ray, Satyajit: *Distant Thunder*, 9
Rebeyrolle, Paul, 112–13
recomposition, 7, 9
Ricoeur, Paul, 26–27
Ross, Kristin, 6
Runia, Eelco, 12
Russia, 46, 78, 92, 115, 149; Soviet Russia, 21
Rwanda, 91

Said, Edward, 4
Saroyan, William, 13
Sartre, Jean-Paul, 13
Sassoun (Sasun), 92
Sèvres, Treaty of (1920), 45
Simmel, Georg, 157
Smyrna (Izmir), 149
Socratic (anamnesis), 12
Soviet Federation, 61
Steedman, Carolyn, 17, 30, 32, 133
Suny, Ronald Grigor, 102–3
Surmelian, Leon, 64
Syrian Desert, 24, 28, 48. *See also* deportations; Der Zor

Talaat, Mehmet (paşa), 100, 103–5, 150
Tbilisi, 44, 77
Toumani, Meline, 141, 168n16
Trail of Tears, 157
Turkey: artisans, 29; capitalist modernization, 36; military, 20; Muslim minorities, 29, 30, 38, 40, 91, 97
Turkification, 91
Turkish Republic, 102
Turkism, 63, 91

unevenness: and combinations, 148; forms of, 3; tensions of, 9
Urfa, 131

Versailles, Treaty of (1919), 45

Washington, DC, 95
Werfel, Franz, 2, 30, 38–39, 95–96, 101, 105, 130
Works Progress Administration (WPA), 52, 134
World Depression, 40, 46
World War I (Great War), 2–3, 24, 30, 34, 40, 93, 96, 100, 102, 122, 129, 130, 149, 151, 153; Turkey's Involvement, 12, 22
World War II, 125–26, 134; displaced peoples, 17–18

Yerevan, 46, 95
Young Turks, 2, 9, 29, 35, 63, 91–94, 100, 106, 124, 128, 130, 150, 151. *See also* Committee of Union and Progress
Yugoslavia, 91

Žižek, Slavoj, 110
Z'vartnots, 159